Avoiding Communication

SOME PAST VOLUMES IN THE
SAGE FOCUS EDITIONS

John A. DALY
James C. McCROSKEY
Editors

Avoiding Communication

Shyness, Reticence, and Communication Apprehension

SAGE PUBLICATIONS
Beverly Hills / London / New Delhi

For information address:

SAGE Publications, Inc.
275 South Beverly Drive
Beverly Hills, California 90212

SAGE Publications India Pvt. Ltd.
C-236 Defence Colony
New Delhi 110 024, India

SAGE Publications Ltd
28 Banner Street
London EC1Y 8QE, England

Printed in the United States of America

Library of Congress Cataloging in Publication Data

Main entry under title:

Avoiding communication.

  (Sage focus editions)
  Bibliography: p.
  1. Bashfulness. 2. Interpersonal communication.
3. Anxiety. I. Daly, John A. (John Augustine), 1952-
II. McCroskey, James C.
BF575.B3A96   1983   153.6   83-27242
ISBN 0-8039-2173-X
ISBN 0-8039-2174-8 (pbk.)

FIRST PRINTING

CONTENTS

Preface

Concern with problems of communication avoidance and anxiety has been present in the literatures of communication and psychology for the past century. Formal research involving these problems first appeared a half century ago and has accelerated to the present. Over the past decade research in this area, as indicated by the extensive bibliography included in this book, has become a prime item on the agenda of communication scholars.

Several booklets have appeared that attempted to bring information in this area to the attention of students and teachers. Similarly, several summary articles have appeared that have attempted to draw together the products of individual research programs within the disparate branches of concern, such as communication apprehension, reticence, or shyness. However, no book has appeared previously that draws together the outputs of the major conceptual, methodological, and research approaches that have developed in this area. The purpose of this book is to do just that.

The editors of this book have discussed putting such a book together for over a decade. We delayed for several years because we didn't believe the various research streams had yet matured to the point that clear and useful distinctions could be made. Once we determined that "the time was right," we confronted a difficult choice. Should we write the book, or should we edit the book? Obviously, we opted for the latter approach. We chose this option because we felt the major goal of the project would best be served in this way. Our goal was to provide, in one place, a clear enunciation of the various views concerning communication avoidance. We are closely identified with one of the approaches that is prominent in the literature, the communication apprehension approach. We were confident that we could represent this approach well. However, we felt, for example, that Phillips could better explain reticence and Buss better explicate shyness. Consequently, we chose to ask such scholars to prepare chapters for this book. All of the authors or senior authors of chapters in this book are leading scholars in their particular areas.

The book is divided into five parts, covering perspectives, measurement, impact, remediation, and implications. In three of these sections — perspective, measurement and remediation — the diversity of approaches is emphasized. In the section on impact this emphasis is absent. Research derived from the various approaches yields similar effects.

Part I focuses on four major perspectives that have guided research and scholarship in this area. McCroskey outlines the communication apprehension perspective, the dominant approach in communication research over the past decade. Buss outlines the shyness perspective, the dominant approach in psychology. Phillips outlines the reticence perspective, an approach that initially was parallel to communication apprehension but that has grown and changed over the years to become very distinct in its own right. Finally, Daly and Buss outline the transitory audience anxiety perspective, the oldest of the approaches in this area and one that continues to the present in both communication and psychology.

Part II considers the critical problem of measurement. Throughout the history of research in this area, three approaches to measurement have had major roles. Each is discussed by authors closely identified with the given approach: McCroskey on self-reports, Beatty on physiological indicants, and Mulac and Weimann on observational techniques.

Part III Daly and Stafford summarize the extensive body of research relating to the effects of communication avoidance and anxiety. Richmond looks at the practical impact of communication avoidance in three critical settings: interpersonal relationships, the work environment, and the instructional environment. Finally, Klopf reports his initial work in cultural settings outside the continental United States, an area of critical importance to the future development of theory in this area if it is to avoid the strong ethnocentric biases of most previous work.

Communication avoidance has long been recognized as a major problem for many people. Consequently, scholars in both communication and psychology have long sought methods of helping people with such a problem. Part IV outlines the three major approaches that have been developed. Friedrich and Goss explain the systematic desensitization approach, the method most commonly applied in the communication field. Kelly explains the skills training approach, the method most commonly associated with those concerned with reticence and a method frequently used in psychology. Fremouw, one of the leaders in psychology in the development of treatment techniques, outlines the behavior therapy known as cognitive modification.

Part V is somewhat unique for this type of book. It is concerned with the implications of all the work that has been done in this area. After all the other chapters had been written, we asked two of the leading scholars in the field of communication to read them and, from their distinctly different perspectives, tell us what it all means. Clevenger, the author of a classic article on stage fright, published 25 years ago, came to the task as a scholar who has spent the majority of a distinguished scholarly career with a central focus in this area. Miller, one of the most published scholars in the history of the field of communication and a recognized leader in theory and research related to interpersonal communication, came to the task as an "outsider," one who has not previously researched or written in the area. We believe their comments help put the efforts of the hundreds of researchers and writers who have done work in this area into better focus for the field as a whole.

The Appendix presents a bibliography on communication avoidance. Payne and Richmond have provided the most extensive bibliography of research and writing available in this area.

There are many people to whom we owe a debt of gratitude for their support leading to the publication of this book. Not the least of these is Max Black and the hundreds of other individual researchers and scholars whose output forms the base for the chapters that appear here. But one individual in particular deserves special mention, our former colleague and teacher, William Lashbrook. Brad spurred us on in our early efforts with frequent jabs suggesting that our "comm ap stuff will never amount to anything." Have we convinced you yet, Brad?

— J.A.D. and J.C.M.

PART I

PERSPECTIVES

1

The Communication Apprehension Perspective

JAMES C. McCROSKEY

The construct of communication apprehension (CA) has been central to the study of communication avoidance since 1970. In this chapter we will examine the evolution of the CA construct and the most current conceptualization of that construct.

The Original Conceptualization

The original conceptualization of CA (McCroskey, 1970) viewed CA as "a broadly based anxiety related to oral communication." Subsequent writings have made only apparently minor modifications of this definition. My more recent papers present the view that CA is "an individual's level of fear or anxiety associated with either real or anticipated communication with another person or persons" (McCroskey, 1977a, 1978).

This seeming consistency across time may be more apparent than real. Two conceptual modifications occurred. The first concerned the oral communication focus of CA and the other concerned whether CA was restricted to a trait conceptualization.

The Oral Focus of CA

In the original article in which I advanced the construction of CA, the focus clearly was on oral communication (McCroskey, 1970). Although in this article "communication" frequently was used without the "oral" qualifier, the earlier work in the areas of stage fright and reticence were acknowledged as the foundations upon which the CA construct was developed. Both of these areas focused exclusively on oral communication at that time.

In some subsequent writings the oral context of CA received less emphasis. Of particular importance were two research programs that were conducted under the general rubric of communication apprehension but that did not focus on speaking. The first was the research concerned with apprehension about writing (Daly & Miller, 1975). This stream of research, led by Daly and his associates, continues currently and has received considerable attention in the field of English. The measure developed by Daly and Miller, the Writing Apprehension Test (WAT), has been employed widely and has been found to have only a moderate correlation with my CA measures. The second research area was that concerned with apprehension about singing. While receiving far less attention than the articles and measures concerned with speaking and writing, research involving the Test of Singing Apprehension (TOSA) also discovered low correlations between the TOSA and CA measures (Andersen, Andersen, & Garrison, 1978).

In sum, over the decade since the CA construct has been advanced it has been broadened substantially. While it was originally restricted to talking, it now encompasses all modes of communication. Consequently, it should be recognized that current instruments labeled as CA measures (notably the Personal Report of Communication Apprehension, PRCA; McCroskey, 1970, 1978, 1982) are restricted to oral CA, specifically apprehension about talking to or with others. My focus in the remainder of this chapter is on this form of CA and when I use the term "CA" this will be my referent. I believe that most of what will follow will apply equally well to other forms of CA, however.

The Trait Conceptualization of CA

The original article that advanced the construct of CA included no explicit mention of whether it is a trait of an individual or a response to the situational elements of a specific communication transaction. However, the implication is clear that the construct was viewed from a trait orientation. Not only was the discussion directed toward a response generalized across situations and time, but also the measures advanced clearly focused on a traitlike pattern.

The overwhelming majority of the research studies employing the CA construct have taken a trait approach (McCroskey, 1977a). Many have referred to CA with terms such as "a traitlike, personality-type variable." More recently, the CA construct has been expanded explicitly to encompass both trait and situational views (McCroskey, 1977a). Some research has been reported that has investigated CA in both the trait and state form (for example, see Richmond, 1978; Prisbell & Dallinger, 1981).

In sum, over the decade since the CA construct has been advanced it has been broadened substantially. While it originally was restricted to a trait orientation, it is now viewed as representing both trait and state approaches. While the original definition of CA restricts the construct to a trait perspective, the revised definition noted above is consistent with the broader view. It should be recognized, however, that the most popular measures of CA are restricted to a trait conceptualization. Research based on more situational perspectives must employ other instruments.

The Current Conceptualization of CA

Minor changes in the conceptualization of CA over the past decade have been noted. Such changes have appeared in the literature in a nonsystematic manner. In addition, some elements of the CA construct have never been spelled out clearly. In the following sections the conceptualization of CA will be enunciated in four major areas: (1) types of CA, (2) causes of CA, (3) treatment of CA, and (4) effects of CA.

Types of CA

Considerable attention has been directed toward the distinction between trait and situational or state CA. This distinction has been quite helpful to researchers in the CA area in their attempt to distinguish older from newer approaches to this subject. Unfortunately, this distinction has come to be viewed as a dichotomy, a false dichotomy. To view all human behavior as emanating from either a traitlike, personality orientation of the individual or from the statelike constraints of a situation ignores the powerful interaction of these two sources. No element of personality yet isolated by psychologists or others has been found to have universal predictability across all situations for all individuals. Similarly, no situation has yet been identified in which we can predict a universal behavior from all individuals. Even in life-threatening situations, people do not all behave alike. Thus it is important that we reject this false state/trait dichotomy and view the sources of CA on a continuum. This continuum can be viewed as ranging from the extreme trait pole to the extreme state pole, although neither the pure trait nor pure state probably exists as a meaningful consideration. Four points along this continuum can be identified. Each of these points represents a distinct type of CA.

Traitlike CA. The term "traitlike" is used intentionally to indicate a distinction between this view of CA and one that would look at CA as a true trait. A true trait, as viewed here, is an invariant characteristic of an individual, such as eye color and height. No personality variable — and traitlike CA is viewed as a personality-type variable — meets this strict interpretation of "trait." After an individual achieves adulthood, his or her true traits are not subject to change. Traitlike personality variables, although highly resistent to change, can be and often are changed during adulthood. That CA is subject to such change is indicated clearly in the substantial research on treatment of people identified as having high CA (for example, see McCroskey, 1972).

Traitlike CA is viewed as *a relatively enduring, personality-type orientation toward a given mode of communication across a wide variety of contexts.* Three varieties of this type of CA have been addressed in the literature — CA about oral communication, CA about writing, and CA about singing. The primary measures of these (PRCA, WAT, and TOSA) are presumed to be traitlike measures, which means that it is assumed that scores for an individual on any one of these measures will be highly similar across an extended period of time, barring an intervention program designed to alter the relevant CA level or a demand characteristic introduced into the CA measurement.[1] This is the type of CA to which most of the research has been directed over the past decade (McCroskey, 1977a).

Generalized-Context CA. Generalized-context CA is one step further removed from pure trait than traitlike CA. CA viewed from this vantage point represents orientations toward communication within generalizable contexts. Fear of public speaking, the oldest of the CA conceptualizations, is illustrative of this type of CA. This view recognizes that people can be highly apprehensive about communicating in one type of context while having less or even no apprehension about communicating in another type of context.

Generalized-context CA is viewed as *a relatively enduring, personality-type orientation toward communication in a given type of context.* Although no taxonomy for generalized-context CA yet has received consensual acceptance in the literature, the one advanced by McCroskey and Richmond (1980) that is based on types of communication settings appears quite adequate. From this view there are four varieties of this type of CA — CA about public speaking, CA about speaking in meetings or classes, CA about speaking in small group discussions, and CA about speaking in dyadic interactions.

The first CA measure to receive wide acceptance by researchers, the Personal Report of Confidence as a Speaker (PRCS) developed by Gilkinson (1942), is illustrative of an instrument designed to tap this type of CA. Subsequent instruments for measuring public speaking anxiety reported by Paul (1966) and McCroskey (the Personal Report of Public Speaking Apprehension, PRPSA, 1970) also fall within this area. More recently, McCroskey and Richmond (1981) have offered instruments to measure each of the four varieties of generalized-context CA that they describe. As was the case with the traitlike CA measures noted in the previous section, it is assumed that scores for an individual on any one of these measures will be highly similar across an extended period of time, barring an intervention program designed to alter the relevant CA level or a demand characteristic in measurement. These measures are distinguished from the previously noted traitlike measures in that they focus more narrowly on communication within a given type of context rather than on communication across contexts. It should not be surprising, however, to find moderate to moderately high correlations between the two types of measures. To the extent that a traitlike orientation toward communication actually exists, an appropriate measure of that orientation should be at least somewhat predictive of orientations within generalized contexts.

Person-Group CA. This type of CA represents the reactions of an individual to communicating with a given individual or group of individuals across time. People viewing CA from this vantage point recognize that some individuals and groups may cause a person to be highly apprehensive while other individuals or groups can produce the reverse reaction. For some people more apprehension may be stimulated by a peer or group of peers. For others, more apprehension may be stimulated by unfamiliar individuals or groups. A school teacher, for example, may be highly apprehensive about talking to her or his principal, but may have no apprehension about talking to a student in her or his own class.

Person-group CA is viewed as *a relatively enduring orientation toward communication with a given person or group of people.* It is not viewed as personality based, but rather as a response to situational constraints generated by the other person or group. Although presumed to be relatively enduring, this type of CA would be expected to be changed as a function of changed behavior on the part of the other person or group. Although people with high traitlike CA or high generalized-context CA would be expected to experience high CA with more persons and groups, knowledge of the levels of neither of these should be expected to be predictive of CA experienced with a given individual or group. In short, this type of CA is presumed to be more a function of the situational constraints introduced by the other person or group than by the personality of the individual. Length of acquaintance should be a major consideration here. While in early stages of acquaintance the personality orientations should be somewhat predictive, in later stages the situational constraints should be expected to overpower these orientations (Richmond, 1978).

Few attempts to measure this type of CA have appeared in the literature. However, the state anxiety measure developed by Spielberger (1966), particularly as modified for this purpose by Richmond(1978), appears to be an excellent tool. It can be adapted readily for use with any person or group within any communication context.

Situational CA. This type of CA represents the reactions of an individual to communicating with a given individual or group of individuals at a given time. This is the most statelike of the types of CA. When we view CA from this vantage point we recognize that we can experience CA with a given person or group at one time but not at another time. For example, a student may experience little or no apprehension when going to a teacher to ask a question about an assignment, but may be terrified if the teacher instructs the student to stay after class to meet with her or him.

Situational CA is viewed as *a transitory orientation toward communication with a given person or group of people.* It is not viewed as a personality based, but rather as a response to the situational constraints generated by the other person or group. The level of this type of CA should be expected to fluctuate widely as a function of changed constraints introduced by the other person or group. Although people with high traitlike CA or high generalized-context CA would be expected to experience high CA in more individual situations than would other people, knowledge of the levels of neither of these should be expected to highly predictive of CA experienced by an individual in any given situation. On the other hand, level of person-group CA should be expected to be moderately highly related to situational CA. Person-group CA primarily is a function of the prior history of the individual with the given person or group. Such a history can be assumed to produce expectations that would influence the level of CA in the given situation involving communication with that person or group.

Measurement of situational CA has received little attention in the previous research. However, the Spielberger (1966) instrument as modified by Richmond(1978), as noted in the previous section, appears to be a very satisfactory tool for this purpose.

Figure 1.1 illustrates the four types of CA. As indicated in that figure, the three components of this conceptualization are context, receiver (person/group), and time. Time should be taken to represent more than just the hour or day of the communication. As conceived here this element includes the variability associated with topic, mood, health, and the like that are seen as changeable over time, as well as the literal element of time itself. Traitlike CA is seen as that which cuts across context, receiver, and time. Generalized-context is seen as that which is associated with a single type of communication context cutting across receiver and time. Person-group CA is seen as that which is associated with a single receiver or group of receivers cutting across context and time. Situational CA is seen as that which is specific to a given context with a given receiver at a given time. It should be recognized that the three components in this model could be combined to generate additional types of CA. However, at present, I do not believe such combinations provide useful insights.

Pathological CA. It is important that we recognize that the four types of CA discussed above do not reference different types of people. Rather, every individual is affected by each type of CA to either a greater or lesser degree. It is a truly rare individual, if one actually exists, that never experiences CA in any communication situation. Such an individual would be seen as evidencing pathological behavior, since fear is a natural human response to a truly threatening situation. Similarly, it is comparatively rare individual who experiences CA in all communication situations, although such people do exist. With the exception of these rare individuals, even people with very high traitlike CA find some situations in which they can communicate comfortably. The most common of these situations involve communication with close friends. It is not so much that close friends produce less apprehension as it is that people who produce less apprehension are allowed to become close friends while more threatening individuals are avoided.

Since in the previous literature much has been made of the pathological nature of high CA, high reticence, and high shyness, we

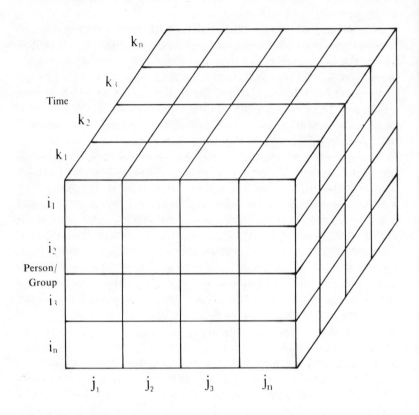

NOTE: Traitlike = grand sum of all $i_x j_x k_x$ cells; generalized-context = j_x across time and context; person-group = i_x across time and context; and situational = each $i_x j_x k_x$ cell.

Figure 1.1 Illustration of Types of Communication Avoidance

need to consider what we should view as pathological, or abnormal, levels of CA. This distinction can be made both conceptually and empirically, although the distinctions are not fully isomorphic.

At the conceptual level, we view abnormal behavior to be that which is nonadaptive, nonresponsive, or nonfunctional in the environment in which it is engaged. Normal individuals are sensitive to their environment, respond to its demands, and adapt their behavior so that they are a functional part of that environment. Experiencing fear or anxiety in a threatening situation and adapting by withdrawing or avoiding the threatening situation is normal. Experiencing no fear or anxiety in a nonthreatening environment and continuing to function in that environment is normal. The reverse responses are abnormal. Experiencing low CA in the face of real danger and experiencing high CA when no real danger is present are both abnormal responses. If such responses become characteristic of the individual, he or she may be regarded as pathological and in need of professional help. The question, of course, is one of degree. Abnormal responses in one or a few circumstances certainly should not generate a judgment of "pathological." Only when such behavior is a consistent pattern of the individual would such a judgment seem warranted. Most important, such judgments should not be restricted to only one end of the CA continuum. Extremely low CA can be just as abnormal as extremely high CA.

Empirically, the distinction between normal and abnormal is a bit more easily determined. I strongly endorse the empirical distinction made most frequently in the previous research. This distinction is based on the normal curve, an approximation of which is generated by scores on most of the common CA measures. People with scores beyond one standard deviation above or below the mean score of the population are identified as high or low in CA. In normally distributed scores, approximately 68% of the population falls within one standard deviation of the mean, with 16% scoring over one standard deviation higher and 16% scoring over one standard lower. The latter two groups are, in fact, statistically significantly different at alpha = .05.

For research purposes, this is a particularly good distinction. The researcher can be reasonably assured that the people classified as "high" are truly different from those classified as "low." These two groups are the ones that theoretically should manifest differential behaviors related to the measure. Those in the middle, the "normals," actually may have no consistent pattern of behavior, particularly if the measure is a personality-type measure. The middle scores most likely indicate that this is a facet of personality not highly associated with the behavior of these individuals. Other personality elements, or situational constraints, may completely dominate their behavior to the exclusion of this particular personality variable.[2]

I originally introduced this system of classification into the literature as a function of observing groups of students brought into rooms for treatment of traitlike CA. I observed that groups of students composed entirely of individuals with scores beyond one standard deviation from the mean simply did not talk. The behavior of individuals in groups composed of people with scores between one-half and one standard deviation above the mean did not have such a consistent pattern. Some were totally noncommunicative, but others were willing to interact.[3] Thus this classification scheme is not purely arbitrary. It does seem to have a behavioral justification.

Two cautions should be stressed, however. First, some samples may not be representative of the overall population. Therefore, the classification-by-standard-deviation procedure should be sensitive to the mean and standard deviation of the population norms rather than the particular sample studied. A sample of successful salespersons, for example, probably would include few people with high CA. Second, while this procedure is excellent for research involving comparatively large samples and based on aggregate data analyses, such a procedure is far too subject to measurement error to be applied to single individuals. Judgments about individuals should never be based on a single score or any scale. Rather, such a score should be only one of many factors to be considered. This is particularly important for people to recognize when developing or implementing intervention programs designed to alter high or low CA.

Causes of CA

The etiology of CA has received comparatively little attention in the literature. Varying writers have presented different views. The differences, however, are not so much a function of disagreement as they are of desperation. The best method of isolating causes of subsequent events generally is considered to be carefully controlled experimentation. Unfortunately, for ethical reasons, this method is highly restricted for investigations of the causes of CA. While we might ethically employ experimentation to investigate situational CA, almost no one would approve such experimentation with traitlike CA. The other types of CA fall within the gray area between these two types. Consequently, most research directed toward the etiology of CA has been performed in naturalistic environments. Such research is useful for establishing correlational associations, but it is fraught with potential error when attempting to infer causality. Much of the writing in this area is based more on speculation than on research. Regrettably, the following causal analysis will also have this characteristic. I hope that future research will provide insight into the validity of my speculations.

Previous causal analyses generally have been restricted to viewing either traitlike CA or situational CA. I will first present my positions in each of these areas and then advance an etiological explanation that I believe may be applied to all types of CA.

Causes of Traitlike CA. Throughout the social sciences only two major explanations of the differential traitlike behaviors of individuals hold sway: heredity and environment. Simply put, we can be born with it or we can learn it. I believe that both of these explanations can contribute to our understanding of the etiology of CA.

Although most early writers discounted out of hand the notion of heredity as a cause of traitlike CA, recent writers have grudgingly acknowledged that there indeed may be a hereditary contribution. Although no one has yet argued that there is a "CA gene," the work of social biologists, particularly their research with twins, has provided compelling evidence that something other than environmentally based learning is having an impact on human behavior tendencies. McCroskey and Richmond (1980, p. 6) summarize the thrust of this research:

Researchers in the area of social biology have established that significant social traits can be measured in infants shortly after birth, and that infants differ sharply from each other on these traits. One of these traits is referred to as "sociability," which is believed to be a predisposition directly related to adult sociability — the degree to which we reach out to other people and respond positively to contact with other people. Research with identical twins and fraternal twins of the same sex reinforces this theoretical role of heredity. Identical twins are biologically identical, whereas fraternal twins are not. Thus, if differences between twins raised in the same environment are found to exist, biology (heredity) can be discounted as a cause in one case but not in the other. Actual research had indicated that biologically identical twins are much more similar in sociability than are fraternal twins. This research would be interesting if it were conducted only on twin infants, but it is even more so because it was conducted on a large sample of adult twins who had the opportunity to have many different and varied social experiences.

It is important that we recognize that the work of the social biologists does not support the argument that heredity is the only cause of sociability, much less of CA, but rather suggests that heredity may be one of the contributing causes. Children, it seems, are born with certain personality predispositions or tendencies. No one has yet argued, not even the most ardent social biologists, that these predispositions or tendencies are unchangeable. Thus what happens in the child's environment will have some impact on the predispositions and tendencies the child carries over into later life. However, because children are born with different predispositions and tendencies, they will react differently to the same environmental conditions. This interaction of heredity and environment, then, is seen as the precursor of adult predispositions and tendencies such as CA.

Although heredity appears to be a meaningful contributor to traitlike CA, most writers allege that reinforcement patterns in a person's environment, particularly during childhood, are the dominant elements. Although most of the views supporting reinforcement as a cause are based primarily on speculation or analogy, some available research is supportive (for example, see McCroskey & Richmond, 1978).

We can view the causal impact of reinforcement in at least two ways. The first is a fairly narrow, behaviorist view. If the child is reinforced for communicating, the child will communicate more. If the child is not reinforced for communicating, the child will communicate less. While this is a rather simple application of the general theory of reinforcement, and may serve to explain many communication behaviors, since it does not address the cognitions of the individual and CA is viewed as a cognitive variable, this explanation is less than satisfactory for our purpose.

The second way we can view the impact of reinforcement is as an adjunct of modeling. Modeling theory suggests that children (and to some extent adults) observe the communication behavior of others in their environment and attempt to emulate it. If their attempts are reinforced, they continue to behave in a similar manner. If they are not reinforced, they alter their behavior. Such an explanation seems to be a very good way of looking at the development of many communication behaviors, such as accent, dialect, and use of nonverbal behaviors. However, this explanation also ignores the cognitive element and thus does not address CA as conceived here.

While I agree that reinforcement is a central component in the development of CA, I do not believe that the behavioristic approaches outlined above can account for this relationship. My view of the place of reinforcement as a causal element in the development of CA will be outlined below when I consider the theory of learned helplessness.

Causes of Situational CA. While causal attributions for elements leading to the development of traitlike CA are based primarily on speculation and rather tenuous analogies, the causes of situational CA appear much clearer. In some cases they have been the subject of direct research, in others strong analogies with similar fears or anxieties can be drawn. I find the causal elements outlined by Buss (1980) particularly insightful. Buss suggests that the major elements in the situation that can result in increased CA are *novelty, formality, subordinate status, conspicuousness, unfamiliarity, dissimilarity*, and *degree of attention from others.* In most instances, the opposite of these factors would be presumed to lead to decreased CA in the situation. Let us examine each of these briefly.

The novel situation presents the individual with increased uncertainty about how he or she should behave. If one almost never has an interview, going to an interview would be novel and the individual might not be sure how to behave, thus becoming more apprehensive. For most people, giving a speech is a novel experience, not something they do every day (or, for many, every year). Approaching such a situation would be likely to increase CA sharply.

Formal situations tend to be associated with highly prescribed appropriate behaviors, with comparatively little latitude for deviation. Less formal situations have less rigid behavior rules and much wider latitudes of acceptable behavior. CA is increased in formal situations because of the narrower confines for acceptable behavior. A similar impact results from interacting from a subordinate position. In such situations, appropriate behavior is defined by the person holding higher status. This is particularly important in evaluative settings, which are common in superior-subordinate communication situations.

Probably nothing can increase CA more than being conspicuous in one's environment. Giving a public speech is a prime example of being conspicuous. So is standing up to make a comment in a meeting or classroom. Similarly, being the new person in a social setting or meeting a new person can make a person feel conspicuous. Generally, the more conspicuous people feel, the more CA they are likely to experience.

Although not all people react to unfamiliarity in the same way, many people feel much more comfortable when communicating with people they know than when communicating with people they do not know. In general, as the degree of familiarity increases, the degree of CA decreases. To some extent, similarity has the same kind of impact. For most people, talking to others who are similar to themselves is easier than talking to people who are greatly different. There are major exceptions to this rule, however. Some people are the most uncomfortable when communicating to similar peers, because they are more concerned with the evaluations such people make than they are with people who are very different from themselves.

A moderate degree of attention from others is the most comfortable situation for most people. When people stare at us or totally ignore us when we are communicating, our CA level can be expected to rise sharply and quickly. In addition, if people become overly intrusive into our private feelings and thoughts, we can become very uncomfortable.

In recent work, Daly and Hailey (1980) have noted two elements that go beyond those advanced by Buss as causes of situational CA. These are degree of evaluation and prior history. When we are evaluated we tend to be more anxious than otherwise. For example, a student giving a talk in a public speaking class for a grade may be more apprehensive than the same student would be if he or she were giving the same talk to the same people at a meeting in the dorm. Of course, not everyone responds to evaluation in the same way. As Daly and Hailey have noted, good writers do better when being evaluated, but poor writers do worse. This may also be true for oral communication, but no research is available that addresses this issue.

The final causative element, prior history, may be the most important of all, as I will note when I consider learned helplessness in the next section. If an individual has failed before it is increasingly likely that he or she will fear failure again, and hence will become more apprehensive. On the other hand, success breeds both success and confidence, and hence less apprehension.

In sum, there are a variety of elements in communication situations that can cause our CA to increase — whether we are high, moderate, or low in traitlike CA. Their absence, likewise, can lower our CA. Most of these elements are at best only marginally under our control. Thus situational CA is produced by others in our communication environment, and, to a large extent, is controlled by them. Often, then, the only method of avoiding the unpleasant aspects of situational CA is to withdraw from or avoid such communication situations.

Learned Helplessness and Learned Responsiveness. Although the above causal explanations are useful in developing a fuller understanding of the etiology of CA, none of them is fully satisfactory. Work in the area of expectancy learning, particularly that concerning learned helplessness (Seligman, 1975), permits a causal explanation that can be applied to all types of CA since it takes into account both traits of the individual and the variety of situational demands the individual can confront.

My approach is a cognitive one. My underlying assumption is that people develop expectations with regard to other people and with regard to situations. Expectations are also developed concerning the probable outcomes of engaging in specific behaviors (such as talking). To the extent that such expectations are found to be accurate, the individual develops confidence. When expectations are found to be inaccurate, the individual is confronted with the need to develop new expectations. When this continually recurs, the individual may develop a lack of confidence. When no appropriate expectations can be developed, anxiety is produced. When expectations are produced that entail negative outcomes that are seen as difficult or impossible to avoid, fear is produced. When applied to communication behavior, these last two cases are the foundation of CA.

Reinforcement is a vital component of expectancy learning. Organisms form expectations on the basis of attempting behaviors and being reinforced for some and either not reinforced or punished for others. The most gestalt expectancy is that there is regularity in the environment. This forms the basis for the development of other, more specific expectations. When no regularity can be discovered in a given situation, either because none exists or there is too little exposure to the situation to obtain sufficient observation and reinforcement, the organism is unable to develop a regular behavioral response pattern for that situation that will maximize rewards and minimize punishments. Anxiety is the cognitive response to such situations, and the behavior is unpredictable to a large extent. However, nonbehavior such as avoidance or withdrawal is probable, since even though this does not increase the probability of obtaining reward, it decreases the probability of receiving punishment in many instances. The organism essentially becomes helpless.

In the early animal research concerning helplessness, dogs were placed in an environment in which rewards and punishments were administered on a random schedule. After attempting behaviors to adapt to this environment but receiving no regular response from the environment, the dogs retreated to a corner and virtually stopped behaving. They became helpless, and some actually died (Seligman, 1975).

An analogue may be drawn with human communication behavior. We learn our communicative behavior by trying various behaviors in our environment and receiving various rewards and punishments (or absence of rewards or punishments) for our efforts. Over time and situations, we develop expectations concerning the likely outcomes of various behaviors within and across situations. Three things can occur from this process. All can occur for the same individual. However, they may occur to greatly different degrees for different individuals. All are environmentally controlled. The three things that can occur are positive expectations, negative expectations, and helplessness. Let us consider each.

When we engage in communication behaviors that work (that is, are reinforced, we achieve some desired goal), we develop positive expectations for those behaviors and they become a regular part of our communicative repertoire. While in the early childhood years much of this occurs through trial and error, during later stages of development cognition becomes more important. We may think through a situation and choose communication behaviors that our previous experience suggests we should expect to be successful. Formal instruction in communication adds to our cognitive capacity to develop such expectations and choose appropriate behaviors. To the extent our behaviors continue to be reinforced, we develop stronger positive expectations and our communication behavior becomes more regularly predictable. In addition, we develop confidence in our ability to communicate effectively. Neither anxiety nor fear — the core elements of CA — is associated with such positive expectations.

The development of negative expectations follows much the same pattern as the development of positive expectations. We discover that some communication behaviors regularly result in punishment or lack of reward and tend to reduce those behaviors. During later stages of development, we may make cognitive choices between behaviors for which we have positive and negative expectations, the former being chosen and the latter rejected. However, we may find situations for which we have no behaviors with positive expectations for success. If we can avoid or withdraw from such situations, this is a reasonable choice. However, if participation is unavoidable, we have only behaviors with negative expectations available. A fearful response is the natural outcome. Consider, for example, the person who has attempted several public speeches. In each case, the attempt resulted in punishment or lack of reward. When confronted with another situation that requires the individual to give a public speech, the person will fear that situation. The person knows what to expect, and the expectation is negative.

The development of helplessness occurs when regularity of expectations, either positive or negative, is not present. Helplessness may be either spontaneous or learned. Spontaneous helplessness occurs in new situations. If the person has never confronted the situation before, he or she may be unable to determine any behavioral options. While this is much more common for young children, adults may confront such situations. For example, visiting a foreign country where one does not understand the language may place one in a helpless condition. Similarly, some people who are divorced after many years of marriage report that they find themselves helpless in communication in the "singles scene." Such spontaneous helplessness generates strong anxiety feelings, and the behavior of people experiencing such feelings often is seen by others in the environment as highly aberrant.

Learned helplessness is produced by inconsistent receipt of reward and punishment. Such inconsistency may be a function of either true inconsistency in the environment or the inability of the individual to discriminate among situational constraints in the environment that produce differential outcomes. For example, a child may develop helplessness if the parent reinforces the child's talking at the dinner table some days and punishes it on other days. If the child is unable to determine why the parent behaves differently from day to day, the child is helpless to control the punishments and rewards. Similarly, the child may be rewarded for giving an answer in school but punished for talking to another child in the classroom. If the child is unable to see the differences in these situations, the child may learn to be helpless. When helplessness is learned, it is accompanied by strong anxiety feelings.

Learned helplessness and learned negative expectations are the foundational components of CA. The broader the helplessness or negative expectations, the more traitlike the CA. Inversely, the more situationally specific the helplessness or negative expectations, the more situational the CA. It should be stressed that helplessness and negative expectations (as well as positive expectations) are the product of an interaction of the behaviors of the individual and the responses of the other individuals in the environment. The development of the cognitive responses of the person, then, may be heavily dependent on the behavioral skills of that person, partly dependent on those skills and partly dependent on the responsiveness of the environment, or almost entirely a result of the environment. Thus any hereditary component that may exist may have either a large or small impact on later cognitions, depending on the type of environment in which the hereditarily predisposed behaviors are performed.

Learned responsiveness is seen as the opposite of learned helplessness. When the individual is able to discern differences in situations and has developed positive expectations for communication behaviors between and across differing situations, the individual has learned to be communicatively responsive. Learned responsiveness is not associated with fear or anxiety, and thus presents a circumstance antithetical to CA. Learned responsiveness can be the product of unsystematic learning in the natural environment or the direct result of formal communication instruction.

Treatment of CA

This explanation of the etiology of CA has taken a cognitive perspective. Before turning attention to possible treatments for CA, I should stress a distinction between what I will call "rational" CA and "nonrational" CA.

Rational levels of CA are produced by combinations of positive and negative expectations and helplessness or responsiveness that are consistent with views of an outside, objective observer's perceptions of reality. That is, the individual, for example, has a positive expectation for a behavior and an outside observer would agree that such a behavior should be expected to produce positive outcomes. Or, as another example, the individual feels helpless and knows of no behavior that would result in a desired outcome, and an outside observer would agree that the individual has no behavioral choice that would result in a positive outcome. Nonrational CA, on the other hand, is seen as the unjustified expectations and helplessness or responsiveness of the individual, as viewed from the perspective of an outside, objective observer. For example, the individual may have negative expectations for a behavior, but an outside observer would see the behavior as highly likely to produce a desired outcome. Or, the individual feels very responsive, but the observer sees the person's behavior as nonfunctional in the situation.

I stress this distinction in order to emphasize the fact that some people feel CA in situations where there is no objective reason for them to do so, while others may not experience CA even in situations in which they should. Past approaches to treatment, for the most part, have failed to make this distinction. It was presumed unreasonable to hold high levels of CA but reasonable to hold low levels of CA, thus only those people with high CA were seen as in need of treatment.

In my view, there are two major classifications of treatments, and they should be applied differentially depending upon whether the CA level is rational or nonrational. Let me explain. Treatments may be directed either toward communication behaviors or toward cognitions about communication behaviors. That is, our treatment focus can be on communication skills within or across contexts or on the apprehension about engaging in communication within or across contexts.

Four general conditions are illustrated in Figure 1.2. The figure represents two levels of communication skill, satisfactory and unsatisfactory, and two levels of CA, low and high. Both low CA/satisfactory skills and high CA/unsatisfactory skills are seen as rational conditions. Low CA/unsatisfactory skills and high CA/satisfactory skills are seen as nonrational conditions. Each condition provides different requirements for effective treatment.

Condition I, low CA/satisfactory skills, requires no treatment. People in this condition have rational cognitions, and most likely are reasonably effective communicators. The goal of all treatments is to move people from the other three conditions to this one.

Condition IV, high CA/unsatisfactory skills, also includes people with rational cognitions. They have unsatisfactory communication skills and are apprehensive about their communication. They have two problems, one behavioral and the other cognitive. No single solution is likely to overcome these problems and move these people to Condition

| | | Communication Skill Level | |
		Satisfactory	Unsatisfactory
	Low	Rational I	Nonrational II
Communication Apprehension Level			
	High	Nonrational III	Rational IV

Figure 1.2 Rational and Nonrational Communication Avoidance Levels

I. If only their skills are improved, they will move to Condition III but will still suffer from high CA. If only their CA is improved, they will move to Condition II but will still suffer from inadequate skills. Thus both their skill deficiencies and their CA require treatment. An analogy with basketball may help to clarify. People in Condition IV are poor foul shooters (say 30% in practice) and are very anxious about shooting foul shots in a game. If we overcome only the anxiety, they still can only shoot 30% in a game. If we only improve their shooting ability in practice, their anxiety will still cause them to miss in the game. To produce a good foul shooter, then, we need to both improve shooting accuracy and reduce anxiety. Returning to communication, people in this condition must develop better skills and reduce their apprehension to become more effective communicators.

Condition II, low CA/unsatisfactory skills, includes people with nonrational cognitions. These are people who should experience high CA, but don't. We could increase their CA, thus making their cognitions more rational, but that would only move them to Condition IV, certainly not solving a problem but only making it worse. The treatment for people in this condition is directed toward improving communication skills. If skill levels are raised, people in this condition move to Condition I, the desired condition. To employ our basketball analogy, these people are poor foul shooters but are not anxious about it. If we raise their skill level (say from 30% to 70%), we will produce good foul shooters in the regular games.

Condition III, high CA/satisfactory skills, also includes people with nonrational cognitions. These are people who should not experience high CA, but do. The treatment for people in this condition is directed toward reducing their CA level, thus moving them into Condition I. In our basketball analogy, these are people who shoot well in practice (say 70%) but choke and shoot poorly in the game (say 30%). If we overcome their anxiety, we will produce good foul shooters in the regular games.

Treatment programs intended to produce effective communicators, then, are of two general types, those directed toward improving communication skills and those directed toward reducing CA. The different types of treatment programs are different solutions to different problems and should not be expected to have major effects on problems to which they are not directed. Reducing CA, for example, should not be expected to be associated with major increases in skill levels. Similarly, improving skills should not necessarily be expected to reduce CA, since CA level may be either rational or nonrational. For people with one problem, one treatment should be chosen. For people with both problems, two treatments should be chosen.

The specific nature of treatment programs is beyond my focus here. However, for skill deficiences regular classroom instruction in communication, individualized skills training, and rhetoritherapy (Phillips, 1977) are recommended. For CA problems, systematic desensitization (McCroskey, 1972; Paul, 1966) and cognitive restructuring (Fremouw & Scott, 1979) seem to be most appropriate. Various combinations of these treatments are possible. The choice of one should not be taken to exclude use of another.

Effects of CA

The effects of CA have been the target of extensive research, particularly concerning traitlike CA, and have been summarized elsewhere (McCroskey, 1977a). My focus here will not be on such specific variable research, but rather on theoretically more global effect patterns. The previous research, although extremely valuable for generating an understanding of how CA is manifested in ongoing communicative relationships of individuals, has been subject to considerable overinterpretation, if not misinterpretation. Effects observed in aggregate data analyses often are seen as regular behavioral and outcome patterns for individual people with high or low CA. Such interpretations fail to recognize the high potential for the individual to deviate from the aggregate norm and the possibility of choosing from numerous behaviors, all of which would be theoretically consistent with the individual's CA level. My concern here, therefore, will be directed toward the internal impact of CA, possible external manifestations of CA, and the role CA plays as a mediator between communicative competence and skill and ultimate communicative behavior.

Internal Impact of CA. As I have noted previously, CA is viewed from a cognitive rather than a behavioral perspective. Although CA indeed may have some behavioral implications, as I will note below, it is experienced by the individual internally. *The only effect of CA that is predicted to be universal across both individuals and types of CA is an internally experienced feeling of discomfort.* The lower the CA, the less the internal discomfort. Since people's cognitions are imperfectly related to their levels of physiological arousal, no physiological variable is predicted to be universally associated with CA across people or across types of CA.

The implications of this conceptualization of CA for both research and treatment cannot be overemphasized. Since CA is experienced internally, the only potentially valid indicant of CA is the individual's report of that experience. Thus self-reports of individuals, whether obtained by paper-and-pencil measures or careful interviews, obtained under circumstances where the individual has nothing to gain or avoid losing by lying, provide the only potentially valid measures of CA. Measures of physiological activation and observations of behavior can provide, at best, only indirect evidence of CA and thus are inherently inferior approaches to measuring CA. Thus physiological and behavioral instruments intended to measure CA must be validated with self-report measures, not the other way around. To the extent that such measures are not related to self-report measures, they must be judged invalid. Currently available data indicate that such physiological measures and behavioral observation procedures have low to moderately low validity.[4]

External Impact of CA. As noted above, there is no behavior that is predicted to be a universal product of varying levels of CA. Nevertheless, there are some externally observable behaviors that are more likely to occur or less likely to occur as a function of varying levels of CA. When examining behavioral outcomes of CA, we must keep in mind the distinction among the types of CA discussed earlier. Traitlike CA, for example, will be manifested in behavior in a given situation only as it interacts with the constraints of that situation. A person with high traitlike CA, for example, may behave in a manner no different from anyone else in a quiet conversation with a good friend. Similarly, a person with low traitlike CA may behave in a manner no different from anyone else if called to a meeting to be reprimanded by a superior. The behavorial manifestations of high CA I will discuss here, therefore, presuppose that CA actually is present to a sufficient degree in a given situation to trigger the behavior. The link is most direct for the most situational type of CA. For traitlike CA the link is most tenuous. The behavioral prediction should be assumed to be correct only when considering aggregate behavioral indicants of the individual across time and across contexts.[5]

Three patterns of behavioral response to high CA may be predicted to be generally applicable and one pattern can be described as sometimes present, but an atypical response pattern. The three typical patterns are communication avoidance, communication withdrawal, and communication disruption. The atypical pattern is excessive communication. Let us consider each.

When people are confronted with a circumstance that they anticipate will make them uncomfortable, and they have a choice of whether or not to confront it, they may decide either to confront it and make the best of it or avoid it and thus avoid the discomfort. Some refer to this as the choice between "fight" and "flight." Research in the area of CA indicates that the latter choice should be expected in most instances. In order to avoid having to experience high CA, people may select occupations that involve low communication responsibilities, may pick housing units that reduce incidental contact with other people, may choose seats in classrooms or in meetings that are less conspicuous, and may avoid social settings. At the lowest level, is a person makes us uncomfortable, we may simply avoid being around that person. Avoidance, then, is a common behavioral response to high CA.

Avoidance of communication is not always possible. In addition, a person can find her- or himself in a situation that generates a high level of CA with no advance warning. Under such circumstances, withdrawal from communication is the behavioral pattern to be expected. This withdrawal may be completed — that is, absolute silence — or partial — that is, talking only as much as absolutely required. In a public speaking setting, this response may be represented by the very short speech. In a meeting, class, or small group discussion, it may be represented by talking only when called upon. In a dyadic interaction, it may be represented by answering questions only or supplying agreeing responses with no initiation of discussion.

Communication disruption is the third typical behavioral pattern associated with high CA. The person may have disfluencies in verbal presentation or unnatural nonverbal behaviors. Equally as likely are poor choices of communicative strategies, sometimes reflected in the after-the-fact "I wish I had (had not) said . . . " phenomenon. It is important to note, however, that such behaviors may be produced by inadequate communication skills as well as by high CA. Thus inferring CA from observations of such behavior is not always appropriate.

Overcommunication is a response to high CA that is not common but is the pattern exhibited by a small minority. This behavior represents overcompensation. It may reflect the "fight" rather than the "flight" reaction, the attempt to succeed in spite of the felt discomfort. The person who elects to take a public speaking course in spite of her or his extreme stage fright is a classic example. Less easily recognizable is the individual with high CA who attempts to dominate social situations. Most of the time people who employ this behavioral option are seen as poor communicators but are not recognized as having high CA; in fact, they may be seen as people with very low CA.

To this point we have looked at the typical behaviors of people with high CA levels. We might assume that the behaviors of people with low CA would be the exact reverse. That assumption might not always be correct. While people with low CA should be expected to seek opportunities to communicate rather than avoid them, and to dominate interactions in which they are members rather than withdraw from them, people with low CA may also have disrupted communication and overcommunicate. The disruptions may stem from pushing too hard rather than tension, but the behaviors may not always be distinctly different to the observer. Similarly, persons who overcommunicate engage in very similar behavior whether the behavior stems from high or low CA. While future research may permit us to train observers who can distinguish disrupted communication resulting from high CA from that resulting from low CA and possibly distinguish between overcommunication behaviors stemming from the two causes, these behaviors are, and probably will remain, indistinguishable by the average person in the communication situation.

CA and Communication Behavior. Without discounting a possible role for hereditary predispositions, I view communication behavior, as other human behavior, as a learned response to one's environment. Since I wish to explore the role of CA as it relates to human communication behavior more generally, it is important to enunciate my assumptions about human learning. Following the lead of contemporary writers in educational psychology, I view human learning as composed of three domains: the cognitive (understanding or knowing),[6] the affective (feeling of liking or disliking), and the psychomotor (the physical capability of doing).

Because of inconsistent and confused use of terms within the communication literature, when I apply these domains to communication learning it is important that I make a distinction between communication "competence" and communication "skill." I see communication competence as falling within the cognitive domain and communication skill as falling within the psychomotor domain. More specifically, communication competence is "the ability of an individual to demonstrate knowledge of the appropriate communicative behavior in a given situation" (Larson, Backlund, Redmond, & Barbour, 1978, p. 16). Communication competence, then, can be demonstrated by observing a communication situation and identifying behaviors that would be appropriate or inappropriate in that situation. Communication skill, on the other hand, involves actual psychomotor behavior. Communication skill is the ability of an individual to perform appropriate communicative behavior in a given situation. To be judged skilled, then, a person must be able to engage physically in appropriate behaviors.

The three components of desired communication learning, then, are communication competence (knowing and understanding appropriate communication behaviors), communication skill (being able to produce appropriate communication behaviors physically), and positive communication affect (liking and wanting to produce appropriate communication behaviors). Any desired impact on long-term behavior of the individual requires that production of all of these types of learning be achieved, whether by the "natural" environment, by a formal instructional system, or by some combination of the two.

CA can have a major impact in all three areas of communication learning, and, consequently, on the long-term behavior of individuals. High CA is seen as a potential inhibitor of the development of both communication competence and communication skill and as a direct precursor of negative communication affect. Low CA, on the other hand, is seen as a facilitator of the development of communication competence and communication skill and as a precursor of positive communication affect.

With regard to communication competence, high CA is projected as a barrier to accurate observation of the natural environment and sufficient experience within it and as a barrier to the formal study of communication. Not only do people try to avoid studying things that cause them discomfort, but such discomfort may inhibit their learning when they do study it. The projected pattern for learning communication skills is seen in the same way. A major facet of psychomotor learning is practice. High CA will lead to less practice and possible misinterpretations of the outcomes of what practice is attempted. The impact of CA in terms of communication affect is even more direct. If we are fearful or anxious about something, we are not given to liking it. On the other hand, things that are not threatening are more likely to generate positive affect.

A major conclusion we can draw from this conceptualization of CA and communication learning is that high CA is highly associated with ineffective communication. As such, CA must be considered a central concern of any instructional program concerned with more effective communication as a targeted outcome, whether the program is labeled a program in communication competence or a program in communication skill. Basic competencies and basic skills cannot be separated from the problem of high CA.

NOTES

1. Criticisms of the 20- and 25-item PRCA instruments have been directed toward a heavy emphasis on items relating to public speaking in those instruments. This problem has been overcome in the most recent form of the measure, PRCA-24 (McCroskey, 1982). For this reason the new form is to be preferred over the earlier versions. This instrument permits four subscores as well as an overall score. The reliability of the instrument (internal) is estimated at .94 and the total score correlates with the earlier forms above .90. Data from over 25,000 subjects indicate that the score form a normal distribution, with a mean of 65.6 and a standard deviation of 15.3.

2. It has been demonstrated repeatedly in the personality literature that any given personality variable may be relevant to behavioral prediction for some people but not for all people. People scoring in the midrange of the measure are least predictable. For such people, the variable may be irrelevant and their behavior may be controlled by the situation and/or other personality characteristics. For a discussion of these problems, see Bem and Allen (1974) and Bem and Funder (1978).

3. These observations were made during data collection for the study reported by Ertle (1969).

4. For earlier research, see Clevenger (1959). More recently, it has been found that although self-reported traitlike CA, as measured by the PRCA, is not highly correlated with physiological arousal, as measured by heart rate, the two combined are able to predict over 80% of the variance in self-reported state apprehension, as measured by a modification of the Speilberger state anxiety measure. The beta weights for the two predictors are nearly equal with little colinearity. See Behnke and Beatly (1981).

5. For suggestions for testing this type of prediction, see Jaccard and Daly (1980). Recent research reports validity coefficients in the neighborhood of .50 for the PRCA and a measure of shyness when tested in this way. See McCroskey and Richmond (1981).

6. My use of "cognitive" previously referred to the distinction made in psychology between "cognitivists" and "behaviorists." This is a broader use of the term than the one relating to the domains of learning. The reader should avoid confusing the two usages.

2

A Conception of Shyness

ARNOLD H. BUSS

This chapter attempts to organize psychological knowledge and understanding of shyness, making various distinctions and attempting to
integrate them into a coherent system. There are four parts: a
description of the various phenomena called shyness, differentiation of
shyness from related reactions, the major causes of shy reactions, and
the personality trait of shyness.

The Reaction

Shyness may be defined as discomfort, inhibition, and awkwardness
in social situations, especially with people who are not familiar. Some of
these aspects are more observable than others. Its most observable
aspect is the *instrumental* or action component. Actually, it is the
relative *absence* of instrumental activity that identifies shyness: withdrawal, reticence, and inhibition. When we are shy, we tend to remain
on the fringe of a conversational group, do not speak up, mumble
minimal replies if addressed, and in general fail to hold up our end of
the social interaction. When the reaction is especially acute, social
behavior can become so disorganized as to produce shaking of the
limbs, clumsy gestures, and stuttering. When possible, we avoid or
escape from social contact that is so aversive.

Less observable than the instrumental component is the emotional
component, which consists of fear, self-consciousness, or both. If fear
predominates, there are likely to be the various somatic reactions that
characterize reactivity of the sympathetic division of the autonomic
nervous system: rapid breathing, quickened heart rate, elevated blood
pressure, and sweating. If awareness of self predominates — in this
instance, awareness of oneself as a social object — the reaction is more
likely to be blushing, which represents parasympathetic reactivity. The

blushing reaction would seem to connote a milder form of shyness, whereas the fear reaction is more intense.

The *cognitive* component is synonymous with what is experienced, which may be fear or self-awareness. If fear predominates, we experience panic in the immediate situation and worry about future social encounters. If excessive self-consciousness predominates, we suffer the intense discomfort of feeling naked, vulnerable, and inept, together with concern about saying or doing something dumb, awkward, or foolish.

All three components ordinarily occur together, though they are not equally discernible. Behavioral inhibition and disorganization are obvious to any observer, but the emotional reactions of fear or acute self-consciousness are more subtle. And the cognitive component, being closed to observation, can be known only if the experiencing person reveals it.

Furthermore, there are individual differences in which component is most salient. For some people, shyness is essentially behavioral inhibition or disorganization, and they suffer little from the emotional or cognitive components of shyness. For others, the somatic reactions and the blushing are most prominent. For the remainder, it is the cognitive or experiential component that marks their shyness. We should not be surprised, then, that there is no uniform pattern of shyness. Rather, when any of the three components occurs in a social context, we can reasonably infer shyness. In this conception, it makes little sense to suggest that any one of the components represents shyness to the exclusion of the other two.

Dividing shyness into instrumental, emotional, and cognitive aspects, though a reasonable expositional device that may help to organize a complex domain, involves little theory. In a more speculative vein, shyness may be divided into the kind that appears early in life and the kind that appears later. The early-appearing form has been called *stranger anxiety* or *wariness* (see Sroufe, 1977, for a review). Occurring in human infants in the first year of life and also in many animals, it consists of a fear of unfamiliar members of the species, a retreat from them, and even a subsequent avoidance of them. The later-appearing form occurs in older human children and requires the prior development of a sense of oneself as a social object, which does not occur in animals or in human infants. There is indirect evidence that this social self first appears during the fourth or fifth year of life (Buss, Iscoe, & Buss, 1979). Thereafter children are susceptible to the kind of shyness that involves acute self-consciousness: They may feel conspicuous and psychologically unprotected. This later, self-conscious shyness, a bashfulness that sometimes includes blushing, seems to be different from the early-developing kind of shyness, which involves the more intense emotion of fear.

Immediate Causes of Transient Shyness

The most important cause of transient shyness is *novelty.* Both animals and humans are cautious in a strange situation, especially in the presence of strangers. We know that most infants react to strangers with fear or wariness (Sroufe, 1977). Most of our lives are spent in familiar surroundings, but when we move to a new city, state, or country or to a new school or job, the strange context is likely to make us inhibited and careful in our social behavior.

More interesting psychologically is novelty of social role. In the course of growing up, we inevitably trade childish roles for more mature ones. Adolescence is a period of rapidly changing roles, when childish roles are no longer rewarded or sought after, and when adult roles are still as new and uncomfortable as a new pair of tight shoes. Adding to the problems of early adolescence are the rapid changes in body height, weight, and secondary sex characteristics, so that adolescents must suffer through the double novelty of both roles and their own bodies. Small wonder, then, that adolescence is the age of greatest shyness.

Formality can also elicit shyness. formal situations are those in which the social script is spelled out in more detail, and we are expected to adhere to the script more closely than in informal situations. The best examples of formal situations are ceremonial, public events: funerals, weddings, graduations, and religious ceremonies. Other examples occur in the world of business, in which bankers and lawyers, for example, are supposed to dress appropriately, use forms of address that connote politeness, and generally follow a rigid code of conduct to the letter. Courts of law and the military also emphasize *status* differences among the participants. Those low in status are likely to be tentative and anxious because they are expected to stick closer to the social rules and will be punished if they make mistakes. Thus the problems with formal situations are that (1) the greater number of rules and the greater insistence of following these rules make it more likely that one will make a mistake, and (2) the public nature of formal situations renders people more exposed and vulnerable.

A major cause of shyness is *social attention*, especially the extremes of the attention we receive from others. No one wants to be ignored; most of us prefer not remaining isolated in a group, and being shunned by others causes a feeling of awkwardness and discomfort (Fenigstein, 1979). Being conspicuous or being stared at also tends to be aversive. Shyness is likely to be the reaction of a girl in a roomful of boys or of a jockey among a team of professional basketball players. Similarly, when all eyes are on us — arriving late at a party, for instance, and finding that everyone present stops to look at us — we are likely to shrink back and look for a place to hide. Only the middle ground of social attention produces psychological comfort: We want our existence to be acknowledged, and we want to be looked at or listened to, but we do not want to receive the excessively focused attention that comes with conspicuousness.

The last immediate cause of shyness consists of *breaches of privacy*. We are strongly socialized to recognize a firm line between acts permitted in private and those permitted in public. A variety of toilet behavior and sexual acts are permitted in private but not in public. When there is a breach of privacy and a private act is made public, the reaction is inevitably one of embarrassment. Such bashfulness may be considered a part of shyness, the part that shades off into blushing and the most extreme awareness of oneself as a social object.

In brief, there are four categories of immediate causes of shyness. Novelty includes not only strangers but also newness in social role, social context, and body. Formality includes not only situations in which rules are more clearly spelled out but also situations in which there is a status discrepancy between the participants. Social attention involves too much attention (conspicuousness) or too little (shunning). Breach of privacy includes those embarrassing occasions when the public-private barrier is inadvertently broken down.

Shyness Versus Related Reactions

Shyness may be regarded as a subcategory of *social anxiety*, which is discomfort and inhibition in social settings. The other major subcategory of social anxiety is *audience anxiety*, which consists of discomfort and inhibition (sometimes disorganization) when performing in front of a group. The performance is usually a speech, and for those interested in speech communication, speech anxiety is equivalent to audience anxiety. We should not forget, however, that performances in front of an audience also include what is done by actors, musicians, clowns, jugglers, dancers, and athletes. Shyness is different from audience anxiety mainly in that shyness occurs only in the context of small conversational or other social groups in which there is a give and take of interaction; there is no audience, no performance, and less evaluation. In conversational groups, one person may occasionally become conspicuous, but conspicuousness is an ever-present and crucial aspect of audience anxiety. Thus, though audience anxiety and shyness share some attributes, they are distinct. Furthermore, it has been estimated that audience anxiety is one of the most common fears, whereas shyness is less frequent. If people were asked to give a speech and to meet a stranger, more people would be apprehensive about the speech than about meeting a stranger. It is a reasonable guess that most shy people also have audience anxiety, but only a minority of those with audience anxiety would be characterized as shy.

Shyness is relatively easy to separate from *test anxiety*, which involves fear of the consequences of having one's achievements or abilities evaluated. Most such evaluations are nonsocial in the sense that the person merely sits down and takes a test. When the evaluation is oral, as in an interview, it shades over into shyness. The difference between shyness and test anxiety, then, is that shyness concerns discomfort when engaging in everyday social behavior, whereas test anxiety involves a fear of failing a test of one's general (usually not social) abilities or achievements.

As a social anxiety, shyness is part of the much larger category of *fearfulness*. Fear is general in the sense that it involves both social and nonsocial contexts. A fearful person is likely to fear not only other people but also airplanes, deep water, hospitals, and a variety of physical dangers. We expect a majority of fearful people to be shy, but only a minority of shy people are expected to be generally fearful; the correlation between the two is .50 (Cheek & Buss, 1981).

Many psychologists have implicitly assumed that shyness is nothing more than low sociability; and, in fact, shyness items may be found on most sociability questionnaires. There is now empirical evidence on this issue (Cheek & Buss, 1981). Sociability was defined as the tendency to affiliate with others and to prefer to be with them. Shyness was defined in terms of the reaction to being with strangers or casual acquaintances: tension, feelings of awkwardness or discomfort, and inhibition of social behavior. Items were constructed that assessed either sociability or shyness as just defined. The questionnaire, consisting of 14 items was administered to 912 college men and women (there were no gender differences). A factor analysis yielded separate factors for sociability and shyness, with only one of the sociability items having a significant factor loading on the shyness scale. The items were as follows:

Sociability

(1)   I like to be with people.
(2)   I welcome the opportunity to mix socially with people.
(3)   I prefer working with others rather than alone.
(4)   I find people more stimulating than anything else.
(5)   I'd be unhappy if I were prevented from making many social contacts.

Shyness

(1)   I am socially somewhat awkward.
(2)   I don't find it hard to talk to stangers. (reversed)
(3)   I feel tense when I'm with people I don't know well.
(4)   When conversing, I worry about saying something dumb.
(5)   I feel nervous when speaking to someone in authority.
(6)   I am often uncomfortable at parties and other social functions.
(7)   I feel inhibited in social situations.
(8)   I have trouble looking someone right in the eye.
(9)   I am more shy with members of the opposite sex.

The shyness and sociability measures correlated $-.30$, which means that sociable people tend to be unshy and unsociable people tend to be shy. The size of the correlation, however, suggests that this linkage is not strong and that there are sizable minorities who are both sociable and shy or both unsociable and unshy. Fearfulness correlated a nonsignificant $-.09$ with sociability but a highly significant .50 with shyness. Self-esteem correlated .18 with sociability and $-.51$ with shyness.

Thus shyness and sociability may be regarded as separate personality traits. This conclusion is based on self-reports, and it was important to demonstrate that these two traits might each affect social behavior. Accordingly, in the same study, college women were selected who were high or low on either trait, yielding four groups of subjects: shy-sociable, unshy-sociable, shy-unsociable, and unshy-unsociable. Pairs of women who were matched on both traits were allowed to get to know one another in a bogus waiting room situation and were surreptitiously videotaped. Shy subjects were more tense than unshy subjects and reported afterward that they were more inhibited, but the trait of sociability also made a difference in their behavior. Most of the differences between shy and unshy subjects were caused, unexpectedly, by the behavior of the shy-sociable subjects; They spent less time talking, averted their gaze more, touched themselves more (nervously), and observers judged them to be more tense than the other three groups. Thus sociable behavior was determined not only by the trait of shyness but also by the trait of sociability. On the basis of the laboratory and self-report data, we can conclude that although shyness and sociability are related, they are separate enough for shyness to be something more than low sociability.

Determinants of the Trait

Inheritance

Strange as it may seem to social scientists who are trained to be environmentalists, there may be an inherited component in shyness. The word "component" is important here, for there is no implication that any genetic disposition inexorably causes shyness, is totally responsible for shyness, or cannot be altered by environmental manipulation. Thus the term "inherited component" means that there is a built-in tendency to act in a way that is likely to lead to shyness, but always in the context of particular environments.

As mentioned earlier, sociability correlates −.30 with shyness. Sociability is known to have an inherited component (Buss & Plomin, 1975), and to the extent that this component is involved in shyness (granted, the correlation of −.30 is moderate), shyness can be said to have an inherited basis. Unsociable people may be mistaken for being shy because they are reticent, are less involved with casual acquaintances, and find social interaction less rewarding them do social people. We are not concerned here with the confusion between sociability and shyness, but with how low sociability might contribute to shyness. Unsociable people have fewer contacts with others and tend to leave social contexts faster than do sociable people (by definition). Thus unsociable children are less likely to habituate to the arousal (often reaching the level of fear) that accompanies strangers and strange social situations. Stranger anxiety is well known in young children. If habituation does not occur, arousal is likely to remain at an uncomfortable level, and such children are likely to feel tense in new social situations and to avoid them if possible. The less time spent with peers, the less likely children are to acquire the social skills that would help them in dealing with others. When children lack the instrumental skills that would facilitate social give and take, they tend to lack confidence, hold back in interacting with others, and feel unconfortable. In brief, unsociability can lead to shyness because, by reducing social contact, it prevents habituation to novelty and slows the learning of the social skills that minimize shyness.

Shyness also correlates .50 with fearfulness. Although we should not infer causation from correlation, in this instance there may be a logical basis suggesting causation. Is it likely that shyness (fear in social situations) spills over and generalizes to all situations, both social and nonsocial? No. It is more likely that children who are generally fearful will tend to be afraid not only in nonsocial situations but also in social situations. Fear seems to lead to shyness, not the other way around. Fearfulness, part of the temperament of emotionality, has been found to have a strong inherited component (Buss & Plomin, 1975).

Children who are physically unattractive tend to be less successful in their sociation interactions, and this is especially true in adolescence when they must deal with the opposite gender. Unattractiveness is likely to cause diminished confidence and, when dealing with members of the opposite sex, a feeling that one may be rejected; unattractive children are often teased mercilessly. Physical attractiveness can be enhanced by a variety of maneuvers, but it is still largely inherent.

In summary, there may be three inherited tendencies that predispose children to become shy: fearfulness, unsociability, and unattractiveness. The correlations among these three tendencies are sufficiently low that some of their effects may be additive. Thus the child who is predisposed by inheritance to be fearful, unsociable, and unattractive is well on his or her way to being shy.

Personal History

Personal history plays a major role in the development of shyness. Children may not be exposed to novel social contexts frequently enough for them to habituate to the arousal or to develop the requisite social skills. Whereas unsociable children may take themselves out of social interaction, sociable children — who are not reluctant to get involved — may be denied the opportunity. Those brought up in isolated communities are more likely to become shy than are those who live in more densely populated areas and who can therefore meet many strangers. Thus lack of experience (leading to no habituation and failure to develop social skills) can occur because the child is deprived of the needed interaction (environment) or because the child chooses not to interact (personality).

Earlier, self-esteem was reported to correlate –.51 with shyness. Shy people tend to hang back when with casual acquantances and therefore come off as dull and uninteresting; their social failures can depress their self-esteem. And those low in self-esteem tend to lack confidence in their social contacts and therefore are timid, bashful, and inhibited. Clearly, shyness causes low self-esteem, and low self-esteem causes shyness, and the two are likely to interact in a vicious cycle. To the extent that low self-esteem causes shyness, however, it may be considered an environmental determinant, for all extant approaches to self-esteem agree that it originates in the *experiences* of each individual.

Awareness of oneself as as social object varies considerably from one person to the next, and there is a self-report instrument (Fenigstein, Scheier, & Buss, 1975) for which there is considerable construct validity (Buss, 1980). Typical items deal with concern about making a good impression and with being aware of appearance and with one's style of doing things. The trait would seem to originate in the way we are socialized, for some parents and other socializing agents emphasize manners, propriety, and the importance of making a good impression. Such socialization varies considerably in both intensity and impact on children, producing marked individual differences in public self-consciousness. This trait correlates .26 with shyness, and therefore it must be added to the list of environmental determinants of shyness.

In brief, it is theorized here that there are three personal history determinants of the trait of shyness: lack of experience, low self-esteem, and public self-consciousness. There are three genetic determinants: fearfulness, low sociability, and lack of physical attractiveness.

Remediation

Shyness need not be a permanent part of anyone's personality. In attempting to remedy shyness, we must recognize the different sources of the problem. If shyness originates in an inherited tendency to become fearful, we cannot hope to alter this tendency much, but we can cope with the stimuli that trigger the fear, for they are largely acquired. One therapy that is specifically designed for fear is *systematic desensitization*, in which the client makes up a hierarchy of feared situations and then is taught to relax to progressively more intense stimuli. If the therapy is successful, the client reacts more calmly to these particular stimuli — in this instance, novel social situations — although other fears may remain.

If the problem stems from low sociability and a consequent lack of experience, the person would have to be informed of the dilemma: Either force yourself to become more sociable or put up with the discomfort of shyness. If the person decides that getting rid of his or her shyness is worth putting up with the negatives of social interaction, some kind of milieu therapy would be advisable. The client would participate with others with similar problems and engage in play-acting in various social contexts to practice social skills under conditions of minimal aversiveness.

The therapeutic approach would be similar if the shyness derived principally from low self-esteem. Such shy people need to develop confidence that they are socially worthwhile and will be accepted by others. Assuming that they have social skills, they should be allowed to use these skills with others who are likely to accept them and respond to them. It must be acknowledged, however, that when the problem is low self-esteem, successful remediation is difficult to achieve, for those low in self-esteem are too ready to believe in their own lack of worth and too ready to accept rejection as their due.

If the problem is a lack of social skills, these can be taught. Young people can learn how to converse on a date, how to join in the fun at a party, and how to make appointments and lunch dates by telephone. Some people need to be taught which social cues are relevant and which responses are appropriate. Normally, such information is available to us, but some people have not managed to acquire it. Information and practice at social interaction should work well if there are no complicating issues.

If it is acute public self-consciousness that underlies the shyness, the optimal solution is to teach the person to divert attention from himself or herself. It would also help to demonstrate that most people are not as aware of us as we may suppose they are. These two procedures — diminishing self-consciousness and diverting attention from self — should markedly reduce bashfulness.

Summary

Shyness is defined in terms of several reactions in social situations, some observable and some not; the major components are instrumental (inhibition), emotional (discomfort or arousal), and cognitive (worry or acute self-awareness). Two kinds of shyness can be distinguished: an early-appearing stranger anxiety, present in animals and human infants, and a later-appearing self-conscious shyness, present only in older human children and adults. Shyness can be distinguished from speech anxiety, test anxiety, fearfulness, and sociability. The immediate causes of shyness are novelty, formality, the extremes of attention from others, and breaches of the public-private barrier.

Shyness is also a personality trait. Its genetic causes are the inherited traits of fearfulness and sociability, and the inherited tendency to be physically unattractive. Its personal history causes are lack of social experience, low self-esteem, and high public self-consciousness. For each of these various cause there is a therapeutic method that is likely to alleviate the shyness, although some causes (especially the genetic ones) may be refractory to intervention.

These various assertions are hypotheses that belong to an integrated conception of shyness. Some represent extrapolations from data, and some are not based on any data but suggest which data we need. Some of the theoretical assertions can be tested easily, but others would required the complexity and difficulty of a longitudinal study. Given the usual fate of theoretical statements, some are likely to be proven wrong, but even the incorrect assertions may help to clarify thinking about shyness.

3

Reticence

A Perspective on Social Withdrawal

GERALD M. PHILLIPS

The Definition of Reticence

When people fear flying, they can stay on the ground. In fact, celebrities like Ray Bradbury and Isaac Asimov surrender possibilities for personal appearances because they refuse to fly. It is a matter of personal choice and of little consequence. There is therapy available for those who fear flying, and sometimes it works, but it is entirely possible to avoid flying and still live a perfectly satisfactory life. Millions of people do it every day.

There are a great number of human activities that cannot be avoided. One can hardly avoid death and taxes, nor is it possible to avoid daily greetings to people, dealing with tradespeople, asking and answering questions, and carrying on one's duties on the job. There are few people who can avoid talk during the course of a day, and there is no way to avoid being evaluated on the way you talk. Talk is the way we convey our personalities. In fact, personality, according to Harry Stack Sullivan (Perry, 1982), is nothing more than the regular interpersonal contacts one carries on — by talking.

Those who fear gliding down slopes can eschew skiing. Those who cannot learn to coordinate eye and hand to hit a ball accurately can find alternatives to golf. There are some things people cannot learn to do, and some things they fear doing. When these fears and incompetencies affect something people *must* do, their quality of life is seriously compromised. This is the premise on which the theory of reticent behavior is based.

Becker (1971) defines speech as the distinguishing characteristic of the human species. Through it, we identify ourselves as singular people and affiliate with our fellow creatures to form families and communities. We carry on our business and govern ourselves through talk. Disputes and their resolutions are composed of talk, as are so many of our entertainments. We share our ideas, express love and hate, maintain the common enterprise, and work for the good of the order as well as for personal fulfillment through talk. We even bind time so our history can affect the future. Instruction is carried on mainly through talk. Our writing is redacted talk, frozen speech (Fry, 1977).

It is important to be able to speak. Speaking well is usually associated with effective living. Our speech connects us with other human creatures, whom we try to influence in order that our own lives can be improved. Recent social commentators (Lasch, 1978; Yankelovich, 1981; Zweig, 1980) have noted a trend in our society toward "narcissism," a situation where self-awareness and personal concern is so great that it interferes with effective contact between people. We are racing toward a sociopathological society (Phillips, 1982), characterized by inconsiderate, hence ineffective, communication between humans. Sophisticated computers and communication devices have separated people from one another and promise to complicate interpersonal interaction materially (Jennings, 1982).

Some people cannot communicate well, and because they cannot communicate well the quality of their life is affected. Sometimes they are consumed with anxiety about their communication. Sometimes they erect defenses against situations that they know they cannot handle. Sometimes they blunder ahead ineptly and take the consequences. Their ineptitude costs them heavily in their careers, for careers are advanced through communication. Their ineptitude costs them heavily in personal relationships, for people are judged by what they say and how they say it. People who do no talk much are not valued much, or they are regarded as conceited and aloof. Either way, it is hard to make friends unless there is some substantial communication.

When people *avoid communication because they believe they will lose more by talking than by remaining silent,* we refer to it as *reticence.* It is an application of Freud's "pleasure principle." Communication causes them pain, so they attempt to avoid it. It provides little pleasure for them, but at least their worst fears of disaster due to poor communication performance are not fulfilled. Gradually, avoidance of communication becomes a style of life. The individual adapts to a pattern of avoidance behavior and acquires a personality based on avoidance of communication. Such people do not comprehend the possibility of pleasure from human interaction. Their relationships, at best, are tenuous. They feel they are allowed to relate to others on sufferance. They are uneasy about their relationships because they do not believe they can do anything about them. They feel their interpersonal fate lies always in the activity of others, and they expect to be disregarded, ignored, patronized, indulged, hurt, and often cast off at the whim of others. So be it! They are reticent. They know what they know and what they know is that they cannot communicate.

The decision to be reticent is a utilitarian formulation. The individual believes it best to avoid losing. Since losing is associated with talking, losses can be minimized simply by avoiding participation. Paradoxically, the notion is based on a utopian premise that says, in essence, some people "got it" and some do not. Speakers are speakers and the other people must take the rap. That, in essence, is the belief structure of the reticent human.

Some, when given a reason to do so, will examine themselves by modifying both beliefs and behaviors. Others never recognize the reason for their lack of success in human relationships. They ascribe their failures on the job to capriciousness of the power structure. Their failures in interpersonal relationships are either chalked up to the deceitful nature of others, or minimized by the construction of walls that keep other people out. They mostly believe that there is some magic formula through which they can become effective people. They may take est or sensitivity training; they may be found in assertiveness groups or in standard psychotherapy. They may drink or take drugs. Whatever, they are not seeking a solution to their problems through communication training, and every illusionary solution takes them further away from the possibility of retraining their communication skills.

Beliefs Associated with Reticent Behavior

Reticent speakers have a belief system replete with myths and unsubstantiated formulas for success. There is a huge "self-help" industry in our society that capitalizes on these beliefs. The popular book by Robert J. Ringer (1978); *Looking Out for No. 1*, made a direct appeal to people who cherished some of these ideas and were willing to part with money for nostrums. Reticent students who come for retraining generally come with a history of seeking relief for their social disqualification. Some have read books or articles about how to be a more effective person. They learn to "dress right," or they have a set of beliefs they seem unable to activate. Many have been in counseling, tried encounter groups and assertiveness programs, and some have even tried Toastmasters or Dale Carnegie. Most of them, adults and students alike, are connected in some way with activities. They join organizations in the hope they will "meet someone." It is interesting to note that those who have no sense of their problem, ones that do not come forward for help, seem oblivious to these social needs. They are characteristic blunderers, appear inept and untrustworthy, and do not earn high grades. There is no way to find out whether they care, but they do not *act* as if they care. Caring is the significant report in the life histories of reticent people.

Effective speakers are born, not made. Reticent speakers report a basic genetic belief in the principle that effective speaking is a hereditary endowment. While many of them keep trying, they excuse their failures on the grounds they "just don't have it." They express envy of people they perceive to be more effective than they, and sometimes indulge themselves in elaborate fantasies of defeating these people in some kind of social game. What they do not understand is how to observe specific behaviors in order to model after them. Most effective speakers can ascribe at least part of their success to imitation of skillful behavior they observe in others. Reticents tend to have heroes like media personalities who are not amenable to imitation.

Learning skillful speaking is unethical because it is "manipulation." Reticent speakers tend to believe in a linear system of influence. They suspect that some people have a "formula" of proper phrases and expressions that invariably "cause" behavior in others. Reticents excuse their own failures on the grounds that they do not know the system, and, furthermore, it would be unethical to learn it, since it is unethical to manipulate behavior in others. The notion of rhetoric as a system of persuasion designed to influence but not cause decisions is hard for them to grasp. They are functional behaviorists locked into a stimulus-response mentality that makes it difficult to administer instruction to them, since they are constantly looking for immediate total change. Once they are trained to pay attention to small gains, instructional progress is possible.

Speech is not important. Most people talk too much. Reticents tend to undervalue oral discourse. They dismiss small talk as a silly waste of time. They claim anyone who makes decisions about other people based on small talk is too stupid to associate with. In this sense, reticents reveal a kind of social arrogance that may play a more important role in their social syndrome than we can presently document. We have always operated on the assumption that reticent behavior was disqualifying, a hardship. There is reason to believe that at least some reticent speakers use their communication withdrawal as an indication of personal arrogance, a form of social superiority somewhat like the intellectual's affectation of refusing to watch television. "Ordinary people talk to one another," the formula goes, "but I am superior enough to be able to make decisions without resorting to something so trivial." The corollary belief is the "vibe," some kind of personal emanation that makes it possible to make infallible decisions about the worth of others. Speech interferes with vibes, it is a sham affected by people who wish to conceal their true personality, and, thus, the tool of those who would unethically control others.

I can speak whenever I want to. But I am a good listener and I don't want to speak very often. This is a deception and consolation indulged in by a great many reticent speakers. It is corollary to the preceding notion. If speech is not important, then it is not important to speak much. Reticents can conceive of some occasions when speech might be important, but they are able to make it seem so simple that they can honestly convince themselves they could handle the situations should they arise. By cleverly avoiding testing themselves, they can preserve their myth and their silence. By ascribing to themselves the quality of "good listener," they assume what they believe to be an important social role. The problem is, they are usually *not* good listeners. Most are locked in their speculative fantasies while other people are talking. Since they know they will not respond, it is not necessary for them to listen with response in mind. This being the case, it is not necessary for them to listen at all, although most know they must *look as if they are listening.* A great many reticent speakers habituate a nodding pattern designed to convince others of their rapt attention.

Better to remain silent and let people think you are a fool than to speak and prove it to them. There is more than just a touch of paranoia associated with reticent behavior. Reticents believe that other people pay a great deal of attention to them. In fact, their anti-Copernican notion of the universe leads them to believe that it is a preoccupation with others to wander about evaluating people according to their speaking patterns. Reticents believe that ineffective speech will lead others to evaluate them as "stupid fools" (a phrase which occurs in virtually every interview with reticents). It is bad to be a "stupid fool," but if one does not talk, others cannot obtain data on which to base the evaluation. Thus, silence is seen as a method of concealment, not of stupidity and foolishness, for reticents do not believe they *are* stupid and foolish, but of inadvertent inept behavior that they believe they indulge in because they do not "have it." Thus, the circle remains unbroken. Reticents can explain *why* they are reticent and why they *stay* reticent. The whole belief system adds up to an effective resistance against modification.

Inherent in the reticent thought system is a firm belief in the medical model. Reticents believe that deviations from normal are pathologies that can be treated. They regard their own disability as a disease, and they seek some form of applied treatment to obtain relief. Two prominent methods of treatment are behavior modification and sensitivity training. Neither seems effective with reticent students because both regard subjects as entirely consistent in problem and needs. Treatments like desensitization, for example, are effective under laboratory conditions, but have little carry-over into life speaking experiences. Reticents can be made less anxious about *thinking about* speaking, although there is little evidence of carry-over. Kleinsasser's (1968) intensive investigations into the effects of desensitization on *actual speaking ability* are highly important. His discovery was that neither treatment nor placebo worked, but those subjects who simply sat around and talked with others while they waited seemed to experience the most improvement.

Sensitivity training was a consummate disaster. Designed to make people more responsive to the needs of others, it created a situation where reticents had lugubrious personal confessions sessions in which they confessed their fears and angers to each other, then became suspicious because other people knew too much about them, and finally lapsed into an even stonier silence than the one that brought them to the experience. Similar results have been observed with programs like est and assertiveness. What happens seems to be the construction of a "monster," voluble and pushy right up to the first failure. Then the whole edifice comes crashing down, everything that was learned (if anything at all was learned) is cast off, and the individual reverts to the comfort of reticent behavior.

Rejection of the medical model is imperative for effective retraining (Phillips, 1977). It is also imperative to recognize the individual differences in the reticent syndrome. Each reticent speaker has his or her own patterns, pressures, and prehistory. The idea is to ignore all of it, to examine the behavior as a technologist might, and to apply whatever informed training systems are available to solve particular performance problems (Varela, 1978). Selection of the term "rhetoritherapy" was more than just a gimmick designed to distract attention from psychological variables. It was a direct effort to draw attention to the singular quality of each case of reticence, to indicate the need to design training systems for the individual, and to evaluate progress in terms of goal accomplishment (Mager, 1972) rather than global feelings. By basing progress assessments on *both* personal report of direct accomplishments and observation of those accomplishments by others, attention can be taken from internal feelings and focused on observable attainment. The process is both empirical and rhetorical; it is *not* psychological or medical. Furthermore, the method contains the qualities of restructuring of the point of view (Beck, 1976) reticents have about themselves and their interactions, as well as inculcating a heuristic capability to solve new problems as they are presented (Phillips, 1981).

Reticent humans see themselves failing at most social enterprises. They will not argue because they know they will lose; they do not ask questions because they despair of getting the syntax right; they avoid social contact because they fear rejection; they choose their work to avoid talk. They are often desperately lonely and bored and they despair of influencing the outcome of events around them. They are also often intrinsically highly intelligent. The reticents who come forward for retraining are measurably more accomplished in their coursework than the norm. What is saddest of all is that society is denied their talents because they choose to conceal them.

The Consequences of Reticent Behavior

People who are not able to communicate well experience a number of depressing emotional states. *Loneliness* refers to involuntary separation from others, inability to make regular human contacts and to sustain desired relationships. *Boredom* refers to a state of ennui characterized by a sameness in activities usually conducted apart from others. *Ineffectuality* refers to inability to influence events or make an impact on the social environment. *Narcissism* is a self-defeating state resulting from a self-perception of centrality. *Sociopathology* is a state characterized by rejection and hostility from people unsuccessfully exploited. All of these are associated with limited communication output similar to reticent behavior.

Psychiatric nosologies have heavy communication components (American Psychiatric Association, 1980; Coles, 1982). Communication can be both cause and cure of many emotional impairments. Remedies are generally acquisition of greater skill characterized by the ability to accomplish interpersonal goals successfully. Psychiatry also aims for improved affect and greater ability to contribute to the society. The Adlerian goal of "social interest" (Ansbacher, 1936) is an important criterion for effective therapy.

Reticence is a highly emotional state. It is often accompanied by anxiety, which impedes improvement. It is not clear whether anxiety is a *cause* of reticent behavior, but in some cases, it must be removed before effective retraining can take place. There are a great number of people so anxious about their communication behavior that they refuse to recognize their impairment and avoid training of all sorts. The problem is that it is not possible to deal with an unwilling trainee. Thus, reticent individuals hampered by anxiety do not usually come forward for help. They remain anxious and their communication problem is intensified.

It must be made clear that anxiety is a subjective and entirely horrifying experience. For Sullivan (Perry, 1982), it was the ultimate dreadful experience for the human. Hyde (1980) describes the phenomenology of anxiety and makes it clear that the ordinary behavior-oriented approaches to personal improvement characteristic of contemporary therapy and training are and will be relatively ineffective against the misinterpretations, restrictions of data, selective perception, and egocentrism characteristic of the anxious person.

Reticent people pose resistance to helpers. Anxiety is a restrictive emotion. It interferes with information input and impedes effective output. Resisting assistance is characteristic of the anxious person who, above all, is unable to trust others. Even when the reticent person understands the need for personal change, he or she has a high stake in retaining the protective behavior habituated over a long time. To strip away defenses without providing new and more effective ones is a dangerous brand of therapy. So many times, reticents find themselves in psychotherapeutic situations where they are compelled to reveal their fears and weaknesses only to discover that there is no remedy offered for their pain. One of the main premises of dealing with reticence is *not* to require self-disclosure. It is simply assumed that the reticent experiences pain; its nature and content are not important to training.

The only important variables are what the individual does and what the individual would like to do. Reasons are not necessary, intense concentration on technology of skills acquisition distracts attention from personal feelings and facilitates enhanced motivation. Thus, naming "disorders" is not helpful since it focuses attention on syndrome and content rather than on behavior and its change (Kelly, 1982).

In addition, reticent humans often appear guilt-laden. They feel they may not be worthy of the skill to be conferred upon them, or they fear they may misuse it. Many will ask their instructors, "but what if I hurt someone?" They have been hurt many times and understand how humans can hurt each other. In addition, resentments built up over years of silence may break through. Sometimes, it has been observed, trained reticents can be like reformed drunks. They become communication zealots, loquacious to the point of being frenetic, appearing to want to make up for lost time, to say what has not been said and to find retribution against the people who once patronized or ignored them. They may even choose to major in speech.

Caution must be exercised throughout retraining to help the reticent accommodate increased competency. Any modification in style or content of discourse results in a personality change that can affect all relationships. The few people who associate with reticents have a stake in keeping them reticent. Often, reticents are associated with stronger people who bully them. Once the reticent begins to become effective, they evoke hostility from the people close to them. There is a kind of iatrogenic effect in the retraining process, for improvement presents new kinds of problems (Phillips, 1977; Phillips & Sokoloff, 1976, 1979). Retrained reticents often find they must move into different social circles, choose new companions, and sometimes entirely modify their career goals. The proper relationship of teacher-student is that of trainer-client, but the trainer has responsibility to show the trainee how to use his or her newly acquired skills.

Identification of Reticence

The most reliable method for identifying reticent humans is self-declaration about the condition (Kelly, 1982). The commonly reported ineptitudes include the following:

— inability to ask and answer questions at work or in school

— inability to present connected discourse in public

— inability to make social conversation and small talk

— inability to make the kinds of talk associated with the development of friendship and intimacy

— inability to interact with the opposite sex

— inability to participate in group activities

— inability to get the attention one thinks one deserves.

— inability to talk with authority figures, parents, teachers, bosses, people with prestige

Reticent people are not inept or fearful in all situations. In more than 4,000 people trained on an individual basis in the last 17 years, virtually none failed to identify some situation in which they felt confident. The problem is that there are so many required situations in which they feel incompetent, and they are unable to carry over their skill in some conditions to new conditions. One of the major problems in training reticent people to be more effective is convincing them that there are some communication skills common to all situations — like goal-setting, organization, responsiveness, and monitoring responses.

Some reticent people will show signs of apprehension. Interviewers can see blotching, perspiring, averted gaze, vocalized pauses, excessively soft voice, trembling, tremolo voice, clammy hands, and fidgetings as some reticents are interviewed. About half will talk about "butterflies in the stomach," "feeling ill or nauseous," "pounding heart," "weak knees," "headache," "dry mouth," and similar symptoms, but it is not clear that these are unusual. Many highly competent performers will report these signs of distress prior to performance. The effects of adrenalin flow are various and hard to predict, but there simply does not seem to be any infallible connection between symptoms and personal reports of incompetence. A number of the people defining themselves as reticent appear quite calm to disinterested observers. In fact, recent studies indicate that in performing simple social tasks, observers cannot detect the difference between self-identified reticents and others not so classified (Kelly, 1982).

We have already identified comments reticents use as personal defenses. One more point must be made: Reticent people are edgy about criticism. They often regard critical remarks as personal attacks. It is important in dealing with reticent people not to criticize anything for which a remedy cannot be offered, since any comment that does not appear completely instructional can be taken as a criticism of a person. For this reason, it is important to avoid getting involved in personal feelings. There is nothing a trainer can do about personal feelings and, therefore, feelings must remain off the agenda lest they be used to drive a wedge between trainer and trainee.

It has been our experience that virtually all trainees can learn two or three new skills in a 10-week training program, so long as there is no effort made to discuss feelings. Follow-up indicates that about 85% retain these skills as long as 5 years after the fact (Oerkvitz, 1975, 1976). The process of carry-over is still obscure. Most trainees seem able to generalize some of the techniques to life situations, but a pedagogy for increasing the probabilities that this will happen, and for developing a theory of how it happens, remains to be found.

Observable Response Formats

There are four main formats in which reticent people respond to others. First and foremost, they do not participate at all. They have learned techniques for avoiding talk. They nod, turn their heads away, move to the fringe of groups, stay at the outside of conversational circles. In the classroom, they would rather receive a low mark than respond to questions. They avoid classes where oral reports are required, and literally seek jobs on a criterion of limited requirements for conduct with others. A study conducted under the auspices of Title III indicated that school teachers could recognize students who handicapped themselves by their unwillingness to participate in required communication activities, confirming the empirical basis for the classification.

A second response pattern is a self-fulfilling prophecy of ineptitude. Many of them have great ability in "snatching defeat from the jaws of victory." When things are going well for them, they do a double take and embark upon a failure track. Many will train hard for a public speech. They prepare a virtually perfect outline, secure first-class documentation, start out like the proverbial house afire, and then, halfway through the speech, it is as if a flash hits them that they are doing well — they proceed to lose their place on the outline, grope for words, leave out large segments of the speech, and eventually fail. There are a large number of reticents who are virtually completely inept, but do not make public notice of it. They are the ones who excuse themselves by saying. "I could do it if I wanted to, but I don't want to."

They do not seek help because the act of being helped would be too threatening to them.

A third response pattern is programmatic activity. Some reticent people habituate standard phrases, clichés, monosyllabic responses, and trivial statements that they use consistently. Some even get reasonably skilled at one topic, and during social engagements spend their time trying to force the conversation in that specific direction. By mastering a few social routines, they absolve themselves for responsibility in conversation. They also label themselves as boring, and eventually push away people who might have been attracted to them.

Finally, a fourth group displays nervous symptoms and mannerisms. This group seems to be soliciting reassurance and pity. Their stark terror is used as a device to solicit more than their share of consideration from the people around them. Manifesting fear can be highly influential in social discourse. It can attract sympathetic attention and public concern. The problem is that it cannot be repeated too often, for people tire quickly of being solicitous and after a while simply refuse to recognize the nervous symptoms as anything more than strategic hysterical manifestations used to manipulate social circumstances.

There is an undeniable quality of narcissism about reticent behavior. It is a defensive narcissism, but it has the capacity to injure people who come close. Reticent people are not reliable associates because they do not play by commonly accepted social rules. They want more reassurance than is normally given, they expect more from their associates than they can possibly get. They excuse themselves from responsibility for reasons not relevant to others. They have no qualms about foisting work off on others because they are unfit to perform it, and when they are criticized, they accept it as part and parcel of the hostility toward themselves they feel comes from the world at large. They can, on one hand, get comfortable with their social evasions, and on the other hand feel miserable because they understand they are not getting what others are getting out of their social lives.

It has not been possible to find specific and consistent causes of reticent behavior. For one thing, people do not remember. For another, what reticents say about themselves is often true of most other people. Reticents can sometimes point to speech traumas like speaking with fly unzipped or being ridiculed; but so can normal speakers. Some talk of a horrible experience with stagefright, such as forgetting lines in a school play; but nonreticent speakers tell these stories as well. There is some reason to implicate parental influence, for some households obviously do not place a high value on speaking. Marginality characterized by inability to learn speaking styles of new social groups may also cause some reticent behavior.

The point is, the causes reticent speakers point to are events, situations, conditions, and problems that affect us all. At the moment, it is impossible to explain why most people seem to surmount these problems, while only a few seem to be imperiled permanently by them. An important concept occurring in talk with most reticents is the idea that they do not really understand the role of communication in socialization. For one reason or another, they have not learned that personhood is expressed through communication. Some almost seem to believe that people can read their minds, even though they do not talk at all. Indeed, reticent demeanors are often downcast, but that comes after years of social defeat and is more likely a response to social rejection than communication ineptitude. The problem is that it is hard to convince reticent people that learning communication skills will do them any good at all. The myth of the vibes dies hard, and reticent speakers do believe in vibes.

It is easy enough to write off reticent personalities with the diagnosis of "low self-esteem" but this inept reification has done considerable damage, for it suggests that by raising self-esteem, reticent people will become competent socializers. There is, however, a tautology implicit in this formulation. Low self-esteem is a function or product of something. It is an evaluation applied to a state of personality resulting from convincing experiences that indicate ineptitude. Self-esteem cannot be restored without acquiring the ability to do the things that the inability to do caused low self-esteem in the first place. It is a chicken-egg problem, and a decision must be made about where to intervene. Reticence instruction has focused on skills acquisition as a way of enhancing self-esteem.

Focus of Retraining

The basis for the retraining is the principle that removal of anxiety alone is not effective. When anxiety is removed, the individuals are likely to plunge into speech experiences for which they are not prepared, suffer defeat, and then encounter even greater anxiety. This reverse process was also observed in that some seemed to behave like Masserman's conditioned cats. As they evidenced greater skill, they suffered greater anxiety. Thus, it appears that a program of persuasion must accompany skills acquisition. The trainee must be convinced of improvement before attempting experiences outside the classroom. The persuasion must include the premise that anxiety can be regarded as performance tension arising from adrenalin flow. Performance tension, goes the message, gets the individual set for quality performance. It is characteristic of athletes and stage actors, and is an important component in skillful performance.

Training then proceeds through application of tools of performance. Trainees are taught to *set goals* for their own performance (*not* for the responses of others). It is possible for people to control their own behavior; by controlling their own behavior, they improve their chances of influencing others. Behavior includes content of talk, organization of talk, delivery, and observation of results. Thus, instruction includes the discovery of things to say, procedures for structuring them, exercises and drill in the use of voice and body in delivering talk, and systems of observation and evaluation of the responses of others. These categories are clearly recognizable as "canons of rhetoric."

It is also important that trainees understand that it is legitimate to plan and rehearse. Based on Winans's (1938) premise that public speech is enlarged conversation, reticents are taught that conversation is reduced public speech. If it is legitimate and possible to prepare for a public speech performance, it is also legitimate and possible to prepare for social interactions. Students are taught how to memorize "lines" usable in interviews, trained in small talk and elementary social discourse, and rehearsed in techniques of asking and answering questions.

They are also taught that they need not take all the responsibility for any failure they might encounter. While a speaker has an obligation not to waste the time of the listener, listeners sometimes have good reasons for not paying attention. Thus, in any given case, failure on the part of the listener might account for failure in the discourse. By learning to share blame, both anxiety and guilt are better managed.

The proposition that people would rather be sick than stupid is countered by teaching reticents some basic principles of rhetorical procedure. They are taught, for example, to analyze communication situations using a modification of Bitzer's *rhetorical situation* (Bitzer, 1968). Personal responsibility for integrity of content and clarity of organization is easy to assume because people can be trained to select material and arrange it. Applying this to standard needs of audiences provides a method of choosing what to include and what to leave out. *Rhetorical sensitivity* (Hart & Burks, 1972) is the basis for understanding audiences. Reticents are taught to do all they can and recognize that other people may simply choose not to comply. Some effort is also made to teach trainees how to observe social situations to discover what is allowable and what is not. This "other directed" (Riesman, 1950) process takes attention off the self and focuses it on actual events and behaviors.

Consideration for audience (or "looking out for number two") is also important. The doctrine of "the fool tells me his reasons, the wise man persuades me with my own" takes emphasis off the narcissistic quality of reticence. Once the reticent learns that no one much cares how he or she feels or why they think the way they do, it is possible to teach how to use topoi systems to select information and appeals designed to meet the needs of listeners. Self-justification is no longer important, and the process of speaking becomes a problem-solving experience.

There are three other premises demonstrably important in instruction. First, the notion of dual perspective permits the reticent the luxury of believing other people feel what he or she feels. By examining their own motives, reticents can discover possible motives in others to which they can appeal. Second, by thinking through a best case, worst case, and most likely case scenario, reticents can equip themselves with alternatives. The idea of forging ahead with a game plan regardless of what the opposition is doing is characteristic of both bad football and bad socialization. In order to learn the necessity to adapt to responses of others, rehearsal is encouraged in scenes played out around the scenarios. Third, vocal training is emphasized. Vocal training has been neglected in recent years. Generations of speech students have been trained without ever learning the capacities of their vocal mechanism. One of the problems with reticents is their delivery is often incompatible with their ideas. By teaching them to improve their vocal range, their possibilities for competent discourses are improved. Training features oral interpretation and various drills designed to enlarge vocal range.

A Brief Summary

In the final analysis, reticence is an eminently practical problem experienced by a great many people. Many do not recognize a need to do anything about it. Those who seek retraining often do so reluctantly and struggle against surrendering their defensive behavior. Reticence cannot be regarded as a psychological problem since it is simply impractical to get involved in personal emotions and confusions and hope for improvement. Focus on skills training accompanied by necessary persuasions that improvement is taking place permits effective retraining of a great many people. This can go on simultaneously with efforts to discover the dynamics and etiology of reticent behavior, and the process of retraining can provide raw data for theoretical interpretation.

4

The Transitory Causes of Audience Anxiety

JOHN A. DALY and ARNOLD H. BUSS

The topic of this chapter is the anxiety a speaker experiences or exhibits when making an oral presentation to an audience. Concern for this anxiety has a long history in the field of speech communication. It is a common issue in textbooks and, according to at least one survey, a major fear of most adults. We propose a series of contextual characteristics of the speaking situation that directly affect the degree of anxiety a speaker feels immediately before and during an oral presentation. There are two major determinants of audience anxiety: the personality traits of the speaker and various aspects of the speaking situation. This chapter omits any discussion of personality traits and focuses instead on the situational determinants of the anxiety. The multitude of these situational determinants requires that they be organized into a coherent scheme. We will discuss events prior to the speech, events that occur during the speech, conspicuousness of the speaker, characteristics of the audience, and novelty. While most of these situational determinants are familiar enough to be recognized, they have not been integrated systematically into a single model.

Before the Speech

One cause of speech anxiety is lack of knowledge about an upcoming speech event. The greater the ambiguity about the speech and its requirements, the greater the audience anxiety. Speakers reflect this relationship when they ask questions like "What kind of an audience will there be?" "How large will it be and what will be it's makeup?" "How long should the talk be?" and "Should the speech be read?" To the extent that these kinds of questions remain unanswered, the speaker faces the audience in a state of doubt and uncertainty, which elevates audience anxiety.

Although greater certainty usually diminishes anxiety, some kinds of advance knowledge may not assuage anxiety but, rather, elevate it. Expectations of a negative reaction from the audience is an example; the expectation that the audience will be tired, bored, or uninterested is another. The anticipation of audience antipathy, though not common, occurs frequently enough to pose a problem. As examples, consider cases such as an abortion advocate planning to talk to an audience of pro-lifers, a Reaganite expecting to speak to a group of liberal Democrats, or an ex-criminal anticipating lecturing to an audience that believes criminals need more punishment. When the prospective audience is known to dislike the speaker personally or his or her opinions, there is good reason for the speaker to dread the occasion.

Another kind of advance knowledge that may elevate audience anxiety is the anticipation of evaluation. The more a speaker feels an audience will be evaluating him or her, the greater the audience anxiety. Obviously, the degree of perceived evaluation is tied to the salience of the likely consequences of the evaluation. If the evaluation is crucial, more audience anxiety occurs. When a speaker believes the audience's judgment will have little impact on him or her, there will be very little audience anxiety. Many speeches are made by candidates for political positions or jobs. Some speeches are made by speakers who represent an organization, and how well they do reflects not only on themselves but also on the organization they represent. When speakers know that a poor performance may affect them negatively — for example, cost them a job or result in censure from a parent organization — they tend to anticipate the worst and dread an upcoming performance.

One way of reducing prior anxiety is through preparation. Speakers usually have adequate forewarning of an impending speech to prepare. If they have little time for preparation, however, they are likely to approach the speech with some trepidation. In the extreme case of no forewarning — a request for a spontaneous, off-the-cuff talk — speakers, especially novice ones, may experience mild panic. When there has been advance notice of a speech, one way of alleviating anxiety is to plan the message, sometimes to the extent of writing out the speech. Planning reduces the uncertainty a speaker may feel about the upcoming performance. In most contexts — especially on formal occasions — it is permissible to read one's speech. In other contexts, however, the speaker is expected to be more spontaneous and talk either from an outline or without any notes. The less the text of a speech is planned, the greater the likelihood of anxiety about the presentation. Speakers know that without preparation there are more opportunities for mistakes (e.g., getting lost, repeating oneself, uttering embarrassing slips of the tongue) that can raise even further the anxiety they experience.

Another way to reduce audience anxiety is to rehearse the speech alone or in the presence of an audience of friends. This process of rehearsal makes the speech more familiar, thus reducing the uncertainty tied to the presentation. Obviously, presenting familiar materials is less anxiety producing that presenting an untried, unfamiliar speech.

During the Speech

Audience reactions during a speech can profoundly affect a speaker's anxiety. The less positive the perceived reactions of the audience, the more the speaker is likely to experience anxiety. One audience reaction that is typically considered negative is boredom, which may be expressed in restlessness, whispering to neighbors, reading books or magazines, repeated yawning, or even falling asleep. Occasionally, a listener may find the speech so dull as to get up and leave. A speaker who notices this boredom is likely to experience greater anxiety even as he or she attempts to recapture the audience's interest.

Apathy, however, is not the worst audience reaction. Audiences may boo, hiss, stomp their feet, and call out nasty comments. Such behavior tends to scare speakers, sometimes to the point of panic. Experienced speakers and speakers high in esteem and low in dispositional speech anxiety tend to handle such reactions better than do their counterparts with little experience, low esteem, or high dispositional anxiety.

Speakers may also become upset and disorganized by disruptions that occur during the speech. There are so many things that can go wrong during a speech that it is rare for a speech to conclude without incident. The house light may fail, the microphone may stop working, the loudspeakers may start wailing, people in adjacent rooms or hallways might talk so loudly that the speaker can barely be heard, carpenters and electricians might start working in an adjoining room, an audience planning on hearing the next speech might arrive early, or visual aids might be out of order. All of these incidents distract audience members and speaker alike. They represent unplanned, disruptive events. The more frequently they occur during a speech, the greater the potential for audience anxiety.

Disruptions can also arise because of actions by the speaker. Speakers sometimes clumsily knock over their lecterns, drop their notes, mishandle their microphones, make obvious mistakes in referring to their hosts, figuratively step on an important person's toes, or merely deliver a malapropism. When speakers become aware that they have made such errors, their audience anxiety intensifies. Experienced speakers cope with such disruptions and disturbances in practiced ways (e.g., laughing, quips about the equipment, humorous self-disparagement, ignoring the event entirely). Inexperienced speakers may be totally flustered by disruptions, letting even a small disturbance create more anxiety as they attempt to recover.

Conspicuousness

The reactions and disturbances just described heighten the conspicuousness of the speaker. Being conspicuous is, of course, part of public speaking, a situation in which all eyes are (or are supposed to be) on the speaker. In everyday conversations, attention is divided among the participants of the exchange. While most people prefer a modicum of attention and no one wants to be totally ignored, there seems to be a limit to the amount of attention that is comfortable. Few people enjoy close scrutiny by others. Yet that is precisely what must be endured by a speaker addressing an audience. In the speaking situation, the audience, by definition, focuses complete and consistent attention on the speaker.

Negative reactions by the audience, disruptions, and mistakes obviously elevate one's sense of being the focus of others' attention. In the speaking situation, two additional conditions promote conspicuousness. The first is being on stage alone in contrast to appearing with several other people, each of whom will also speak. The second condition involves the degree to which the speaker is completely open to inspection by the audience. Speakers — especially inexperienced ones — often prefer remaining behind a lectern or some other prop, which provides physical support as well as a barrier between audience and speaker. Being alone on stage and being completely exposed to the audience tend to elevate conspicuousness to its greatest extent, and the knowledge that one is exposed is a strong cause of audience anxiety.

Characteristics of the Audience

Certain characteristics of an audience can affect speakers' anxiety. These characteristics include the size and heterogeneity of the audience, its status relative to the speaker, and the degree to which the speaker differs from the audience.

Speaking to a small group of people involves a moderate degree of conspicuousness. As the number of people who are looking and listening grows, the speaker's feeling of conspicuousness also increases. This may be the reason why larger audiences cause more anxiety for speakers than do smaller audiences. Larger audiences heighten anxiety for a number of reasons. The speaker cannot relax as much; he or she senses a need for more audience management skills with the bigger group; and there is less predictability, and consequently less control, with big audiences.

Large audiences are more likely to consist of a mixture of diverse people. Audience members may vary in intelligence, knowledge about the topic, or even command of English, so that some will understand the speech and others will not. They may vary in age and gender, so that if the speech is pitched toward one group, another group will be left out. Or they may vary in whether they are motivated to listen, and, if motivated, their goals may vary, so that if the aims of one part of the audience are satisfied, the desires of another part may be frustrated. A large, heterogeneous audience poses an especially acute problem for the speaker. If the speech is oriented toward the bright members of the audience, it will be over the heads of the less intelligent members; if the level is low enough for the less intelligent, the more intelligent are likely to become bored. If the speech is directed toward the middle of any dimension, people at either end of the dimension will be frustrated. Faced with this insoluble problem, the speaker who is aware of the heterogeneity of the audience may well become anxious.

An important audience characteristic is its status relative to that of the speaker. A teacher lecturing to students is superior in status and therefore tends to experience little audience anxiety. If the same teacher were speaking to a group of educators of national prominence, however, their higher status would tend to elevate audience anxiety; this would occur even if the speaker was not actually being evaluated. Presumably, this feeling of tension in the presence of higher-status people is learned as part of childhood socialization. In dyadic interaction, an ordinary person may become tongue-tied in the presence of the president, a member of royalty, or a Nobel laureate. Similarly, when the speaker is clearly of lower status then the audience, the likely consequence is tension during the speech. Such speech anxiety is especially likely when the high-status audience is also more experienced and more knowledgeable than the speaker in his or her own field of expertise.

Even when status is not an issue, differences that cause the speaker to feel conspicuously different from the audience can elevate audience anxiety. Consider a woman speaking to an audience of men, a Black speaking to an audience of Caucasians, or an American speaking to an audience of English-speaking Japanese. In each instance, the speaker must be keenly aware of how sharply he or she differs from the audience, an awareness that gives rise to feelings of conspicuousness and an inability to bridge the gap.

Novelty

As mentioned earlier, most people seldom speak before an audience. The infrequency of the act means that any fear associated with it is unlikely to habituate over time. That is, because practice is so infrequent for most people, the fear of the experience is unlikely to lessen over time. Aside from the variables mentioned above, what has the speaker to fear? One answer is the unknown. Infants and children are afraid of strange situations and strangers, and to some extent this fear is also present among adults. In a novel situation, a person is confronted with the feeling of tension and wariness common to both humans and animals, but which kinds of novelty are specific to audience anxiety?

First, there is novelty of environment. The less familiar the setting for the speech, the greater the audience anxiety. This is especially important for the novice speaker, who has spoken in public so seldom that virtually any environment is novel. It is also a problem for the more experienced speaker who is called on to give a speech in a different room, different city, different building, or even outdoors. For someone who has always used a microphone, speaking without one might pose a problem; the problem would be more severe, of course, for the person who is confronted with a microphone for the first time. Unless one is in a deep rut in their speaking, novel situations keep appearing. Teachers who have taught for many years and therefore have virtually no speech anxiety may experience at least mild panic when giving their first lecture at a new school. Only after time has been spent in the new locale, in the new room with the new chairs, lights, and room arrangements, does the anxiety wane. Experienced speakers recognize this and try to familiarize themselves with the speaking environment and its characteristics prior to the speech.

Second, there is novelty of audiences. The less familiar the audience, the greater the speaker's anxiety. When the audience is a new one, the speaker cannot be sure of its makeup, background, or possible reactions to his or her message. Not only is the speaker confronted with an unknown audience that may be sufficient to elicit anxiety, but he or she is also unlikely to know the techniques and approaches that will work with that group. While the speaker is attempting to find out how to approach the audience, his or her anxiety level will be high. Only after becoming familiar with the audience will the speaker's anxiety dissipate.

Third, there is novelty of role, which is a problem in many kinds of social interaction. A novel role generates anxiety. Speakers are less anxious if the role they are playing is a familiar one. Switching or changing to a new one creates ambiguity and consequently anxiety. Novice speakers are unaccustomed to being the focus of an audience's attention. Because they are unfamiliar in this role, they are more likely to experience anxiety than are their counterparts with more experience. When students are training to become teachers, they are comfortable in their role as students. When they graduate and assume the role of teacher, initially they may experience audience anxiety because of the novelty of the teacher role. Even those with experience at speaking may become uncomfortable when they try a new speaker's role, such as introducing the main speaker of a program, being a discussant, or having to present an unfamiliar kind of speech (e.g., delivering a humorous monologue).

All three kinds of novelty share two sources of audience anxiety: fear of the unknown and uncertainty about how to act. For most people, giving speeches is an infrequent act, which means that there is little opportunity for them to become sufficiently acclimated to the experience for the novelty (and, therefore, the fear) to wane. Furthermore, since fear of public speaking is common, most people tend to avoid making speeches, which means that novelty is a continuing cause of audience anxiety.

We have posited a group of variables that cause audience anxiety. Taken alone, each may contribute to the amount of audience anxiety an individual experiences. Together, they can cause panic, disorganization, and an overall poor speaking performance. However, the magnitude of their impact is affected by a speaker's personal characteristics. For an experienced speaker or one with little dispositional speech anxiety, the different causes may have little impact. These individuals may have devised coping strategies that even allow them to take advantage of the different factors. On the other hand, inexperienced speakers or those with high dispositional anxiety may find that the different factors exacerbate their nervousness. In the next two sections we briefly discuss two related issues that need clarification in the literature on audience anxiety: (1) the difference between anxiety and excitement and (2) the similarities and differences between the immediate causes of shyness and speech anxiety.

Anxiety Versus Excitement

This chapter focuses on determinants of transient audience anxiety. There is an additional issue that needs to be mentioned in any discussion of audience anxiety: the difference between anxiety and excitement. It is common to hear that one requirement of a good speech or performance is some degree of stage fright. Entertainers such as Johnny Carson say that a good dose of stage fright is an absolute necessity when getting "up" for a performance. While it is true that most speakers and performers experience arousal prior to their performances, this everyday observation confuses the arousal of *anxiety* with the arousal of *excitement*. This chapter has focused on the arousal of anxiety when speaking to an audience. We have discussed the various transient determinants of this anxiety and need add only that it is typically experienced as an uncomfortable or even unbearable problem by speakers.

Excitement, in contrast, involves no discomfort or other negative experience; the feeling is different from anxiety. Consider watching a movie such as *Raiders of the Lost Ark* and being caught up in the adventure of the protagonist; viewing the Super Bowl wind down to the final minutes with only two points separating the teams; eagerly awaiting a telephone call informing one of whether a contest has been won; or preparing for a social evening with an attractive companion. What these examples have in common is an elevated arousal of suspense as one eagerly awaits the outcome of a gripping situation. Now consider a speaker about to face an audience. For speakers who are neither anxious nor confronted with most of the determinants of speech anxiety discussed previously, the situation can be neutral or even pleasant. Any arousal they feel is probably the same anticipatory excitement runners experience just before a race. In both running and speaking, the issue is not so much one of fear but rather the "rush" of arousal that occurs just before the impending event.

How can the two kinds of arousal be distinguished? In fear, there is a strong activation of the sympathetic division of the autonomic nervous system, which is reflected in sweating, tremors, and a dry mouth. Such reactions do not occur in excitement. For the person who is about to speak, the experiential component may offer the best means of distinguishing between anxiety and excitement. The speaker's feeling of anxiety is dread, as he or she frets about the outcome of the performance. The speaker's feeling of excitement is some combination of eagerness, pleasurable arousal, and an optimistic expectation about the outcome of the performance; at the very least, the excitement is merely neutral (but not aversive).

The distinction between the two kinds of arousal bears on the commonsense idea that stage fright is necessary to a good performance. This idea appears to be correct only when limited to excitement, which can make a speaker more lively, spontaneous, and perhaps even larger than life. True stage fright (audience anxiety) does not facilitate a speech but rather disorganizes and degrades it. Such anxiety causes speakers to stammer, inhibit natural gestures, forget their place, and perhaps even freeze into immobility. Thus when people suggest that some degree of stage fright is necessary to a good performance, they are confusing the rush of anticipatory excitement with the worry or panic of stage fright. The first may be helpful, but the second can only be detrimental.

As separate distinction can be drawn between the anxiety a speaker experiences immediately before and during the speech and anxiety experienced in preparation for the speech. The former is the focus of this chapter and we consider it an uncomfortable and negative experience. On the other hand, the latter, to some degree, may be positive insofar as it enhances an individual's level of preparation. The anxiety is motivating when it spurs the speaker's preparation of the speech. Conscientious preparation tends to reduce procrastination and laxness, eliminating or limiting many of the immediate causes of audience anxiety described in this chapter. But even this anxiety can be detrimental if it leads the person to be overwhelmed by the stress of preparation.

Shyness and Audience Anxiety

The focus of this chapter is on the immediate causes of transitory audience anxiety. Speaking to an audience is different from most communicative acts, in that the speaker is highly conspicuous and is responsible for the event. In everyday social interactions the speaker is less conspicuous and, in essence, lacks an audience; every member of the conversation actively participates. Some reactions of participants in a conversation, however, resemble the negative reactions of speakers when experiencing audience anxiety. In the case of a speech, the discomfort is called *audience anxiety*, while the discomfort experienced in social interactions is labeled *shyness*. The purpose of this section is to compare the causes of each.

In shyness, the variables that play a role prior to an interaction are primarily the knowledge components. Typically, ambiguity about an upcoming conversation — particularly when it is an important one — will result in more shyness. As a general rule, clarity in expectations reduces anxiety about an interaction. Just as with public speaking, this generality has its limitations. If a conversationalist expected a negative response, that knowledge would probably generate shyness. Similarly, knowledge of a salient evaluation would elevate an individual's shyness about the interaction. While prior knowledge is a cause of both shyness and audience anxiety, preparation, planning, and rehearsal appear to be specific to audience anxiety. Seldom do people actively prepare, plan, and rehearse normal conversations. When they do (for instance, in a job interview) the conversation begins to resemble a public speaking situation. Except in unusual cases, however, preparation, planning, and rehearsal are not relevant factors in generating shyness.

As with a speech, during a conversation the responses of others can cause shyness. Apathy and negative responses often make a person more reticent. Similarly, mistakes such as inappropriate phases and words, an unknowing insult, an unintentional but overbearing or too boisterous utterance can make a person reticent for a period of time in the conversation. While the responses of others and embarrassing mistakes create greater shyness, environmental disruptions are less likely to create a reaction in a conversation than they do in a speech. Any external disruption in a dyadic or small group setting is usually shared and coped with by everyone present. Furthermore, it is typically more easily controlled in conversations than it is in a speech. Conversations ordinarily involve no particular settings or equipment, whereas speeches do. In summary, like audience anxiety, shyness is often instigated by the responses of others and by errors made by the speaker. In contrast to audience anxiety, disruptions play only a small role in creating shyness in a conversation.

Conspicuousness is a major component in our model of the immediate causes of audience anxiety. In the case of shyness, conspicuousness usually plays a minor role. In a typical conversation, no one individual is the focus of attention for very long. Rather, the focus of attention shifts back and forth and is shared by all involved. Obviously, there are exceptions. In a job interview or a panel discussion being watched by others, participants may feel conspicuous. A conversationalist who makes a major error may experience a sense of conspicuousness as other members of the exchange note (or too obviously ignore) the mistake. But these are extreme cases. In contrast to audience anxiety, conspicuousness does not play a leading role in everyday social interaction.

Two of the major characteristics of audiences that engender anxiety also play roles in creating shyness: status differentials and homogeneity. In the case of status differentials, an individual will generally experience more shyness when interacting with someone higher in status. In the case of homogeneity, when two interactants perceive a good deal of difference between one another, more shyness is expected. Both status and diversity would seem to generate shyness for only a limited time in a conversation. As the conversation progresses (assuming both members are cooperating in making each other feel comfortable), status differences and heterogeneity become less important. Audience size is obviously irrelevant to shyness in conversations, for seldom do social exchanges include more than three or four members.

The final component relevant to audience anxiety was the degree of novelty involved in the speaking situation. Three sorts of novelty were identified: environment, audiences, and role. Each plays a similar role in the creation of shyness. In an unfamiliar setting, in speaking with an unfamiliar partner, or in a novel role, participants experience more shyness than when familiar with environment, partner, and expected role.

Audience anxiety and shyness share a number of causes, the most prominent of which are novelty and conspicuousness. Some causes of audience anxiety, however, are not causes of shyness; audience characteristics is an obvious example. The similarities are to be expected, for audience anxiety and shyness are both social anxieties. But the differences are also to be expected, for each represents a different kind of social anxiety.

Summary

In theorizing about the situational causes of audience anxiety, we have divided them into two classes. *Before* the speech, ambiguity about what is expected and anticipation of evaluation are potential causes of audience anxiety. *During* the speech, audience anxiety originates in, or is intensified by, negative audience reactions, disruptions, conspicuousness, audience characteristics, and novelty. We also suggest a distinction between the aversive anxiety that may precede a speech and the neutral or pleasurable excitement that may precede it. Finally, we distinguish two kinds of social anxiety. One kind (shyness) occurs mainly in conversational groups, in which each member participates and receives attention from the other(s). The other kind (audience anxiety) occurs when a speaker is responsible for a presentation to an audience and receives virtually all of their attention. All these statements should be regarded as hypotheses; some have been confirmed in research, but others await empirical test.

PART II

MEASUREMENT

5

Self-Report Measurement

JAMES C. McCROSKEY

For over fifty years, communication avoidance, anxiety, and fear have constituted a major concern of social scientists who study communication. In fact, this area represents the oldest continuing research effort in the field of communication. Throughout this half century of research, continuing attention has been directed toward the issue of measurement.

Three major approaches to measurement initiated in the early days of the research continue to the present. Lomas (1934) and Gilkinson (1942) began the stream of research that employs self-report measures. Henning (1935) initiated research using observer ratings. Redding (1936) launched the research that focuses on measurement of physiological arousal.

Almost exactly midway in this five decades of research, Clevenger (1959) published a major review of the research done to that time. He found that all three approaches to measurement generated highly reliable scores. However, he observed that the scores did not seem to be related to each other meaningfully. As he put it:

> Surprisingly, instruments which are so reliable display comparatively poor intercorrelations. Results of comparisons of various indices of stage fright suggest that the emotional disturbance which is recorded on physiological measuring devices is different from both the emotional disturbance which the speaker reports having experienced, and the emotional disturbance which a group of judges report having observed, and that the latter are different from each other. (Clevenger, 1959, p.137)

The overwhelming concern of this early research was anxiety or fear relating to public speaking, or, more commonly, stage fright. In recent years communication avoidance, anxiety, and fear have been examined in other communication contexts. However, a survey of that literature indicates that Clevenger's conclusion in 1959 could as well be drawn today. Self-reports, physiological arousal indicants, and observer ratings, while often significantly correlated, are not measures of the same thing. Isomorphism, concurrent validity, and interchangeability simply are not present.

While Clevenger's (1959) conclusion, as well as the one I draw above, is based on the empirical findings of research, careful conceptualization prior to that research would have made the findings expected rather than surprising. In most cases, such care in conceptualizing communication avoidance, shyness, communication apprehension, and reticence has not been present prior to instrument development. Of particular importance for conceptualization in this area is the trait-state distinction advanced by Spielberger (1966). While this dichotomy is now discredited by many writers, the underlying concept of the distinction is critical for our understanding of measurement in this area.

Human behavior is the product of at least two interacting factors: characteristic predispositions of the individual (traits) and situational constraints on behavior at a given time (states). Individual traits are relatively enduring over time, whereas states are highly variable. Applying this to the common problem of stage fright, a person may be generally apprehensive about giving speeches and thus will experience considerable anxiety when forced into giving a speech. Another person may generally enjoy and not fear giving speeches, but if asked to give a speech on television with insufficient time to prepare may experience a comparable amount of anxiety. The anxiety of one stems primarily from the trait of the individual, the anxiety of the other is primarily the result of the situation itself. Depending on how we choose to measure stage fright in this instance, two measures may be either highly correlated or totally uncorrelated.

Communication avoidance, shyness, communication apprehension, and reticence can all be measured by self-report, observer rating, or physiological arousal indicant at either a trait or state level. However, the three measurement approaches are not equally useful for all purposes or at all levels. The primary thing we must determine before we select or construct a measure is what we want to measure. The three primary options available are physiological arousal, behavioral disruption, and cognitive discomfort. I will consider each measurement approach below and suggest when each may be most useful.

Choosing Measurement Approach

Indicants of Physiological Arousal

If one wishes to measure physiological arousal, the many instruments that record indicants of physiological arousal are an obvious choice. The case for such measures appears strong, at least on the surface. Physiological responses are hard to fake and the instruments, if handled by competent professionals, are not as subject to such human frailties as demand characteristics and experimenter biases as are other instruments. However, there are many pitfalls in the use of such instruments. Few scientists and even fewer teachers are trained in the appropriate use of the technology involved. This equipment in the hands of the untrained individual is worse than useless and very likely to lead to false knowledge claims that are difficult to identify in research reports. In addition, use of such instruments for screening large numbers of students would seldom be economically or strategically feasible. Finally, as Beatty notes in Chapter 6, many issues are not yet settled among even the experts on how such data should be analyzed and interpreted.

The usefulness of physiological measures, for all intents and purposes, is restricted to state issues. Because of the difficulty of calibrating such equipment to each individual, the possibility of using such measures across a sufficient variety of communication settings to generate an estimate of a trait arousal level is extremely remote and, in the case of some instruments, completely impossible with current technology.

Finally, we must address the question of whether we should attempt to measure arousal at all. Arousal does not equal anxiety; arousal simply equals arousal. Considerable research indicates that people who report experiencing anxiety and people who report feeling exhilaration can have highly similar arousal levels. The measures of arousal, then, have insufficient face validity as indicants of communication avoidance, shyness, communication apprehension, or reticence to deserve research attention from researchers concerned with these constructs. The sole exception would be research that employs previously validated measures of these constructs along with measures of physiological arousal in the attempt to discover the physiological impact of these constructs in various communication settings. Physiological measurement, then, is the least useful approach for measurement in this area.

Behavioral Observation

Most scholars concerned with shyness, communication apprehension, or reticence profess their concern as a result of the presumed relationship between these constructs and potentially observable human behaviors that may have important positive or negative effects in the life of an individual. While I share this concern, I also believe that communication apprehension (in particular as it is conceptualized in Chapter 1) can have important effects on the individual that are not observable in behavior. Nevertheless, much of the research in this general area is amenable to the use of behavioral observation.

As reticence is currently conceptualized (the inability to perform competent communication behaviors), behavioral observation probably is the most valid and useful approach to measurement. Predispositional and physiological arousal factors are only marginally related to this construct. Thus, whether one is interested in a general trait of reticence or reticence in a specific state setting. observed behavior is the only indicant with strong face validity.

Communication avoidance and shyness (which I see as virtually isomorphic constructs) are also amenable to measurement by behavioral observation. Both envision the person who is shy or avoidant as engaging in less communication, either generally (trait) or in a given situation (state). Thus observation of behavior should provide a measure with strong face validity if carefully administered.

Behavioral observation is least useful as a measure of communication apprehension because there are no behaviors that are specifically predicted from the communication apprehension conceptualization. Rather, this conceptualization envisions a variety of options available to the individual, many of which are not observable. In short, measurement by behavioral observation has little or no face validity for communication apprehension.

To say that behavioral observation is potentially very useful for measurement of reticence, communication avoidance, and shyness is not to say that it should always be the measure of choice. This approach has several limitations that may force its rejection for some purposes.

Observing behavior is often, although not always, an intrusive approach to measurement. The observer may, and often does, alter the behavior being observed. This is particularly true in dyadic communication settings, but can apply to any setting. One method advocated for overcoming this problem is use of video recording. However, as one who has carefully debriefed subjects who knew they were being videotaped, this is only a "better than nothing" improvement. Intrusion is still there.

The most difficult problem for the researcher considering the use of behavioral observation is the determination of what behavior is to be observed. For example, if reticence is the reverse of communication competence, what behaviors shall be taken as evidence of reticence? As a field we are in far from complete agreement about the nature of what we shall call "competent" communication. We simply have not yet come to agreement on the set of behaviors that will operationally define this construct. Some believe we never will. In the absence of such general agreement, we have operationalism at its worst — reticence is whatever my measure measures. Such an approach is unlikely to lead to major advance in knowledge.

Behavioral observation probably is most useful for assessing states and least useful for assessing traits. This is not inherent in the technology of the method, but is a function of the limitations on the practical application of the method. Behavioral observation is highly time consuming and expensive in most instances. It usually is difficult to apply appropriately even to assess states, since resources typically are more limited than would be desirable. To assess traits requires extensive observation across many settings to generate valid data. Resources are seldom available for such careful observation. Even the use of this method where it may be most appropriate, the screening of students for reticence/competence for purposes of assignment for communication instruction, is seldom economically feasible. Thus the practical alternatives we often confront are to choose another method or to use this method in an inappropriate and invalid way. Unfortunately, the over-reaction of our society to the need to assess communication competence often leads us as individuals as well as our professional associations to accept the latter alternative.

Self-Report

The most widely employed approach to measurement in the areas of communication avoidance, shyness, and communication apprehension is that of self-report scales. There are several reasons for this clear preference on the part of both researchers and practitioners — some good, some not so good.

Many people argue that the best way to find out something about someone is simply to ask her or him. I cannot argue with that logic, except to point out that it is only correct if the person knows the answer and if the person is willing to tell you the truth. To illustrate: If you ask me how many ounces of blood there are in my body, I can't give you the correct answer because I don't know. However, if you ask whether I feel apprehensive about interviewing with a university president for a position, I can give you a correct and precise answer. In addition, if you are a good friend of mine and you ask me whether I fudge on my income tax return, I know the correct answer and probably will tell you the truth. But if you are a tax auditor and ask me the same question, it is most likely I will tell you I don't, whether I do or not.

Self-report measures, then, are most appropriate when they are directed toward matters of affect and/or perception in circumstances where the respondent has no reason to fear negative consequences from any answer given. They are least useful when they are directed toward matters of fact that may be unknown or unknowable by the respondent. For research involving the constructs of communication avoidance, shyness, communication apprehension, and reticence, these distinctions are critical to the decision of selection of this type of measure.

Self-report measures are the most useful for measuring communication apprehension. Since this construct is directed toward the cognitions of the individual, it is uniquely suited to self-report measurement, if care is taken to avoid causing the respondent to provide false answers. Such measures have strong face validity (some have other strong indications of validity as well) and are the only measures isomorphic with the communication apprehension construct. Physiological and observation measures lack such isomorphism, and thus must rest their case for validity upon observed correlations with previously validated self-report measures.

Self-report measures are amenable to either trait or state concerns with communication apprehension. Respondents can report their general feelings, their feelings in broad categories of communication situations, and their feelings in specific situations with equal ease.

Self-report measures probably are the least useful for measuring reticence. While subjects can report whether they *feel* competent in general or in specific settings (probably an indirect and imprecise measure of communication apprehension), they are not likely to be in a position to know whether they *are* competent. Most likely such self-reports would be overwhelmingly influenced by the respondent's self-esteem. Respondents with high self-esteem would report being competent, while those with low self-esteem would report being incompetent. Such reports might even be somewhat correlated with observed competence, but they would still lack face validity. It has been my experience, for example, that many people who consider themselves the most competent in interpersonal communication or public speaking (often experts and teachers in the area) are, in fact, among the least competent.

The use of self-report instruments to measure shyness or communication avoidance is problematic. The question that must be addressed is whether respondents actually know how much they talk compared to others. On the one hand, Bernard and Killworth (1977) present convincing evidence that people cannot accurately report with whom they talk on a given day (the basic data for much network research). On the other hand, at least one measure of shyness has generated a respectable validity quotient when assessed against observer ratings (McCroskey and Richmond, 1982a). With this limited information, we may infer that self-reports of shyness may be more valid for trait measurement than they are for state measurement. However, more research is needed before we can hold that conclusion with much confidence.

While determining advice for or against the use of self-report scales for shyness or communication avoidance is difficult at best, the decision probably should be based on two considerations: (1) Does the self-report measure have a substantial case for validity compared to observer ratings? and (2) Is it practically feasible to use observer ratings as an alternative?

As I noted previously, behavioral observation has strong face validity for the measurement of shyness and communication avoidance. Such face validity is lacking for the other measurement approaches. Thus behavioral observation, other things being equal, should be the measure of choice. However, in many instances it is not feasible to employ this method. When this is the case, the researcher should turn to self-report measurement with extreme care. There are a number of shyness measures available in the literature, many of which really are measures of communication apprehension, and most of them have only modest data supporting validity, if any at all. One of the most widely used measures of shyness (Zimbardo, 1977), for example, has a modest case for predictive validity, but I have been unable to generate acceptable validity quotients against observer ratings for this measure. It is probable that this measure is simply a crude and imprecise measure of communication apprehension, since it generates moderate correlations with established communication apprehension measures, and the Zimbardo conceptualization of shyness is very similar to the conceptualization of communication apprehension outlined earlier in this book.

All in all, self-report measures are potentially very useful for researchers concerned with communication avoidance, shyness, and communication apprehension. They represent an inexpensive and efficient method of assessing large numbers of respondents with minimum effort or imposition. Of course, the choice of self-report instrument must hinge on the instrument's demonstrated validity. The use of unvalidated instruments should be avoided carefully. Validated instruments for most purposes are available and should be chosen over the many others that have appeared in the literature.

Available Measures

A wide variety of self-report measures related to communication avoidance, shyness, and communication apprehension have been reported in the literature. Many of these have been used only once or have negative indications of validity, so these will not be considered here. The ones that are discussed below are instruments that are widely used, have a good case for validity, and/or show some promise for future use. These are grouped in four categories: measures of communication avoidance or shyness, measures of communication apprehension in generalized contexts, measures of traitlike communication apprehension, and measures of state communication apprehension.

Measures of Communication Avoidance or Shyness

As noted previously, I am considering shyness to be the tendency to avoid communication and talk less. Shyness has been defined in other ways by other scale developers. Scales that measure "shyness" conceptualized in a different way are considered in another section.

The Predispositions Toward Verbal Communication (PVB) scale was developed by Mortensen, Arntson, and Lustig (1977). This is a 25-item, 7-step scale with good reliability and substantial indications of validity, even though it has received little use from researchers other than its developers. Although a few of the items on the scale appear to be more appropriate for a measure of communication apprehension, the bulk of the items appear to measure a traitlike orientation toward initiating, maintaining, and dominating communication. In general, the PVB appears to be a very good measure of a trait approach-avoidance orientation. This conclusion is supported by substantial relationships between PVB scores and both observer ratings and actual coded behavior in controlled settings.

The Unwillingness-to-Communicate Scale (UCS) was developed by Burgoon (1976). The scale has been found to have two independent dimensions, one measuring communication apprehension and the other measuring perceived communication rewards. The apprehension dimension is not relevant here and is measured better by other scales to be discussed in a later section. The reward factor is promising as a measure of the construct of concern. However, there is little support for the validity of the instrument available at this point. It has received little attention from researchers since its publication. One major concern about the scale is the *lack* of correlation between the two factors. Conceptualizations of communication apprehension and communication avoidance, as well as the conceptualization of unwillingness to communicate itself, suggest that there should be a substantial relationship. The PVB does evidence such a relationship, and thus probably should be selected in preference over the UCS.

The Stanford Shyness Survey (SSS) developed by Zimbardo (1977) is the best known measure of shyness. However, its use has been limited primarily to its originator and his students. In any event, it is very difficult to determine what the SSS actually measures. Results reported from use of the measure are a close analogue to results of studies employing communication apprehension measures. At present, there is little evidence to support this measure's use as a measure of communication avoidance. The PVB clearly should be preferred over the SSS for this purpose.

The measure of communication avoidance (SHY) that I developed (McCroskey, Andersen, Richmond, and Wheeless, 1981) was generated as an artifact of attempting to develop a measure of communication apprehension with simplified wording that could be used with preliterate children. Preliminary work indicated the presence of two factors that although substantially correlated (around .60), were clearly distinct. The items on the measure relate specifically to the amount a person believes he or she talks compared to others.

The SHY measure is a 14-item, 5-step scale with good reliability and face validity. Its validity also is suggested by moderately high correlations between SHY scores and observer ratings. Also, in unpublished research I have found PVB and SHY to be correlated above .80, suggesting concurrent validity for the two measures. In general, then, either measure can be chosen with some confidence. However, if length of scale or simplicity of wording is an important concern, the SHY scale should be preferred because it is shorter and simpler.

Measures of Communication Apprehension in Generalized Contexts

Most of the early measures that fit in this category of instruments were concerned with communication apprehension in the public speaking context, commonly called "stage fright." Only recently have measures appeared that attempt to measure communication apprehension in other generalized contexts. All of these measures attempt to tap a traitlike orientation that applies only to a specific type of communication context (as opposed to a traitlike orientation that cuts across contexts, which will be considered in the next section).

The first widely used measure of traitlike stage fright was the Personal Report of Confidence as a Speaker (PRCS) developed by Gilkinson (1942). Numerous shorter versions of the PRCS have appeared in the literature, the most commonly used being one reported by Paul (1966). Both the longer and the shorter versions have been demonstrated to be highly reliable and numerous research studies point to their validity.

Since the PRCS employs a forced true-false response option, I developed the Personal Report of Public Speaking Anxiety (PRPSA), a 34-item, 5-step, Likert-type scale, to increase precision of measurement (McCroskey, 1970). This scale is highly reliable and was found to maintain that reliability, in subsequent research, with only half as many items (Hensley and Batty, 1974). The concurrent validity of this scale was demonstrated by correlations above .80 with the PRCS. Those same correlations, of course, question the need for the scale, at least in its long, 34-item form. It is essentially equivalent to, not superior to, the PRCS. It might be preferred to the PRCS if the short form (17-item) is used when length of measurement is a problem.

Buss (1980) reports use of two scales that appear to measure communication apprehension in separate categories of communication contexts. One is referred to as a measure of audience anxiety, a 5-item scale with a reliability of .73. Unfortunately, three of the items relate to public speaking and two relate to talking in class, two contexts that have been found to be correlated yet distinct in terms of the level of generalized communication apprehension they generate. Consequently, this scale is not recommended for use.

The second scale is referred to as a shyness scale, a 9-item scale with a reliability of .78. While this scale clearly does not measure shyness as conceptualized here it does appear to be a fairly good measure of communication apprehension in dyadic and small social group contexts. The problem, as with the audience anxiety scale, is that the contexts of dyadic and small group communication are confounded in the scale. Apprehension concerning these two contexts has been found to be correlated, but the levels are distinct from each other and often dramatically different for a given individual. Consequently, this scale is not recommended for use.

Leary (1982) also has developed two instruments that appear to measure communication apprehension in separate categories of communication contexts. Unlike the Buss (1980) scales, these are clear measures of two distinct contexts. The first scale is the Interaction Anxiousness (IA) scale. This is a 15-item, 5-step, Likert-type scale tapping apprehension about interpersonal, primarily dyadic, communication. The second scale is the Audience Anxiousness (AA) scale. This is a 12-item, 5-step, Likert-type scale tapping stage fright, primarily in the public speaking context. Both instruments generate good reliability and there is some evidence for validity.

As can be seen from the above discussions, we have several instruments that appear to be very satisfactory measures of communication apprehension in the public speaking context, but we have no widely used or strongly validated measures of traitlike communication apprehension for the contexts of talking in meetings or classes, talking in small group settings, or talking in dyadic settings. The only measures that seem to hold some promise for these purposes, other than the Leary IA scale, are those I developed with Richmond (McCroskey and Richmond, 1982a). Each scale is a 10-item, 5-step, Likert-type instrument. The reliabilities we have obtained have been very satisfactory and the face validity of the instruments is good. However, at present no other indications of validity have been established. Thus I recommend the use of these scales only on the basis of the absence of other scales and the promising outlook for the validity of these scales, yet to be verified.

Measures of Traitlike Communication Apprehension

The Personal Report of Communication Apprehension (PRCA), in its various forms, has been the self-report measure employed in the overwhelming majority of studies involving traitlike communication apprehension. There are 20-item (McCroskey, 1970), 10-item (McCroskey, 1978), 25-item (McCroskey, 1978), and 24-item (McCroskey, 1982) versions of this instrument available. All use 5-step, Likert-type response formats. The reliability of all of the forms is very high, usually above .90. The forms are correlated around .90. There is overwhelming evidence for the predictive validity of the measures.

The 10-, 20-, and 25-item versions of the instrument have been criticized for their inclusion of a disproportionate number of items relating to public speaking when the instruments purport to tap traitlike communication apprehension across communication contexts. The most recently developed, 24-item, version of the instrument overcomes this criticism since it includes 6 items for each of 4 contexts: public speaking, talking in meetings or classes, talking in small groups, and talking in dyads. This version also permits the generation of 4 subscores (1 for each context) as well as an overall score. In some as yet unpublished research, the subscores have been found to differ in their predictive power for a variety of dependent variables. Thus the clear choice of which form to use is the 24-item version.

Another measure of traitlike communication apprehension that may be recommended for some uses is the Personal Report of Communication Fear (PRCF; McCroskey et al. 1981). This measure is not completely isomorphic with the various forms of the PRCA, hence its slightly different name. It was designed to employ a much smaller vocabulary than the PRCA so it could be used with preliterate children. With older children and adults the two measures correlate around .80, suggesting substantial concurrent validity but not isomorphism. This measure can be used with small children, but the PRCA-24 should be used with all older groups. One problem with the PRCF when used with young children is that many of the items are worded in a negative way to avoid response bias. Young children have considerable difficulty handling the double-negative response of disagreeing with a negatively worded item. Hence, since this measure must be presented orally to the young children, the administrator of the instrument must take great care to be certain that the correct response from the child is determined and recorded. Carelessness in administration will lead to greatly reduced reliability and validity of the scores.

The Measure of Elementary Communication Apprehension (MECA) was designed to overcome the wording problems in the PRCF (Garrison and Garrison, 1979). The MECA is a 20-item, 5-choice, Likert-type instrument. It is unique in that the response options are presented in the form of faces, ranging from a broad smile to a broad frown. The problem of response bias is controlled by presenting the faces in reverse order for half of the items. Concurrent validity with the PRCF is very good and fairly good with the PRCA-10. Discriminate validity was also established. This measure should be the instrument of choice when working with small children, but probably should not be used with older children, who may feel the "smiling faces" response options are a bit beneath them.

Measures of State
Communication Apprehension

In the past most measurement of traitlike and generalized-context communication apprehension has employed self-report instruments. In contrast, most state measurement of communication apprehension has employed physiological indicants or behavioral observation. The weakness of the latter two approaches for measuring communication apprehension has led recently to the use of self-reports.

The State Anxiety measure developed by Spielberger (1966) has been employed most frequently. This measure can be used to tap any state anxiety, not just state anxiety about a communication situation. It is a 20-item, true-false type of instrument. It has very good reliability and strong face validity. Richmond (1978) employed a modified version of the instrument with good results. She adapted the instructions for the instrument to apply specifically to a communication situation and converted the response options to a 5-step, Likert-type format. She obtained high reliability and a strong indication of validity.

This instrument can be recommended strongly for use as a measure of state communication apprehension. However, the instrument is under copyright (which I do not hold) and fees for use are unusually high. As an alternative the State Communication Apprehension Measure (SCAM) is recommended. This measure was developed by Richmond and I to avoid copyright infringement (McCroskey and Richmond, 1982b). Unlike the Spielberger instrument, the SCAM is a 20-item, 5-step, Likert-type instrument. It has high reliability, around .90, and good face validity.

Conclusion

Self-report instruments are readily available for use as measures of communication avoidance, shyness, and communication apprehension (both triat and state). Many have both good reliability and support for validity. Care must be taken to determine that self-report measurement is appropriate for the task at hand. Self-report instruments, when properly developed and validated, and when employed for legitimate purposes, can be invaluable tools to both researchers and practitioners concerned with communication avoidance, shyness, and communication apprehension. The use of poorly developed or invalid self-report measures or the use of self-report instruments when other measurement approaches are more appropriate are abuses that both researchers and practitioners must avoid.

6

Physiological Assessment

MICHAEL BEATTY

The mere notion of communication apprehension (CA) evokes images of certain physiological reactions. For example, elevated heart rate and increased muscle tension for apprehensive persons caught in communication situations comes to mind. What speech teacher has not observed the trembling hands or blushed neck of nervous students during public speaking assignments? At the base of physiological communication research is the assumption that physiological arousal underlies these observable behaviors. There is some evidence that apprehensive communicators recognize the influence of physiological changes in their overall reaction to communication. Beatty and his colleagues (1976) interviewed undergraduate students who described themselves as anxious about public speaking. Statements concerning increased heart rates, respiration, and tension were common among the descriptions and survived subsequent test analyses. However, the path to defining the precise nature of the communication-physiological activation relationship is replete with methodological and theoretical pitfalls. In this chapter, selected research concerning the measurement of physiological activation relationship between activation and CA will be summarized. Additionally, some complications related to the body of research will be discussed.

How Has Physiological Activation Been Measured in Communication Research?

Covert responses are releases of energy that subjects can not control easily. The task for the physiological researcher is to measure accurately these responses. Communication apprehension researchers focus on those covert responses that are most likely associated with fear or anxiety reactions in communication settings. Perhaps the most popular responses measured in this line of research are those related to the circulatory system. As early as 1951, Dickens and Parker found significant differences in blood pressure before and after subjects gave speeches. Fluctuations in blood pressure in response to stressful situations are due to constriction of blood vessels, an effect of the homeostatic process. When the constant volume of blood is forced through the reduced vessels, pressure is increased.

Kelly, Brown, and Shaffer (1970) measured, among other variables, heart rates of anxious patients and normal persons. They reported that resting heart rates were significantly higher for the anxious patients. Although the Kelly et al. study was not communication apprehension research, it paved the way for subsequent communication research, establishing the assumption that heart rate is a useful index of a speaker's emotional response to public speaking. For example, Behnke and Carlile (1971) measured speakers' heart rates continuously during a public speaking performance. Heart rates were recorded during one-minute intervals before, during, and after the speech. These researchers observed four distinct patterns that occur during a speaking episode, in chronological order: (1) anticipation — a small elevation in average heart rate during the one-minute period prior to the speech; (2) confrontation — a dramatic elevation in average heart rate during the one-minute period after the student begins to speak; (3) adaptation — a marked but not dramatic elevation in average heart rate during the last minute of the speech; and (4) release — a small elevation in the average heart rate during the one-minute period after completion of the speech. These periods have served as operational definitions of heart rate in most physiological communication studies (Porter, 1974; Behnke, Carlile, & Lamb, 1974; Behnke & Beatty, 1981).

A second response commonly used to evaluate physiological arousal is skin conductivity. Perhaps the most popular measure of skin conductivity is the galvanic skin response (GSR). The GSR is generally considered a highly sensitive measure (Behnke, 1976, p.17). Several studies have employed skin response to assess the impact of a stimulus Burnstein, et al. 1965) on apprehension or anxiety (Moroney & Zenhausern, 1972; Hyman & Gale, 1973). Myers (1974) used GSR as a dependent measure to validate both visualizations and the effects of systematic desensitization.

The analysis of palmar sweating as a measure of arousal stems from the work of Kuno (1934). Briefly, Kuno established that human perspiration falls into two categories: (1) thermal sweating, the result of extreme temperature changes, which is unrelated to emotional conditions; and (2) emotional sweating, which results from emotional arousal (p. 29). Furthermore, Kuno posited that thermal and emotional sweating are discrete autonomic functions. Thermal sweating is not stimulated by noxious stimuli and emotional sweating is not stimulated by temperature changes. Of course, both types of sweating may occur simultaneously. It is the use of palmar sweat analysis that allows researchers to distinguish emotional sweating from thermal sweating. Palmar sweat analysis has been employed by Silverman and Powell (1944), Davis (1957), and Bixenstein (1955) as a measure of autonomic response in psychological research. Palmar sweat analysis also has been employed in communication research. In 1963, Brutten used the procedures as an index of stress in an investigation of disfluency and expectation. Later, Bode and Brutten (1963) used palmar sweating as their operational definition of speech anxiety.

The most recent development in evaluating physiological responses to communication events is the indirect measurement of brain temperature. Brain temperature is measured by inserting a thermister probe, which is a hearing-aid-like device, into the ear. The thermister senses brain temperature via the external auditory meatus of the dominant ear. Temperature in the meatus is correlated with temperature at the typanic membrane and, in turn, with the temperature of the hypothalamus (Dickey, Ahlgren, & Stephen, 1970). Increased blood volume in the hypothalamus leads to decreased brain temperature because blood is cooler than brain tissue and tends to act as a coolant. Conversely, increased brain temperature indicates blood flow away from the brain. The measurement of brain temperature has important implications for psychophysiological-oriented communication research. Basically, brain-related variables are related to central nervous functioning, whereas the first few measurement techniques reviewed in this chapter index autonomic nervous activity. Integration of brain-related variables with other physiological measures will be discussed in more detail in later sections.

Other physiological variables include muscle tension, respiration depth and frequency, skin temperature, and brain wave activity. Since these measures have not been used as measures of communication-related anxiety, they will not be reviewed in this chapter. However, future research employing these variables might provide valuable information about covert responses to communication situations.

What Is the Relationship Between
Physiological Arousal and Communication Apprehension?

A review of the research literature shows that the relationship between physiological arousal and CA is indeed complex. Different and often conflicting empirical generalizations apply, depending on several factors. For example, several published studies have reported significant moderate correlations between heart rate and scores on self-report inventories measuring how subjects actually felt during public speaking performances (Behnke & Carlile, 1971; Behnke et al., 1974; Behnke & Beatty, 1981). The generalization stemming from this limited body of research is that there is a moderate correlation between heart rate increases and self-reported state anxiety when both physiological and self-report scores refer to the actual event.

The body of published research concerning the relationship between CA, conceptualized as a trait, and physiological measures is scant. Available research for the most part shows no meaningful relationship, particularly for heart rate. However, one published study sheds some light on this relationship. Among other things, Behnke and Beatty (1981) studied the relationship between elevations in heart rates during public speaking assignments. The results indicated no relationship with trait CA. However, they reported a significant negative correlation ($r = -.499$) between brain temperature during performance and PRCA scores collected in a prior class period. In physiological terms, these results suggest that the higher a subject's level of CA, the lower the brain temperature. As discussed earlier, these findings also indicate that the higher a subject's level of CA, the more blood volume or flow there is in the hypothalamus during communication performances. The correlation between brain temperature collected in absence of a communication stimulus and PRCA scores is nonsignificant ($r = .031$), discounting the possibility that there is an inherent physiological difference between high and low CAs.

An important theoretical question, of course, concerns the obvious discrepancy between the heart rate-CA research and the brain temperature-CA research. Why is brain temperature correlated with trait CA whereas heart rate is not correlated with trait CA? Answering this question is necessary to generalize about CA and physiological responses.

Understanding the role various physiological responses play in emotions may illuminate the issue. Schachter and Singer (1962) proposed a paradigm for explaining emotional response that appears to explain why heart rates are correlated with anxiety reported during speaking yet uncorrelated with trait CA. They postulated that "an emotional state may be considered a function of a state of physiological arousal and of a cognition appropriate to the state of arousal" (p. 380). Physiological arousal engenders pressure to understand and label sympathetic nervous activity (p. 380). How an individual labels this arousal depends on past cues "as interpreted by past experience" (p. 380). According to Schachter and Singer, neither physiological arousal nor cognitive perception alone would account for the emotions experienced during communication. Individual levels of emotion during specific communication experiences are contingent on the presence of a physiological activation along with an interpretation of the arousal as being caused by the communication situation. For example, a person who perceives himself or herself to be a high CA would interpret increased heart rate during communication as fear or anxiety, whereas a confident low CA might interpret the arousal as excitement. Therefore, CA serves as the predisposition to interpret arousal during communication as anxiety or fear. Viewed in this context, CA does not cause — nor is it caused by — increased heart rate.

Behnke and Beatty (1981) tested a regression model derived from Schachter's theory. Using PRCA scores and elevations in heart rate as predictors, they accounted for 79.60% of the variance in self-reported speech state anxiety experienced during public speaking. The beta weights for the CA variables and the heart rate variable were essentially equal, and there was no significant collinearity.

If CA does not cause arousal, where does the elevated heart rate originate? Increased heart rate serves to energize persons whether in approach or avoidance situations. The approach or avoidance decision itself is cognitive, whereas the arousal is dependent on perceived properties of the situation. For example, the social facilitation research (Zajonc, 1965) shows that the presence of strangers increases arousal in humans. Moreover, the effect tends to increase as the number of strangers increases. A need for social approval (Crowne & Marlowe, 1964) also seems to result in increased heart rate (Adams, Beatty, & Behnke, 1980). Although few other causes of arousal during communication have been documented, elements such as novelty, formality, and conspicuousness, outlined by Buss (1980), probably are likely candidates. McCroskey (1981) pointed out that these causal elements are particularly insightful with respect to CA. Clearly, the presence of strangers, need for approval, novelty, formality, and conspicuousness are integrated into the experience of a novice public speaker during a graded performance in a normal classroom setting. The published research in which heart rate is monitored continuously demonstrates the impressive physiological impact of public speaking (Behnke & Carlile, 1971; Porter, 1974; Behnke & Beatty, 1981). While the impact may be similar for experienced performers (Behnke & Beatty, 1981), the arousal is interpreted as fear or anxiety by high CAs. Currently there is no research investigating low CAs' perceptions of physiologically arousing communication experiences.

In sum, it can be argued that the cognitive predisposition evaluates whether or not a particular emotion is experienced in a specific situation. Evidence has been cited to support the belief that CA constitutes such a predisposition. However, it is feedback in the form of physiological arousal — heart rate in particular — that determines the magnitude of the emotional response. Consequently, a subject self-perceives tremendous fear related to communication because he or she is a high CA and experiences elevated heart rate during a communication encounter. A cycle is created in which the self-perception is assimilated into the predisposition, thereby reinforcing an individual's level of CA (Beatty & Behnke, 1981). Thus CA, heart rate, and self-perceived fear in communication situations are entwined in a system of attitudes and responses.

Why does brain temperature correlate directly with trait CA if other physiological variables such as heart rate do not? First, it is crucial to recall that brain temperature measures central nervous activity, whereas heart rate is associated with autonomic activity. Second, it is difficult to argue that CA is free from any physiological basis. After all, cognition and perception are phenomena normally associated with brain activity (Popper & Eccles, 1977). Physiological reductionists maintain that all mental process can be reduced and are identical to physical operations in the brain. Accordingly, reductionism posits that mental states are merely images projected by specific brain activities. Interactionists, on the other hand, hold that mental states and brain behavior are not identical but do influence one another. In other words, thought is more than the reflections of brain activity.

Philosophically opposite of reductionism is mentalism. Mentalists argue that brain activity is the result of the mind that exists independently of the physical brain. In this perspective, the human mind has essence or soul qualities. However, recent brain research connecting specific brain functioning with cognitive activities has lead to the abandonment of mentalism with respect to learning theory. Popper and Eccles (1977) accurately referred to the reductionist-interactionist-mentalist controversy as the "brain-mind problem" (p. 134). The preceding discussion leads to the conclusion that unless some type of brain activity-CA relationship is expected, CA is either not a cognitive phenomenon or mentalism is correct and CA is a soullike quality.

The fact that hypothalamic temperature,in particular, relates to CA is important because such a relationship bridges two bodies of literature. Arnold (1967) postulated an "affective memory" committed to the hypothalamus in which the perceptions of stimuli are processed and a search for affective responses based on past experience with the stimuli is conducted. The stronger the affect associated with a stimulus, the more hypothalamic activity during confrontation with the stimulus. Conversely, stimuli to which affect has not been strongly attached produces little hypothalamic activity. CAs could be viewed as persons who have stored strong negative reactions to communication situations in affective memory. Therefore, when forced to communicate, the search narrows and focuses on negative emotions, resulting in hypothalamic activity indexed by increased blood flow and decreased hypothalamic temperature, hence the negative brain temperature-CA correlation. As with heart rate, brain activity is not the emotional response. Rather, it is merely a function that facilitates the processing of information relevant to the person's adaptation to situations.

This concept of affective memory fits neatly into Schachter and Singer's paradigm outlined previously. Central to this theory is the contention that increased arousal, such as heart rate, is interpreted based on past experience. However, when previous experience fails to provide an appropriate label, the person must work creatively to explain the aroused state. Arnold's (1967) construct of "affective memory" provides a physiological explanation for Schachter and Singer's model, positing the hypothalamus as the central mechanism that stores and controls the labeling function.

Although the previous theorizing is highly speculative, the results of existing physiological research are consistent with expectations derived from the perspective. In addition, some evidence drawn from studies directly testing a Schachterian model has been published. Perhaps even more important for future research, a theoretical framework has been offered that can be supported or rejected. Most physiological research in the field of communication has been atheoretical and merely correlational. The outcome has been correlations between physiological arousal and self-report measures that rule out mentalism but reduce uncertainty about little else. In any case, the relationship between self-reported communication anxiety and physiological activation is far more complex than was depicted by Clevenger (1959) in his early review of research on stage fright.

What Problems Complicate CA-Physiological Research?

The difficulties that plague CA-physiological research concern both theoretical and methodological issues. Moreover, the theory-method overlap has greater import on resulting research findings than in other lines of communication research. For example, the method used to calculate factor scores can be critiqued independent of the variable being measured. Measures of homophily or speaker credibility in and of themselves place no demand on factor score computation. Whether a factor score represents the sum of all weighted items or merely the sum of the raw scores for the five highest items is determined by methodological convention. In contrast, how physiological data are reduced to numbers *is* tied to assumptions about physiological response.

Physiological measurement results in data that takes various forms, and the continous monitoring of responses results in an enormous amount of data. Measuring rate, for instance, produces a continuous wave form on literally yards of paper per subject. How should these numbers be collapsed into a single subject's score? If a subject's heart rate is monitored during a fifteen-minute speech, should average heart rate for the entire period be used or should multiple intervals be analyzed? In the communication literature these questions seem to be answered by arbitrary selection from a variety of techniques. Seldom, if ever, have theoretical justifications for the approach selected been provided, nor is evidence offered to support the belief that the data reduction technique was appropriate to the data at hand.

Communication research focused on physiological responses has not dealt with the Law of Initial Value (LIV) in an adequate manner. As summarized by Wilder (1957), the law states:

> Not only the intensity but also the direction of a response of a body function to any agent depend to a large degree on the initial level of the function at the start of the experiment. The higher this "initial level," the smaller is the response to function-raising . . . . agents. At more extreme initial levels there is a progressive tendency to "no response" and to "paradoxic reactions," i.e., a reversal of the usual direction of the response. (1957, p. 73)

The explanation for LIV resides in understanding the body's homeostatic process. As a matter of nature, living organisms regress toward the mean any extreme physiological response. Therefore, a student experiencing an abnormally high level of heart rate prior to a public speaking performance may show no change or a decline in heart rate even though the experience is having a substantial impact on the student. However, suppose the student finds that the experience is not as bad as anticipated and actually becomes more at ease during the performance. In this case the student may show no change or perhaps a decline in heart rate. Thus a decline in heart rate may indicate separate and conflicting states.

The existence of LIV has been recognized by researches in the field of communication. Although Wilder (1957) is usually cited, physiological responses to communication-related stimuli actually have not been adjusted or corrected in the sense implicated by LIV. Porter and Burns (1973) first raised this issue about a decade ago. Unfortunately, the issues raised at that time have not been addressed in the communication field.

Any attempt to account statistically for LIV must accomplish two goals. First, the technique must free response scores from initial-level scores. Of course, this issue has hounded researchers interested in studying changes of all kinds. Many different approaches for dealing with change scores have been offered in measurement texts (Ferguson, 1971, pp. 386-387). Second, the scoring procedure must deal with the nonlinear relationship between initial and stimulus scores implicated by LIV. By far the most popular approach to LIV is due to Lacey (1956). Lacey advanced the following formula (p.139) as a method for computing autonomic lability scores (ALS), which is touted as complying with the LIV assumption:

$$ALS = 50 + 10 \frac{Yz - Xz \; rxy}{(1 - rxy_2)^{1/2}}$$

In this formula, Yz represents standardized response scores, whereas Xz represents standardized initial-level scores. There is little doubt that ALS frees response scores from intial levels or that it assigns higher scores for increases from relatively higher initial levels. For example, assuming an initial-level-stimulus correlation of .50, a subject moving from a standard scores of 1.00 to 2.00 would receive as ALS equal to 67.32. A subject moving from 2.00 to 3.00, although the change is also one standardized unit, would receive an ALS of 73.09.

The problem with ALS relates to the nonlinear initial-level and stimulus-level relationship. According to Wilder's conception of LIV, decreases in observed phenomenon may indicate increased arousal, but such occurrences may also be indicative of decreased arousal. Obviously, the ALS formula cannot accommodate both empirical outcomes. For example, a .50 correlation between initial and stimulus levels may indicate substantial curvilinearity, in need of correction, or it may indicate only a moderate degree of linear dependence requiring only the calculation of change scores. ALS cannot discriminate between these two cases. To deal fully with LIV, it must first be determined that the relationship between initial and response levels is in fact not linear. It is worth noting here that Wilder (1957), in his original studies, reported that the effect attributed to LIV does not occur in 25% of experiments. Second, the degree of curvilinearity must be determined so that some estimate of how much correction is needed can be calculated. Third, some method for correcting the nonlinearity must be applied. If the data in a particular study, determined to be curvilinear, is corrected using a linear transformation appropriate to the shape of the relationship or higher-level polynomials are incorporated into the ALS formula, then the spirit of Wilder's LIV might be met. However, simply applying ALS to data as a matter of convention and footnoting Wilder and Lacey, as is currently in vogue in the communication literature, does not account for LIV. At best, such a practice is successful in those cases where LIV is not occurring. At worst, the curvilinear component to LIV is omitted from the data analysis, and all of the confounding problems outlined by Wilder occur unbeknown to the researcher or the unsuspecting consumers of the research. Porter (1974) is one noteworthy exception in a body of research where empirical justification for using or not using ALS is lacking.

Conclusion

Three decades of research have produced some important insights concerning physiological reactions to stressful communication situations. For example, it is now known that public speakers experience considerable autonomic arousal during performances. It has been reported that arousal during this period correlates significantly with certain self-report measures of state anxiety. Research has shown that individual levels of communication apprehension are used by communicators to define and interpret arousal that is experienced during communication episodes. Published studies have also reported that high CAs demonstrate differentiated brain functioning in contrast to low CA counterparts but only while anticipating a stressful communication experience. However, physiological research holds considerably more potential to yield valuable information about emotional responses to communication. Theoretical advances concerning physiological aspects of communication apprehension are required to guide research efforts and to reap more abundant yields.

7

Observer-Perceived Communicator Anxiety

ANTHONY MULAC and JOHN M. WIEMANN

Communication apprehension is clearly a multifaceted phenomenon. However, researchers who have investigated communication apprehension or anxiety have typically been concerned with the experience of the speaker, as reported by the speaker. In this chapter we focus on the audience. More precisely, we hold that during the act of communicating, the speaker's experienced anxiety is consequential only to the extent that the audience perceives that anxiety and makes attributions about the speaker based on those perceptions. In the following we develop a rationale for the importance of observer-perceived communicator anxiety in the study of communication anxiety, discuss methods for its measurement, present guidelines for determining the quality of that measurement, and offer suggestions for further study.

Rationale

Clevenger (1959) recognized that audience members' perceptions of anxiety are conceptually different from both the cognitive and physiological experience of that anxiety. Behavioral speech anxiety was defined by Mulac and Sherman (1975b, p. 276) as "the degree of assumed speaker anxiety perceived by observers on the basis of manifest speaker behavior." Thus it is the manifest behavior which observer — whether members of a lecture audience, an interviewer, or cocktail party conversation partners — base their judgments about speakers. This aspect of apprehension thus becomes paramount to speaker "success."

Being apprehensive and acting apprehensive are very different experiences. Speaker success vis-à-vis the audience depends on the latter even though the quality of the experience for the speaker is probably somewhat related to the former. And it is also likely that, to an extent, being apprehensive in the cognitive-physiological sense translates into acting apprehensive, although this is not necessarily the case. Further, if specific behaviors manifested by the speaker are the product of his or her experienced apprehension, but the audience construes them differently (e.g., "He's sweating because it's hot in here"), then the speaker's apprehension has no pragmatic effect on the audience or their evaluation of that person as a speaker. The converse can also be argued, of course. A speaker can feel calm and anxiety-free. Yet if he or she engages in behaviors the audience construes as cues of anxiety, then the practical effect is that the speaker and message will be discredited to some degree.

Argyle (1969, p. 325) described the social behavior of an anxious person as "ill at ease, flustered and embarrassed, tense and awkward, and generally unable to cope." Goffman (1959) suggested that such behavior in and of itself is dysfunctional to an encounter, whether a public speech or a social interaction, especially in that it puts a strain on everyone involved, not just the anxious person. Following Goffman's line of thinking concerning participants' "obligations" to maintain each others' face (i.e., presented self) we surmise that a visibly anxious person makes unusual demands on those with whom he or she interacts. Because one's interlocutors may not always be willing or able to tolerate such demands, the anxious person runs several communicational risks, including limited opportunities to interact, diminished credibility, and diminished opportunities to influence and lead in groups. Obviously anxious behavior can be considered no more than faulty self-presentation if it is an unusual performance for a particular person or if the situation is one where anxiety is more or less the norm (e.g., an interrogation). But when anxious behavior is displayed in many contexts — especially in encounters that are defined by other participants to be "relaxed" — the anxious person is considered abnormal to some degree, with diagnoses ranging from unpleasant to psychotic (Trower, Bryant, & Argyle, 1978).

The point is that it is anxious behavior that results in negative attributions, not merely feeling anxious, and these attributions have consequences. In addition to the work in person perception and implicit personality theories that demonstrates in a general way the behavioral base of attributions (see Schneider, Hastorf, & Ellsworth, 1979, for a review of this literature), several communication scholars have noted the particular consequences of apprehensive behavior.

One group of studies that highlights the importance of observers perceptions-attributions divides subjects into high and low apprehensive groups based on self-reports and then assess how these different groups are judged by observers. Since these studies do not evaluate the behavior of the subjects (only their perceptions of their own behavior), we do not know what the subject did which resulted in negative attributions (i.e., they might have acted anxious or they might have behaved in other nonrewarding ways). They are interesting to us because they demonstrate that on at least some occasions experienced anxiety becomes manifest. For example, Quiggens (1972, reported in McCroskey, 1976) found that group members perceived high apprehensives as less competent and socially attractive than low apprehensives. Apprehension has also been found to result in people being perceived as less interpersonally attractive (McCroskey, Daly, Richmond, & Cox, 1975) and less credible (McCroskey and Richmond, 1976). McCroskey (1976; also see McCroskey, 1977) refers to this phenomenon as the "effects of communication apprehension." It is clear that when self-experienced apprehension is made public by unrewarding and possibly anxious behavior, negative evaluations result.

Studies of the effects of communication apprehension do not provide direct evidence of the behavior-attribution relationship. But another line of work has made this relationship its focus. The importance of perceptions-attributions is demonstrated empirically by their negative correlation with measures of speech skill (Price, 1964) and credibility (Berlo & Lemert, 1961). Mulac and Sherman (1975a) found that perceived anxiety, as measured by their Behavioral Assessment of Speech Anxiety Scale (BASA; see Mulac & Sherman, 1974, was negatively correlated with perceptions of speech skill ($r = -.81$ for men and $-.45$ for women). In the same study they reported BASA ratings were negatively correlated with perceptions of trustworthiness ($-.63$) and competence ($-.75$) for men.

Similar results have been obtained in interpersonal settings. Displays of anxiety-related behaviors have been linked to attempts to deceive (Mehrabian, 1971), to perceptions of low communicator skill (Argyle, 1969; Trower et al., 1978), and to perceptions of relatively low communicative competence (Steffen & Redden, 1977; Wiemann, 1977).

The obvious importance of observer-perceived communicator anxiety argues for a measurement strategy that places those perceptions at its center. Researchers concerned with communication performances have developed procedures to assess what communicators do and the impact their behaviors have on others.

Measurement

The assessment of enacted communication anxiety — that is, the measurement of observers' perceptions of how anxious another is — has taken two courses. One approach has been to construct rating instruments on which observers indicate whether, or how severely, a relatively large number of specific behaviors have occurred during a given time. Most commonly, the observers check or rate any of the behaviors that occur during a segment, and performances are not replayed for the rating of other variables. The other approach uses coders to count the frequency of the display of a smaller number of specific behaviors during an encounter, with the audio or videotape replayed for each variable to be coded. The former has been used most frequently in public speaking situations, while the latter has been employed more commonly in the assessment of social, interpersonal behaviors. These approaches differ mainly in the amount of responsibility given the observer in terms of behaviors they score at any one time and level of inferences they are asked to make.

In an attempt to establish the factor structure of the "visible symptoms of stage fright" in the public speaking setting, Clevenger and King (1961) devised a checklist of 18 visible behaviors, drawn from speech textbooks and previous research and judged to be useful by a group of experienced speech teachers. The researchers noted that they used the term "symptom" to denote "behavior considered characteristic of [stage fright], and should not be construed as equivalent to 'indicator'; there was no assumption that any of the symptoms reflected the inner feelings or physiological states of the speakers" (p. 296). These behaviors (e.g., hands tremble, sways, deadpan expression) were measured during beginning speech students three-minute informative speeches by three experienced observers present in the classroom. The instructions read: "Place a check mark beside each of the following actions that you notice the speaker doing, regardless of degree" (p. 296). For each speaker the researchers noted the number of judges who observed each behavior and assigned a 4-point "severity" score for the number of judges noting a particular behavior: none, 1, 2, or 3. Factor analysis of the data revealed three factors: Fidgetiness (shuffles feet, sways, swings arms, etc.), Inhibition (deadpan, knees tremble, hands in pocket, etc.), and Autonomia (moistens lips, plays with something, blushes, etc.).

Although the Clevenger and King (1961) checklist does not appear to have been used in other research, a revision of it by Paul (1966) —

the Timed Behavioral Checklist for Performance Anxiety (TBC) — has seen frequent use. Like its predecessor, the TBC provides a list of observable behaviors that are marked if they occur during a segment of the speech. Paul's modifications of the Clevenger and King list included (1) rewording of some items (e.g., "deadpan expression" was changed to "face 'deadpan'"); (2) "plays with something" and "swings arms" were combined to form "extraneous arm and hand movement"; (3) "returns to seat while speaking" was dropped; (4) four items were added ("clears throat," "perspires [face, hands, armpits]' " "voice quivers," and "speech blocks or stammers"). In addition, Paul changed the coding procedure so that the observers looked for each of the 20 behaviors every 30 seconds, rather than only once during the speech. Thus a four-minute speech was assessed eight times for the presence or absence of the behaviors. To compute a total score, Paul simply summed the number of times each variable was checked as occurring during the eight time periods, and then summed the total checks (0-8), which were marked for all 20 variables. No factor analysis was attempted by Paul, and none of the approximately 20 published studies using the original checklist or a modification reported factor analysis of its data. The TBC has been employed in its original 20-item version (e.g., Blom & Craighead, 1974; Slutsky & Allen, 1978; Weissberg & Lamb, 1977). However, it has more often been reduced to 12-14 items for ease of completion during the 30-second time intervals (e.g., Fremouw & Harmatz, 1975; Kirsch & Henry, 1977; Trexler & Karst, 1972).

The Behavioral Assessment of Speech Anxiety (BASA; Mulac & Sherman, 1974) represents a modification of Paul's behavioral items in the form of deletions and additions, as well as a substantial change in the coding procedure. Furthermore, unlike the Clevenger and King (1961) checklist and the Paul (1966) TBC, which were designed to be used in coding live behavior, the BASA was intended for use with videotape-recorded behavior. Several but not all of the changes in the behavioral items reflect this fact: (1) Because the initial testing and use of the BASA was with black-and-white videotape recording, "face pale" and "face flushed (blushes)" were dropped, (2) Similarly, the recordings carried insufficient information to observe "perspires (face, hands, armpits)," and it too was dropped. (3) During the pilot testing, none of the university students speakers displayed "moistens lips'" thus leading to its omission from the list. (4) Several other items added to the preliminary 32-item instrument and supported during pilot testing were retained on the final 18-item BASA: "too fast (voice)"; "too soft (voice)"; "monotonous, lack of emphasis (voice)"; "vocalized pauses (e.g., ah, er)"; and "hunts for words, speech blocks." A final item was added requiring a holistic judgment on the part of the observer: "overall anxiety estimate." Table 7.1 summarizes the items constituting the BASA, with variable weights and summary statistics derived from its initial testing (Mulac & Sherman, 1974).

Of greater significance, the BASA requires that the trained observes rate the severity or degree of occurrence of each behavior for a given

TABLE 7.1
BASA Variables with Weights, Means, Standard Deviations, and Intraclass Reliability Coefficients[a]

Category BASA Variable	Weight	Mean[b]	S.D.[b]	Reliability
Voice				
1. Quivering or tense voice	1.33	7.49	3.84	.82
2. Too fast	1.03	3.11	3.18	.82
3. Too soft	0.40	2.05	3.27	.88
4. Monotonous, lack of emphasis	0.66	7.85	4.34	.84
Verbal fluency				
5. Nonfluencies, stammers, halting	1.42	9.35	5.65	.92
6. Vocalized pauses	1.13	11.58	7.40	.96
7. Hunts for words, speech blocks	1.28	4.83	3.33	.81
Mouth and throat				
8. Swallows	0.82	1.13	1.02	.35
9. Clears throat	0.68	0.28	0.81	.94
10. Breathes heavily	0.98	4.12	2.09	.71
11. Lack of eye contact, extraneous eye movements	1.18	12.84	5.84	.91
Facial Expression				
12. Tense face muscles, grimaces, twitches	1.22	4.98	3.45	.70
13. "Deadpan" facial expression	0.73	6.06	4.53	.83
Arms and hands				
14. Rigid or tense	1.20	9.72	4.33	.80
15. Fidgeting, extraneous movement	1.39	8.92	5.46	.90
16. Motionless, lack of appropriate gestures	0.55	11.41	5.38	.84
Gross bodily movement				
17. Sways, paces, shuffles feet	1.00	8.53	6.29	.95
Overall				
18. Overall anxiety estimate	1.00	20.36	4.07	.91
Total weighted score	—	142.00	38.10	.95

a. Based on analyses reported in Mulac and Sherman (1974).
b. Means and standard deviations for the 18 variables are based on the summation of unweighted scores across four segments of each speech.

speaker, as compared to the other speakers being rated, using a 10-point scale. Instructions printed at the top of each form are as follows:

Behavioral Assessment of Speech Anxiety

Following is a list of ways in which speech anxiety may be behaviorally manifested during a public speaking performance. Each behavioral manifestation may occur in varying degrees of severity, which may be quantified according to the following rating scale:

0	1	2	3	4	5	6	7	8	9
not at all			slight			moderate			strong

For each behavioral manifestation of speech anxiety that occurs during a given time period, mark your rating (from 1 to 9) to indicate how severe it was. Be sure to provide an "overall anxiety estimate" for each time period in addition to rating specific manifestations.

Thus on the first page of this rating booklet, observers indicate the extent to which each behavioral variable occurred during the first minute and give an overall judgement of displayed anxiety; they then proceed to turn to the next page in the booklet and rate the behaviors that occurred during the second minute of the speaker's speech, and so forth. Variables not given a severity rating during a segment are later coded as 0.

Furthermore, the BASA assumes that variables rated are of differing importance in terms of indicating to a receiver that the speaker is anxious, and therefore provides a set of variable weights (see Table 7.1). Scores for each variable are simply summed across the four one-minute time periods and then multiplied by the respective item weights and summed to provide a total BASA score.

Because of the conceptual importance and possible clinical utility of determining the underlying factor structure of observer-perceived speaker anxiety, the BASA items have been factor analyzed and preliminary factor makeups indicated (Mulac & Sherman, 1974, pp. 140 – 142). Four factors emerged: Rigidity, Inhibition, Disfluency, and Agitation. To compute dimension scores for these four factors, scores for the items comprising each are multiplied by the corresponding variable weights and summed.

The BASA has been used most often in its 18-item version (Goss, Olds, & Thompson, 1978; Jaremko, 1980; Jaremko, Hadfield, & Walker, 1980; Mulac & Sherman, 1975a, 1975b; Sherman, Mulac, &

McCann, 1974). However, on the basis of Mulac and Sherman's (1974) results of factor analysis Fremouw and Zitter (1978) used a 14-item version and Trussell (1978) a 13-item version.

Other behavioral measures have been employed in a small number of studies, either separately or in combination with the TBC or BASA instruments. The number of disfluencies, parallel to an item on the BASA, has been used (Fremouw & Harmatz, 1975; Hamilton & Bornstein, 1977). Duration of silence has been employed by Jeger and Goldfried (1976) along with a modified TBC, as well as by Fremouw and Zitter (1978) with a modified BASA. Freimuth (1976) made use of rate of output (in utterances per minute) and proportion of abstract words as behavioral measures. Tesser, Leone, and Clary (1978) provided four global questions regarding the speaker's apparent lack of pleasure in speaking to the group, degree of embarrassment, and quality of performance. In other studies, overall speech anxiety — an item on the BASA — has also been employed in combination with the TBC (Fremouw & Harmatz, 1975; Trexler & Karst, 1972).

Reliability and Validity
of Observational Measures

Since they are designed to be employed by several observers, the most meaningful estimates of reliability for observational measures assess agreement across judges. Because of the multidimensional nature of the construct, estimates of internal consistency of item scores are clearly inappropriate. In general, reported estimates of the reliability of observational data have been high. Clevenger and King (1961) did not report reliability estimates for their data. However, Paul (1966) indicated that the reliability of his total TBC scores was .93 and .96 for two rounds of speeches. Other researchers have generally reported high reliability for the total TBC scores, ranging from .79 (Osberg, 1981) to .99 (Kirsch, Knutson, & Wolpin, 1975), with a median reliability of .88. Reliability estimates for individual TBC item do not appear in the literature. Mulac and Sherman (1974) demonstrated similarly high reliability for the BASA, .95 for the weighted total scores (see Table 7.1 for the reliability of individual item scores). Ratings of the four factors were also consistent across judges: Rigidity, .86; Inhibition, .94; Disfluency, .96; and Agitation, .96. The lowest reliability for BASA data reported to date had a mean of .82 for two judges (Jaremko, 1980);

the highest by researchers other than Mulac and Sherman was .92 for two judges (Trussell, 1978).

Although no formal validation of TBC data has been reported, the TBC's thorough grounding in the work of Clevenger and King (1964) and the wide-spread acceptance of the majority of behavioral items may be seen as evidence of the instrument's content validity. The fact that a number of studies (e.g., Gatchel & Proctor, 1976; Kirsch et al., 1975; Trexler & Karst, 1972) have found predicted gains in TBC scores after remediation provides evidence of its criterion-related validity.

Unlike the TBC, the BASA has been subjected to substantial, albeit initial, validity testing (Mulac & Sherman, 1974). Evidence of its content validity comes from the fact that two-thirds of its items directly parallel those of the TBC. Of the remaining six unique items, two (Hunt's words; Speech blocks and vocalized pauses) represent a further breakdown of the disfluencies variable generally accepted as communicating anxiety. The overall anxiety estimate is also consistent with the literature. Evidence of criterion-related validity has come from several sources. The correlation of weighted total BASA scores with overall speech anxiety scores given by expert judges (university faculty and advanced teaching assistants) showed substantial correspondence ($r =$ .88; Mulac & Sherman, 1974). Also, several studies have demonstrated improvement in public speaking student's BASA scores brought about by the course itself (Jaremko et al., 1980; Mulac & Sherman, 1975a, 1975b; Sherman et al., 1974). Others have reported changes in BASA scores predicted on the basis of remediation programs (Fremouw & Zitter, 1978; Goss et al., 1978; Jaremko et al., 1980).

Evidence of the construct validity of data generated by the BASA is less unambiguous. Using data from male speakers only, Mulac and Sherman (1974) provided results of their factor analysis that yielded four factors: Rigidity (rigid or tense arms and hands; motionless, lack of appropriate gestures; tense face muscles, grimaces, twitches); Inhibition (monotonous, lack of emphasis [voice]; "Deadpan" facial expression; too soft); Disfluency (hunts for words, speech blocks; quivering of tense voice; nonfluencies, stammers, halting; breathes heavily; vocalized pauses); and Agitation (fidgeting; sways, paces, shuffles feet; lack of eye contact, extraneous eye movements). These factors are similar to those obtained by Clevenger and King (1961), where similar items existed on both instruments. Also, weighted scores for these four factors were found to be similarly and significantly related to overall anxiety estimates (Mulac & Sherman, 1974), and each of the factors differentiated speakers from the top and bottom overall anxiety groups (Mulac &

Sherman, 1975b). More recently, however, Goss and his associates (1978) failed to confirm this four-factor solution in a study of male and female speakers measured under slightly different circumstances, and it remains to be seen whether the structure found by Mulac and Sherman is viable with different speakers across communication settings.

In interpersonal settings, some researchers have asked observers to make more general assessments of anxiety, and have occasionally included assessments of relaxation as well. In a study of communicative competence, for example, Wiemann (1977), developed a Likert-type, five-item subscale as part of a general instrument to assess competence (e.g., "The subject likes to use her voice and body expressively"; "The subject is relaxed and comfortable while speaking").

A more microscopic procedure for assessing anxiety in interpersonal contexts involved identifying and counting specific behaviors indicative of anxiety and its interactional counterpart — social relaxation. In two studies Mehrabian (1971b; Mehrabian & Ksionzky, 1972a) constructed, on the basis of their earlier research, a set of behaviors considered important in social interaction with the intent of identifying "categories of social behavior." Behaviors were scored by counting their frequency per minute and rating their severity when appropriate (see Mehrabian, 1972, appendix A, for details). Factor analyses of these and similar studies (e.g., Mehrabian & Ksionzky, 1972b; Mehrabian, 1972) revealed a consistent, stable factor structure for this set of "social behaviors." Of interest to us are the factors labeled "relaxation" and "behavioral index of distress." Behaviors negatively related to relaxation were rocking movements per minute and leg and foot movements per minute; body lean was related positively. The distress factor, which may appropriately be seen as observer-perceived anxiety, was defined by percentage duration of walking, object manipulations per minute, and arm position asymmetry (this late behavior was later dismissed as an artifact of the situation and not a true indicant of distress; see Mehrabian, 1972).

This series of studies is important for our purposes for two reasons. First, these studies identify a set of nonverbal behaviors that serve as cues of anxiety or relaxation in social situations. Second, and more important, they demonstrate that anxiety and relaxation can be seen as separate, although obviously related, dimensions of social behavior. Assessment of one or the other exculusively does not necessarily present an accurate estimate of perceived communication anxiety. Rather, it appears that people enact both relaxed behavior and anxious behavior in the same brief episode (Mehrabian examined two-minute encounters) and that perceptions of overall anxiety-relaxation is some combination of perceptions of both sorts of behaviors. That is, perceived relaxation is probably not caused by the mere absence of anxiety-related behaviors.

In addition to percentage duration of walking (i.e., pacing) and rate of object manipulations, several other behaviors have been identified and used as cues of anxiety. These include a variety of disfluencies: speech error rate (Harper, Wiens, & Matarazzo, 1978; Mahl, 1959; Mehrabian, 1981; Seigman & Pope, 1972); halting quality of speech (Mehrabian, 1969a, 1972); incomplete sentences (Kasl & Mahl, 1965); and repetition of words (Kasl & Mahl, 1965). High pitch has also been used as an anxiety cue (Apple, Streeter, & Krauss, 1977). Additionally, Mehrabian (1971, 1972, 1981) has identified the following behaviors as cues of anxiety, tension, and distress: infrequent nodding, gesturing, and leg and foot movements; forward body lean; talking less and more slowly than comparable others in a given situation; and more smiles. Glogower, Fremouw, and McCroskey (1978) also used amount of talking, in the form of frequency and length of utterance, as well as the Tension factor bipolar scales from the Interaction Behavior Measure (IBM; McCroskey & Wright, 1971).

Conversely, arm- and leg-position asymmetry, sideways lean, hand and neck relaxation, reclining body position (backward lean), self-manipulations, and rocking movements have all been related to relaxation in social situations (Mehrabian, 1969b, 1972, 1981; Mehrabian & Williams, 1969; Wiemann, 1981).

Mehrabian (1972) illustrated how behaviors can be combined to form a single index for the general social category they cue, resulting in ease of subsequent analysis. Similarly, Wiemann (1981) demonstrated the viability a single relaxation-anxiety index for evaluating subjects' behavior.

Difficulties in using a behavioral taxonomy for assessing relative anxiety arise from two intertwined characteristics of nonverbal behavior: Its meaning in most instances is simultaneously ambiguous and context-bound. For example, in summarizing his work, Mehrabian (1972) reports that he had found rocking movements to load negatively on relaxation factors in several studies but to be positively related to relaxation in another. The differentiating circumstances is that in some studies, research participants were standing (rocking indicated anxiety) and in others were sitting. The social task in which people find themselves engaged, as well as their "emotional states," also influence how specific behaviors will be interpreted. High-risk deceit, which is assumed to be tension-arousing (Mehrabian, 1981), is accompanied by displays of anxiety. Such deceit is also accompanied by increased self-manipulations (Knapp, Hart, & Dennis, 1974; McClintock & Hunt, 1975; Mehrabian, 1981), but in other research these behaviors have been associated with relaxed, dominant behavior (Mehrabian, 1972). It is likely that different varieties of self-manipulation were observed in different studies (e.g., liars might scratch themselves, while dominant people smooth their hair). Whatever the specifics of the self-manipulation as a cue, researchers using it and similar behaviors must make inferences about its meaning in the specific context they are studying. Other behaviors — body lean, body asymmetry, disfluencies, less bodily activity — are less ambiguous and can be used with more confidence.

Guidelines for Measurement

Based on our review of past and current research practice in measuring observer-perceived communicator anxiety, we believe that any procedure or instrument should take into account the following realizations:

(1)   A relatively large number of behaviors are generally perceived as indicating that the communicator is anxious. Therefore, many variables should be assessed. (There may, of course, be situations where the research question will be best answered by measuring a subset of these variables.)

(2)   Each behavior exists in varying degrees among speakers, and those degrees are perceived as indicating different degrees of communicator anxiety. Therefore, each variable should be measured in terms of its extent of occurrence, using either its frequency or, where possible, its rated severity of occurrence, not simply whether it occurred in a given period.

(3)   Different behaviors are perceived as differentially indicative of communicator anxiety. Therefore, different weights should be applied to each variable if variables are to be combined in any way.

(4)   Where important conceptually or remediationally, the variables should be explainable on the basis of a smaller number of underlying factors. Therefore, provisions should exist for computing dimension scores.

(5)   An overall impression or holistic assessment may be important in a given situation. Therefore, provisions should exist for computing a total (weighted) score.

(6)   Videotape-recorded communication events should be assessable, given the potential for reduced reactivity in the communication setting and the ability to control for time of assessment (e.g., pretreatment or

posttreatment). Therefore, testing and validation should be undertaken using videotape recordings.

(7)   Resulting data should pass the usual tests of reliability and validity.

Suggestions for Future Research

Although no longer in its infancy, the measurement of observer-perceived communicator anxiety clearly has not reached maturity. Researchers interested in the phenomenon as it occurs in public speaking, or conceivably television broadcasting, may find it useful to test further the applicability of the BASA for selected contexts in its present form or with modifications. Among other things, the BASA should be tested for its utility with female as well as male speakers. On the basis of reported differences in linguistic and nonverbal output of male and female speakers (Eakins & Eakins, 1978; Thorne & Henley, 1975), it is reasonable to suppose that male and female communicators might display apparent communication anxiety in different ways. It is, of course possible that gender-linked behavioral differences might be assessable using the BASA items. This possibility seems all the more likely given the moderate number of published studies using the BASA with male and female speakers, and the large number using the TBC (with its comparable items) for speakers of both sexes.

Second, the factor structure underlying the BASA requires further research. In the process, however, it should be acknowledged that some behaviors may exist that are important indicators of communicator anxiety and yet may not co-occur with other indicators, and hence not "fit" into a traditionally determined factor structure. For these it may be necessary to generate and test additional variables, rather than discarding the variables failing to meet standard criteria. Unlike semantic differentials, where items are established to be redundant, the BASA items were established on the basis of experience and research. Individual items should not be dropped without evidence that they fail to be perceived as indicators of speaker anxiety.

Third, the variable weights of the BASA should receive scrutiny. The current weights, although empirically established and verified (Mulac & Sherman, 1974) must be tested further to determine their predictive reality in other communication settings.

Fourth, other variables should be tested as possible additions to the BASA. For example, the TBC items of "face pale," "face flushed (blushes)," and "perspires (face, hands, armpits)," which were dropped during pilot testing of the BASA because they could not be discerned on black-and white videotape recordings, might be re-introduced for use with color television.

Finally, improved videotape-recording techniques should be employed where possible. Recording in color is recommended for increased resolution. Also, Lamb (1978) recommends recording with two cameras, one showing the face and the other showing the entire body, using two recorders and television monitors. In cases where synchronization of playback is impossible, an alternative would be use of two cameras and split-screen (by means of a special effects amplifier), recorded on one recorder and played back on one monitor.

A second major area for further research involves the expansion and further testing of variables used to assess observer-perceived interactant anxiety in interpersonal settings. It would be useful to determine whether additional variables — over and above those currently in use (e.g., Mehrabian, 1972; Wiemann, 1977) — convey interactant anxiety to other interactants or to third-party observers.

A third area for additional research involved the interaction of positive relaxation cues with negative anxiety cues. Wiemann (1981) included an assessment of relaxation as part of an overall anxiety-relaxation index. Given existing evidence that relaxation cues and anxiety cues are displayed in the same episode, further research should determine the relative importance of the two and the extent to which positive judgments of relaxation attenuate negative judgments of anxiety. This extension of conceptualization could lead to a more complete evaluation of perceived anxiety.

Finally, we recommend that all major programs of research on communicator anxiety, under whatever label, include the measurement of behaviors interpreted by observers as indicating communicator anxiety. The theoretical importance of this construct, as indicated earlier, is too great, and its proven impact on the communication process too profound, for it to be overlooked. Such a combined approach of measuring behavioral indices, as well as self-report and in many cases physiological indices, has become the standard for research on communication anxiety remediation (usually public speaking) conducted in psychology and related disciplines. In these studies, a common but by no means universal finding is that particular remediation procedures bring about improvement in one facet of the target phenomenon but not the other. For example, some studies have found significant treatment-related improvements in self-report, but not observer-perceived, anxiety (Cradock, Cotler, & Jason, 1978; Kirsch & Henry, 1979; Weinberger & Engelhart, 1976). On the other hand,

Weissberg (1977) reported significant improvement on behavioral indices of anxiety but not on self-report. Marshall, Stoian, and Andrews (1977) and Osberg (1981) found that differences among treatment group effects differed depending on whether one viewed the self-report or the behavioral indices.

The value of acknowledging these separate elements of communication anxiety, each important and only partly related to the others, is as great now as it was when first articulated by Clevenger (1959). Summarizing his own findings, Paul (1966, p. 90) states:

> The necessity of including criterion measures of improvement from sources other than the involved participants (therapists and clients) was also evident. External behavioral criteria did, in fact, appear to be the most useful, and certainly the most reliable. However, continued use of self-report and multiple criteria is still necessary in outcome studies.

Despite the difficulties of locating and training raters, dubbing video-tape-recorded communication acts, and conducting rating sessions, we must concur with Clevenger and Paul: Observer-perceived indices of communicator anxiety must be measured in any program of research dealing with communication anxiety.

PART III

IMPACT

8

Correlates and Consequences of Social-Communicative Anxiety

JOHN A. DALY and LAURA STAFFORD

This chapter focuses on the correlates and consequences of the dimension of personality that emphasizes people's willingness to approach or avoid social interaction. The disposition has a number of labels, such as communication apprehension (McCroskey, Chapter 1), reticence (Phillips, Chapter 3), shyness (Buss, chapter 2; Zimbardo, 1977), social anxiety (Leary, 1983), audience anxiety (Daly & Buss, Chapter 4), unwillingness to communicate (Burgoon, 1976), predisposition toward verbal behavior (Mortensen, Arnston, & Lustig, 1977), social reticence (Jones & Russell, 1982), and social-communicative anxiety (J. Daly, 1978), among others. While the constructs associated with each of these labels differ in emphasis, the general thrust of all is the differing proclivity of people to participate in and enjoy, or avoid and fear, social interaction. In this chapter we refer to the disposition as "social-communicative anxiety." We choose that term because it seems sufficiently inclusive to incorporate the extensive literature on the topic and because it is not tied to any particular measure or theoretical perspective.

This chapter is divided into five sections. First, some preliminary considerations that frame our review of the disposition's correlates and consequences are examined. Research on the specific correlates and consequences of the disposition is summarized in the sections covering *developmental correlates, personality correlates, social perceptions,* and *behavioral correlates.* While we try to include all of the major strands of past research, space limitations obviously preclude complete coverage of every investigation completed on this topic. The amount and variety of scholarship on the topic of social-communication anxiety is immense. What we seek to do in this brief review is summarize the major currents of research, providing to the interested reader an introduction to the literature.

Preliminary Considerations

There are three considerations that affect the way anxiety and its correlates are understood: (1) multiple constructs, (2) disposition-behavior relationships, and (3) situation-disposition distinctions.

Multiple Constructs

The literature on social-communicative anxiety is dotted with a plethora of labels and assessment measures. Virtually every major investigator interested in the topic seems to find it necessary to create both a new assessment instrument and a new referent for the disposition. There are, for instance, at least thirty different self-report questionnaires purporting to tap the construct. This legacy presents a knotty problem for the person seeking to understand the research: the proliferation of instruments, and supposedly new constructs, mitigates any opportunity for developing a sophisticated and integrated synthesis. One is essentially forced to choose between narrowly tying each research finding to a specific operationalization or broadly summarizing the corpus of materials, ignoring the varying conceptual and instrumental distinctions. In this review we gravitate toward the latter, more liberal, choice. We do so because there is considerable evidence suggesting that, by and large, the many different constructs within this area tap a single, broad disposition. The average intercorrelation among the various constructs is relatively high (Daly, 1980; Daly & Street, 1980; Kelly, 1982). Further, when findings based upon different operationalizations are compared, no major inconsistencies emerge. In no case do different constructs make diametrically opposed predictions. Differences between varying operationalizations are always ones of magnitude rather than direction: One construct might propose a strong positive relationship while its conceptual cousin suggests only a moderate one. Thus, for purposes of this brief review, we collapse findings across measures and labels. Don't misunderstand: Conceptually, many of the differences among constructs are important. The wealth of perspectives offered by the varying construals of the anxiety provides fertile ground for much valuable work. However, to date, that sort of work has not been well enunciated empirically.

Relating Disposition to Behavior

There has been considerable debate about the relationship between personality and behavior in recent years. Spurred by Mischel's (1968) critique, a number of scholars have questioned the validity of individual differences on two major grounds. First, research linking personality variables with specific behaviors that are theoretically relevant to the variables has discovered relationships of only low to moderate magnitude. Second, the average correlation among behaviors, supposedly representative of a personality dimension, tends to be relatively low. Critics of personality marshal these two observations to argue that individual differences, as they are currently construed, have relatively little value in understanding human behavior. Disputing these critiques are a number of investigators who propose that personality is meaningfully related to behavior. Their responses take a number of forms. One response highlights the interplay between situations and traits in predicting behavior. It suggests that while neither a trait nor a situation is singularly a good predictor of a behavioral response, the interaction among the two provides good behavioral prediction (Magnusson & Endler, 1977). Another approach supposes that a particular trait is relevant to only some people. When it is relevant, the correlation between behavior and disposition is high; when it is irrelevant, the correlation is small (Bem & Allen, 1974). Similarly, certain situations elicit high trait-behavior correspondence while others preclude any meaningful link (Monson, Hesley, & Chernick, 1982). A third response asserts that a different conceptualization of the behavioral criteria is necessary if large trait-behavior relationships are to be obtained. Epstein (1979) demonstrates that taking an extensive sample of behavior over time yields more reliable indices of behavioral tendencies that, in turn, produce stronger associations with traits (however, see Day, Marshall, Hamilton, & Christy, 1983, for limits to this technique). Also focusing on the behavioral criteria, Jaccard (1974) and others (for example, Buss & Craik, 1981; McGowan & Gormly, 1976; Moskowitz, 1982) find that correlating a trait with a group of trait-related behaviors (a multiple act criterion) yields correlations substantially larger than those obtained when a single behavior is related to a trait.

Scholars interested in social-communicative anxiety have not ignored the trait-behavior problem. Hewes and Haight (1979) and Parks (1980) have suggested that there is little cross-situational consistency among trait-related behaviors, thus casting doubt, in their minds, on the disposition's validity. Hewes and Haight (1979) note small average correlations among a group of verbal behaviors. Parks (1980) reports that while communication apprehension is substantially correlated with self-reported behaviors in settings where people are relatively unacquainted, there is no significant correlation between the disposition and reported behaviors in contexts where people are well acquainted. Hewes and Haight (1980) also indict the use of a multiple act criterion in the case of social-communicative anxiety. They argue that the correlations between trait and behavior remain relatively small.

In communication, these challenges to the behavioral validity of the construct are not unanswered. J. Daly (1978) and Jaccard and Daly (1980) successfully applied the multiple act criterion to communication apprehension. They found that when the trait was correlated with a large group of self-reported behaviors considered over time, the magnitude of relationship was substantial. Furthermore, Jaccard and Daly (1980) note serious problems in the Hewes and Haight (1980) critique of the application of the multiple act approach. In a different vein, Monson et al. (1982) demonstrate that situational pressures affect the magnitude of the relationship between the extroversion trait (in their study, the trait was, in essence, social-communicative anxiety) and behavior. When situations strongly constrain behaviors, there is a very small relationship between trait and behavior. But, when situational constraints are relaxed, the correlation improves markedly. Finally, some scholars argue that the trait is only relevant to some portions of the population — notably, those who are high or low in the disposition (Fong & Markus, 1982). Using these extreme groups, a strong trait-behavior link emerge; for those in the middle range, where the trait is less relevant, the correlations should be smaller.

Situation Versus Disposition

This chapter focuses on the *disposition* of social-communicative anxiety. Inherent in the research on the disposition are the typical assumptions tied to personality traits: that individuals (1) can be ordered reliably along the continuum that the construct represents and (2) are generally consistent in their behavioral tendencies as they relate to the construct. Obviously, the trait alone does not entirely account for a person's behavioral response. A number of situational or transitory factors also play important roles. It is not our purpose, however, to review the small body of theory and research on transitory social-communicative anxiety (Buss, 1980: Daly & Buss, Chapter 4; Schlenker & Leary, 1982). We limit our review to the correlates and consequences of dispositional social-communicative anxiety. We will consider, in turn, developmental, personality, perceptual, and behavioral correlates of the disposition. The exposition of these results is, by necessity, quite brief. Our catalogue is meant to summarize the main currents of study and provide, to the reader, a starting point for further study.

Developmental Correlates of Social-Communicative Anxiety

Understanding the developmental correlates of social-communicative anxiety provides critical points of departure for the integration and understanding of research, theory, and remediation strategies related to the anxiety. There are four major, interrelated clusters of correlates: (1) genetic predisposition, (2) reinforcement, (3) skill acquisition, and (4) modeling. Each cluster offers some explanatory account for the anxiety's etiology through the specification of correlates. No single explanation accounts for the development of the anxiety; rather, they operate interactively shaping an individual's level of worry or enjoyment of communication. In each case, once the disposition is established people high in the anxiety avoid situations where communication appears to be required and, when placed in them, respond anxiously. Alternatively, people low in the anxiety seek out and savor situations that demand communication. For purposes of brevity, we do not cite the specific literature sources for each finding summarized in this section. The references are readily available in other recent summaries (Daly, 1977; Daly & Friedrich, 1981; Van Kleech & Daly, 1982).

Genetic Predisposition

Some portion of the anxiety is genetically based. In studies of twins, as well as adopted children, investigators consistently find that sociability and its variants (one of which is the anxiety) has an inherited component. The fact that various genetically determined physical characteristics are linked to anxiety-related behaviors also suggests a role for heredity in the development of the anxiety. Although some genetic contribution exists, its role is probably minimal in the entire scheme of events contributing to an individual's level of anxiety. The three remaining components — reinforcements, skills, and models — contribute much more (see Van Kleeck & Daly, 1982 for references).

Reinforcement

The most common explanation for the anxiety's development emphasizes the reinforcements and punishments a child receives for communication attempts. Based on general learning models, the approach suggests that individuals seek situations and engage in behaviors predicted to result in positive consequences. They avoid activities and situations that hold aversive consequences for them. Thus, for some people, avoiding social and communication activities is rewarding since participation is expected to lead to punishment; for other people, engaging in the same activities is perceived as rewarding and thus sought out. These expectations are formed early in life. Over time, the positive and negative consequences associated with communication become internally mediated, removing the necessity for external events to elicit a response. Research on operant conditioning of infant vocalization, language delays, mother-infant interaction, verbal abilities of children, and specific verbal skills such as question asking all evidence the power of this explanation. Further, studies on the modification of social withdrawal in children and the modification of the children's talk through reinforcement contingencies also demonstrate the role of reinforcements in shaping an individual's anxiety level (see Van Kleeck & Daly, for references).

An adjunct to this interpretation is McCroskey's (1982) hypothesis for the development of communication apprehension. He proposes that its development lies in the expectancies people come to have about communication. Individuals who are highly anxious about communication become so either because they form negative expectancies about social interaction (a strict reinforcement model) or because they experience a random pattern of responses to their communication attempts, resulting, over time, in a sense of helplessness (Seligman, 1975). In either case, they come to avoid communication.

Skills Acquisition

A third explanation for the development of social-communicative anxiety is the poor development of skills related to communication. In most cases the problem lies not in the absence of skills per se, but rather in either insufficient acquisition of the skills or slower than average development of the skills. When highly anxious children are compared to their nonanxious peers, their social and communicative skills are not as well developed. Relevant research on this explanation focuses on the development of referential communication skills, peer interaction, language use, reciprocity skills, sensitivity to social cues, interaction management, and the use of verbal rewards. The skills explanation garners further support through research showing that popular children are more socially skilled than are unpopular children and that the availability of multiple social stimulations is positively related to the development of better social skills and lower communication apprehension (see Van Kleeck & Daly, 1982, for references).

Modeling

A final explanation emphasizes the role and importance of models in the development of the anxiety. Research supportive of this position centers on the reduction of social isolation in children through the use of models. There is also evidence that children tend to imitate their parents' communicative styles (see Van Kleeck & Daly, 1982).

Obviously, no single explanation sufficiently accounts for the genesis of the anxiety. Rather, the explanations blend together, shaping an individual's level of anxiety. For instance, children whose communication skills are poorly developed probably receive fewer rewards for their communication attempts. Receiving fewer rewards discourages the active development of skills, which leads, in turn, to further lack of reinforcement.

Personality Correlates

A large body of research relates various personality and demographic variables to the disposition. This research falls into four categories: (1) sex differences, (2) self-esteem, (3) social-personality variables, and (4) other personality variables.

Sex Differences

Some research suggests that social-communicative anxiety and sex are, in a very minimal way, related. The direction of the effect is unclear. Females report slightly more anxiety than males in some studies (Andersen, Andersen, & Garrison, 1978; Bruskin Associates, 1973; Clevenger, 1959; Feldman & Berger, 1974; Friedrich, 1970; Gilkinson, 1942; Lazarus, 1982b; Porter, 1974), while in others males report being shyer than females (Mortensen et al., 1977; Van Kleeck & Daly, 1982; Pilkonis, 1977a; Watson & Friend, 1969; Zimbardo, 1977). Whatever the direction, the magnitude of difference is quite small — so small as to suggest that the difference is probably inconsequential. Further, the direction appears to depend heavily on the particular operationalization used to assess the person's anxiety (McCroskey, Simpson, & Richmond, 1982). Studies also link the anxiety to a person's psychological sex type. Greenblatt, Hasenauer, and Freimuth (1980) and McDowell, McDowell, Hyerdahl, and Steil (1978) report that highly feminine subjects are more apprehensive than either androgynous or masculine subjects.

Self-Esteem

Research consistently demonstrates an inverse relationship between social-communicative anxiety and self-esteem. Using general measures of self-esteem, Cheek and Buss (1981), Comrey (1973), Hamilton (1972), Jones and Russell (1982), Lazarus (1982a), Leary (1983), Lustig (1974), McCroskey, Daly, Richmond, and Falcione (1977), McCroskey and Richmond (1975), Mortensen et al. (1977), Santee and Maslach (1982), Snavely and Sullivan (1976), and Snavely, Merker, Becker, and Book (1976) find this relationship. A number of investigators note a similar relationship using measures tapping various aspects of self-esteem (Bormann & Shapiro, 1962; Cacioppo, Glass, & Merluzzi, 1979; Crozier, 1981; Ekert & Keys, 1940; Fenton & Hopf, 1976; Giffin & Heider, 1967; Gilkinson, 1942; Low & Sheets, 1951; Muir, 1964; Smith & Sarason, 1975; Zimbardo, 1977). This relationship is one of the most consistent in the literature of social-communicative anxiety. Regardless of how either anxiety or esteem is operationalized, the inverse relationship holds.

Social Personality Correlates

A number of studies link social-communicative anxiety to other personality variables that are related to social behavior. Overall, these correlates suggest that the greater the anxiety, the less socially oriented the individual.

Social-communicative anxiety, in its various forms, is inversely related to an individual's level of individuation (Santee & Maslach, 1982), tendency to self-disclose (Miller, Berg, & Archer, 1983; Morris, Harris, & Rovins, 1981) and elicit self-disclosure (Miller et al., 1983), self-monitoring (Briggs, Cheek, & Buss, 1980; Gabrenya & Arkin, 1980), innovativeness (Hurt & Joseph, 1975; Hurt, Joseph, & Cook, 1977; Hurt, Preiss, & Davis, 1976; McCroskey & Richmond, 1976; Richmond, 1980; Witteman, 1976; Witteman & Andersen, 1976), dominance (Mortensen et al., 1977), argumentativeness (Infante & Rancer, 1982), assertiveness (Bell & Daly, 1983b; Jones & Russell, 1982), perspective taking among females (Davis, 1983), and social responsiveness, attentiveness, and perceptiveness (Cegala, Savage, Bruner, & Conrad, 1982).

The anxiety is positively related to loneliness (Bell & Daly, 1983b; Jones, Freeman, & Goswick, 1981; Jones & Russell, 1982; Cheek & Busch, 1981; compare Zakahi & Duran, 1982), situational communication anxiety (Kearney & McCroskey, 1980; Lohr, Rea, Porter, & Hamberger, 1980; Richmond, 1977), public self-consciousness (Bell & Daly, 1983b; Cheek & Buss, 1981; Fenigstein, Scheier, & Buss, 1975; Heinemann, 1979; Jones & Russell, 1982; Leary, 1983; Pilkonis, 1977a), maladaptive self-consciousness (Christensen, 1982), receiver apprehension (McDowell & McDowell, 1978; Wheeless, 1975), touch avoidance (Andersen & Leibowitz, 1976), writing apprehension (Daly & Wilson, in press), personal distress, empathic concern, and ability to fantasize in men (Davis, 1983), social isolation (Mortensen et al., 1977), anomie and alienation (Burgoon, 1976; Burgoon & Burgoon, 1973), and fear of negative evaluation (Leavy, 1980; Watson & Friend, 1969).

Other Personality Correlates

Research also links the anxiety to personality dimensions less related to social behavior. The anxiety is positively related to dogmatism, locus of control, trait anxiety (McCroskey, Daly, & Sorensen, 1976; Porter, 1979), test anxiety (Scott, Wheeless, Yates, & Randolph, 1977), neuroticism (Pilkonis, 1977a), avoidance of risk taking (Rocklin & Revelle, 1981), dependency, self-criticism, inefficacy, and depression (Blatt, Quinlan, Chevron, McDonald, & Zuroff, 1982), intolerance of ambiguity (Lashbrook, Lashbrook, Bacon, & Salinger, 1979; McCroskey et al., 1976), and constricted cognitive control (Ludwig & Lazarus, 1982). Some studies use multidimensional inventories of personality, seeking to encapsulate, in a single thrust, the personality of the highly anxious individual. For instance, McCroskey et al. (1976) link communication apprehension with Cattell's 16PF, a general personality inventory. They report that communication apprehension is inversely related to self-control, adventurousness, surgency, emotional maturity, cyclothmia, dominance, character, and confidence. There was no relationship between apprehension and sophistication, self-sufficiency, sensitivity, eccentricity, or radicalism. Davies (1982) also used the 16PF with a measure of social-communicative anxiety (Fenigstein, Scheier, &

Buss, 1975). In that study social anxiety was negatively related to tendencies to be outgoing, emotionally stable, assertive, happy-go-lucky, venturesome, and suspicious, while it was positively correlated with dimensions assessing tenseness and apprehensiveness. Rosenfield and Plax (1976) correlated reticence with measures included on the CPI, TSCS, and EPPS. Highly reticent college students are low in dominance, nurturance, affiliation, socialization, aggression, and social and physical self, but high in deference, consistency, and achievement via conformity.

Research consistently finds little or no relationship between intelligence and the anxiety (Bashore, 1971; McCroskey et al. 1976; compare Davis & Scott, 1978). However, if educational achievement and performance are considered rather than intellectual ability, the anxiety is relevant. McCroskey and Andersen (1976) demonstrate a significant relationship between communication apprehension and scores on standardized test such as the ACT. They also find that extremely high apprehensives have, on average, a significantly lower college grade-point average than do extremely low apprehensives. Powers and Symthe (1980) and Scott and Wheeless (1977b) found that low anxious college students received significantly higher grades on assignments in communication classrooms than did high anxious students. Hurt et al. (1976) and Hurt and Preiss (1978) note a similar grade-anxiety relationship among junior high school students. On the other hand, Garrison, Seiler, and Boohar (1977) do not find any relationship between apprehension and performance in classes in the life sciences and both Davis and Scott (1978) and Porter (1979) detected minimal relationships between the anxiety and college student achievement.

Social Perceptions

In this section we examine the social perceptions held by individuals as they relate to the anxiety. Three major emphases exist in the literature: the judgments others have of the anxious individual, the judgments of others made by individuals varying in the anxiety, and the feelings highly anxious people have about themselves.

Others' Perceptions of Anxiousness

A sizable body of research indicates that the amount an individual talks, vocal activity, is positively related to a broad variety of positive person perceptions (for reviews, see Daly, McCroskey, & Richmond,

1976, 1977; Hayes & Meltzer, 1972). This research frames studies exploring the link between the anxiety and social judgments. In these studies there are two predominant methods: In some, people are asked to evaluate individuals described in verbal portraits as high or low anxious; in others, people whose anxiety has been assessed are asked to interact and then are evaluated by others who either participated in or observed the interaction. Whichever method is used, compared to the low anxious individual, the high anxious person is perceived as less socially and interpersonally attractive (McCroskey, Hamilton, & Weiner, 1974; McCroskey, Daly, Richmond, & Cox, 1975; Richmond, 1977; Quiggins, 1972; Bliese, Fenton, Benhower, & Neff, 1976; Burgoon & Koper, 1983; Jones & Russell, 1982; McCroskey & Richmond, 1976), less credible (Burgoon & Koper, 1983; Fenton & Hopf, 1976; McCroskey & Richmond, 1976; Richmond, 1977; Wissmiller & Merker, 1976), less physically attractive (Pilkonis, 1977b; compare Burgoon & Koper, 1983), less friendly, attentive, and relaxed (Pilkonis, 1977b; Porter, 1982), less dominant (Porter, 1982), less assertive and responsive (Knutson & Lashbrook, 1976; Kearney & McCroskey, 1980), more nonimmediate, detached, and submissive (Burgoon & Koper, 1983), more tense and less expressive (Slivken & Buss, 1983), less trustworthy (Mulac & Sherman, 1975; compare McCroskey & Richmond, 1976), less competent and effective in communication (Arnston et al., 1980; Freimuth, 1976; Jablin & Sussman, 1978; Mulac & Sherman, 1975; Wells & Lashbrook, 1970), less likely to be an opinion leader (Hurt & Joseph, 1975; McCroskey & Richmond, 1976), and less of a leader (Arnston et al., 1980; Bliese et al., 1976; Fenton & Hopf, 1976; Jones & Russell, 1982; Wenzlaff, 1971). Conversationally, they are seen as more tense, inhibited, and unfriendly (Cheek & Buss, 1981). The only exception to this generally very negative group of perceptions is McCroskey and Richmond's (1976) finding that high apprehensive people are perceived as higher in character than low apprehensive individuals. Indirectly, Daly et al. (1976) suggest that the high anxious person (as operationalized via low vocal activity) may also be perceived as a better listener than the low anxious individual.

This negative bias generalizes to the educational environment and employment setting. Teachers have less positive regard for students who they believe are high in the anxiety, whether the students are presented as hypothetical prototypes (McCroskey & Daly, 1976; Powers & Dunathan, 1978) or are actual students who vary in the anxiety (Symthe & Powers, 1978). In organizational and business settings, social-communicative anxiety also affects perceptions. For instance, Daly, Richmond, and Leth (1979), in a series of studies, report that in a personnel selection analogue, highly apprehensive applicants are less positively regarded than their low apprehensive counterparts.

Anxiety Affects Perceptions

While social-communicative anxiety affects how an individual is judged, the anxiety also affects judgments made by individuals who vary in the anxiety. Individuals with high anxiety trust others less (Giffin & Heider, 1967), perceive greater differences between stimulus persons with the labels "talkative" and "quiet" attached to them (Daly, 1979), and find others less attractive than low apprehensives (McCroskey et al., 1975). Highly apprehensive students fail to differentiate, in terms of evaluative ratings, between interactants who either continuously gaze or avert their gaze during conversations. Low and moderate apprehensives, on the other hand, are more sensitive and make a distinction. They respond more positively to the continuous gaze (Andersen & Coussoule, 1980). Groups composed of high apprehensives perceive greater status differentials within their groups than groups of low apprehensives (Jablin, 1981; Jablin, Seibold, & Sorenson, 1977). In work settings, communication apprehension of subordinates is positively related to perceptions that supervisors are more dominant and coercive in their use of power (Richmond, Wagner, & McCroskey, 1983) and inversely related to satisfaction with work and supervision (Falcione, McCroskey, & Daly, 1977). In classrooms, highly apprehensive students perceive their teachers as less animated, impression leaving, dramatic, friendly, open, affiliative, and immediate than low apprehensives (Andersen, 1979). Highly anxious teachers make significantly greater discriminations between students sitting in high and low interaction seats than low apprehensive teachers (Daly and Suite, 1982), perhaps because of the greater salience of communication-related behaviors (such as seating choice) to the high anxious teachers. While research generally suggests differences between high and low apprehensives in how they respond to others, there are studies that fail to find this effect. For instance, Daly et al. (1979) find that people's apprehension has no impact on their evaluations of individuals who vary in the anxiety. Regardless of a judge's apprehension, a highly anxious stimulus individual is rated less positively than the low anxious. Richmond (1977) reports a similar pattern. Also, high and low anxious individuals do not differ in their preference for various compliance-gaining strategies (Lustig & King, 1980).

Three other bodies of literature are of some relevance here. First, studies demonstrate that a person's expectation that he or she is conversing with another individual who is introverted or extroverted leads him or her to ask questions that elicit behaviors confirming the expectancy. For instance, if an interviewer believes that the person he or she is talking with is extroverted, the interviewer will ask questions that seek extroverted responses. Because the questions are framed to generate a particular sort of response, they serve to confirm the original expectancy (Christensen & Rosenthal, 1982; Synder & Swann, 1978; Swann, Giuliano, & Wegner, 1982). Implied in this research is that if an individual believes he or she is interacting with someone with high social-communicative anxiety, he or she is likely to establish, via his or her talk, a confirming behavioral response by the other person. Second, research suggests that the anxiety may affect a perceiver's judgments only when the anxiety serves as an organizing construct, or schema, for the perceiver. People who think of themselves as either high or low in the anxiety tend to be more confident in their judgments of other people's extroversion than individuals who think of themselves as neither particularly shy nor particularly outgoing (Fong & Markus, 1982). Presumably, this is so because, for the highs and lows, the anxiety is part of their person schema. The moderates, on the other hand, are aschematic when it comes to using the trait in judging others.[3] Third, highly anxious people differ from others in what they focus on, and how they process information, in social settings. For instance, under social-evaluative stress, anxious individuals are more concerned than others about the evaluations of them by others (Smith, Ingram, & Brehm, 1983). In public speaking contexts, the anxiety is inversely related to memory for incidental environmental cues (Daly & Lawrence, 1983), while it is positively related to the number of errors made in recalling previous conversations (Stafford & Daly, 1983).

Self-Perceptions

High and low anxious individuals differ in their self-perceptions. Major differences in self-esteem correlates were noted in a preceding section. In addition, there are studies indicating that high anxious people, when compared to their low anxious counterparts, feel less physically attractive (Prisbell, 1982), less competent, confident, and understood in communication settings (Freimuth, 1976; Low & Sheets, 1951; Prisbell, 1982), and less involved and less influential in group interactions (Arnston et al., 1980). They underestimate their ability in, and quality of, speaking when compared with observer ratings (Gilkinson, 1943), feel audiences see them as less expert and dynamic (Infante & Fisher, 1978), perceive the same evaluative feedback more negatively (Smith & Sarason, 1975), expect more negative evaluations (Muir, 1964; Smith & Sarason, 1975), feel more isolated in academic settings (Hurt et al. 1976), feel they know fewer faculty members in college (McCroskey & Sheahan, 1978), are less certain in social settings (Parks, Dindia, Adams, Berlin, & Larson, 1980), feel more inhibited and awkward in conversations (Cheek & Buss, 1981), believe they self-disclose less (McCroskey & Richmond, 1977; Miller et al., 1983), feel less pleasant and comfortable when speaking (Pilkonis, 1977b), consider themselves less assertive (Crozier, 1981; Kearney & McCroskey, 1980), feel less nonverbally expressive (Friedman, Prince, Riggio, & DiMatteo, 1980; but see Nicholls, Licht, & Pearl, 1982), are less satisfied with their abilities to express self, to lead, to meet people, and to make decisions (Crozier, 1981), are less satisfied with their group products and performance (Burgoon, 1976; Fenton, 1976; Jablin, 1981) and their school performance (Hurt et al., 1976; McCroskey & Sheahan, 1978), and, generally, when entering settings where communication occurs, experience greater nervousness, anxiety, and expectations of failure (Morris et al., 1981).

In occupations, highly anxious individuals are less satisfied in their work and with their supervisors (Falcione et al., 1977; Richmond, McCroskey, & Davis, 1982). They have less desire for advancement and believe they are less likely to advance (Scott, McCroskey, & Sheahan, 1978). The anxiety affects people's preferences for, and choices of, occupations. Highly anxious individuals prefer positions that are perceived to require little communication, while low anxious individuals select and find desirable jobs that demand communication (Daly & McCroskey, 1975; Scott et al., 1978; compare Porter, 1979).

Attributionally, high and low anxious people offer different explanations for their behaviors. When failing, socially anxious individuals attribute more responsibility to themselves than do socially nonanxious people. On the other hand, nonanxious people assume significantly more personal responsibility for success than for failure. Socially anxious individuals respond to social evaluations with modesty, while nonsocially anxious people respond more actively, offering a favorable self-presentation (Arkin, Appelman, & Burger, 1980). Shy people make significantly fewer internal-stable attributions for positive outcomes and more internal-stable attributions for outcomes with negative consequences than do nonshy people. Shy individuals feel less intense positive affect than do nonshy people when outcomes are favorable, but report significantly more intense negative affect in cases with unfavorable outcomes (Teglasi & Hoffman, 1982). In essence, highly anxious individuals make attributions that tend to confirm their anxiety, thus preventing them from incorporating positive experiences into their lives. This consequently limits their opportunities to modify their anxiety. Research also shows that people's attributions can affect their performance. By changing attributions, one may modify behavior. For example, if shy individuals can be convinced to misattribute their performance to nonpsychological sources, the nervousness associated with the shyness fails to interfere with their performances (Brodt & Zimbardo, 1981; compare Cotton, Baron, & Brokovec, 1980; Slivken & Buss, 1983). Also, if individuals receive false physiological feedback about their anxiety, they respond in ways that match the false feedback, especially when the feedback suggests a low level of arousal (Motley, 1976).

In educational settings, the anxiety plays a role in the choices and judgments people make. Highly anxious individuals select majors having significantly fewer perceived communication demands than those selected by low anxious people (Daly & Shamo, 1977). High apprehensive students, when compared with low anxious students, are more likely to choose to drop out of courses containing many communication demands (McCroskey, Ralph, & Barrick, 1970) and prefer mass-lecture classes over smaller classes (McCroskey & Andersen, 1976). Indirect evidence suggests that highly anxious students take fewer study breaks, prefer less crowded and noisy studying environments, and view socializing, during studying, as less important and preferred than low anxious students (Campbell & Hawsley, 1982). Among junior high school students, as well as college students, communication apprehension is inversely related to positive attitudes toward school and instructional activities involving oral communication (Hurt & Preiss, 1978; McCroskey & Sheahan, 1978; Scott & Wheeless, 1977).

Behavioral Correlates

The behavioral correlates of the anxiety are described in this section. The research suggests that people who vary in the disposition also differ in their social and communicative behaviors.

Social Behaviors

The anxiety plays only a limited role in settings where the individual is well acquainted with those with whom he or she is interacting. Its predominant role is in social contexts where people are relatively unacquainted (Burgoon & Koper, 1983; Parks, 1980; Pilkonis, 1977b; Zimbardo, 1977). In the area of social relations, there are substantial differences between anxious and nonanxious individuals. The anxiety is inversely related to dating frequency (Jones & Russell, 1982; McCroskey & Sheahan, 1978; compare Parks et al., 1980), in line with a good deal of research on heterosexual social anxiety (for example, see Curran, Wallander, & Fischetti, 1980). Further, high apprehensives see themselves as possessing fewer heterosexual social skills, more heterosexual social anxiety, and less physical attractiveness than low apprehensives (Prisbell, 1982). High anxious people are more likely to date one person to the exclusion of others and are less likely to go on blind dates than their low anxious counterparts (McCroskey & Sheahan, 1978; Parks et al., 1980). Highly reticent individuals have significantly fewer friends than their less reticent counterparts (Jones & Russell, 1982). In groups, social anxiety and shyness are significantly and positively related to an individual's likelihood of conforming with others (Santee & Maslach, 1982) and is inversely related to the likelihood of assuming leadership positions (Crowell, Katcher, & Miyamoto, 1955). The anxiety is inversely related to the ability of individuals to describe strategies for getting others to like them. Furthermore, the anxiety is positively related to tendencies to concede control and inversely related to tendencies to assume control or use dynamism as a means of generating affinity (Bell & Daly, 1983a). Some recent studies suggest that there may be serious negative societal correlates associated with the anxiety. Wilson and Cox (1983) report that members of a paedophile club in Great Britain are significantly more shy than a control group of nonpaedophiles. Lee, Zimbardo, and Bertholf (1978) find that 80% of an admittedly small sample of "sudden murderers" describe themselves as dispositionally shy. Garvin (1979) found that a large majority of child neglecters were high communication apprehensives. Perhaps less extreme, but still not a societal plus, is Sheahan's (1976) finding that high apprehensives are less likely to register, in person, to vote, than low apprehensives.

Nonverbally, in predicting behavioral indices of anxiety (such as self-manipulations and gaze avoidance), shy but sociable women exhibit the most anxiety cues (Cheek & Buss, 1981). In comparison to low anxious people, high anxious individuals show more anxiety, bodily tension, and disinterest (Burgoon & Koper, 1983); maintain less eye contact with listeners and fidget more (Clevenger, 1959; Clevenger & King, 1961; Pilkonis, 1977b); gaze significantly less when talking (S. Daly, 1978); nod less, lean away more, and exhibit less facial pleasantness (Burgoon & Koper, 1983); have greater personal space needs (Gifford, 1982; Pilkonis, 1977b), especially when with those they dislike; prefer traditional classrooms over more socially interactive designs (McCroskey & McVetta, 1978); and select seats in small group settings and classrooms, as well as homes, that involve fewer communication demands (McCroskey, 1976; McCroskey & Sheahan, 1976).

Communicative Behaviors

Studies also explore the communication correlates of social-communicative anxiety. A consistent finding is that the anxiety is inversely related to the frequency and duration of talking done by people (Arnston et al., 1980; Boster, Fryrear, Mongeau, & Hunter, 1982; Burgoon, 1976, 1977; Cheek & Buss, 1981; S. Daly, 1978; Fenton & Hopf, 1976; Jordan & Powers, 1978; Lerea, 1956; Lustig, 1974, 1980; Lustig & Grove, 1973; Mortensen & Arnston, 1974; Mortensen et al., 1977; Natale, Entin, & Jaffe, 1979; Paivio & Lambert, 1959; Pilkonis, 1977b; Wells & Lashbrook, 1970). Further, it is inversely related to an individual's ability to interrupt successfully (Natale et al., 1979; Pilkonis, 1977b), likelihood of reciting and participating in dramatic activities within classrooms (Paivio, 1961), ability to initiate or control a conversation (Arnston et al., 1980; Pilkonis & Zimbardo, 1979), and speed of speech when in front of audiences compared to when alone (Paivio, 1965).

The anxiety is positively associated with listener cues (such as backchannel responses; Natale et al., 1979), disfluencies and speech errors (Baker, 1963; Hunter, 1935; Lerea, 1956; Levin, Baldwin, Gallway, & Paivio, 1960), nervous smiling in speeches (Slivken & Buss, 1983), longer latencies of verbal response and greater silences (Fenton & Hopf, 1976; Pilkonis, 1977b; compare Bliese et al., 1976), and more verbal repetitions (Jordan & Powers, 1978).

When the content of what is uttered is examined, research shows that high anxious people, compared to low anxious people, make more negative and fewer positive self-statements (Glass, Merluzzi, Biever, & Larson, 1982), are less comprehensible (Freimuth, 1976), exhibit greater tension (Burgoon & Burgoon, 1974; Sorensen & McCroskey,

1977), engage in less information seeking and giving (Burgoon, 1977), offer more irrelevant statements (Wiener, 1973; Wells & Lashbrook, 1970) and fewer ideas (Jablin et al., 1977; Jablin & Sussman, 1978) in small group exchanges; and in conversations (Stafford & Daly, 1983), use less immediate language (Conville, 1974), exhibit more restricted and unvaried language (Lerea, 1956), utter more rhetorical interrogatives (such as "You know?" and "You see?"; Powers, 1977), make more submissive statements in conversation (Arnston et al., 1980; Ellis, 1978), and offer less self-disclosure (Hamilton, 1972; McCroskey & Richmond, 1977; Wheeless, Nesser, & McCroskey, 1976), which, when offered, is likely to be more negative, less honest, and felt to be less under their control regarding its depth (Bradac, Tardy, & Hosman, 1980; McCroskey & Richmond, 1977). Further, higher anxious people recall fewer of their previous interactions (Hatvany & Zimbardo, 1977) and make more errors in what they recall (Stafford & Daly, 1983).

Conclusions

In this chapter we have explicated much of the research on the correlates and consequences of social-communicative anxiety. Some brief conclusions are in order. First, we believe that it is reasonable, in a review such as this, to subsume the many different constructs purportedly representing the anxiety under a single broader construct. As we noted previously, the patterns of research are complementary. There are very few disagreements among findings derived from different operationalizations. Second, there is sufficient research to suggest that the trait is predictive of a number of behavioral correlates given some necessary limitations. It is most predictive in early acquaintance situations, when multiple act criteria are applied, and when the behavior in question is distinctly related to communication or social activity. Clearly, the disposition, by itself, is insufficient to predict completely any specific behavior. The magnitude of effects observed in the studies reviewed in this chapter are typically moderate, with correlations ranging from .20 to .50. That is the portion of the variance attributable to the trait. The remaining variability is probably due to situational characteristics, other traits, and the relevant interactions. The trait does predict a number of important social behaviors and personal characteristics.

Third, in terms of its correlates, the genesis of the anxiety can be subsumed by four major components: some genetic factors, the reinforcements a person receives for early communication attempts, the amount and timing of skill acquisition, and the availability of good models of social and communicative behaviors. Further, the anxiety is related to a number of other personality dimensions. The portrait these personality correlates paint is of a socially anxious individual with tendencies to be lower in self-esteem, less socially oriented, less assertive and dominant, less achieving academically, and more lonely, withdrawn, and self-conscious than a socially nonanxious person. Perceptually, highly anxious people are perceived, and perceive themselves, less positively than do nonanxious individuals. Attributionally, they tend to take less credit for their successes and more credit for their failures than their counterparts low in the anxiety. Behaviorally, the anxiety is positively related to avoidance of social experiences and, when communication is required, reduced involvement both in terms of quantity and quality.

9

Implications of Quietness

Some Facts and Speculations

VIRGINIA P. RICHMOND

Throughout the chapters in this book, it has been noted repeatedly that a primary characteristic of highly communication-apprehensive (ca) people is their desire to avoid communication. In fact, the highly communication-apprehensive person often will go to extreme lengths to avoid communication, such as giving an inappropriate or wrong answer to a question that they could answer correctly, not talking when they should, and not joining in at social gatherings.

These patterns of behaviors have led researchers to study the perceptions others have of the highly communication apprehensive. The general consensus in the research is that characteristically the high CA is perceived as being less competent, less attractive, and less likely to be a leader. For a more extensive review of the effects and correlates, see Chapter 8. Additional research has illustrated that high CA is strongly associated with low self-esteem and loneliness.

In American society, life is an almost continuous series of communication encounters. While many of the communication experiences are mediated and others can be avoided, there still remains environments in which the highly apprehensive or quiet person must communicate. Hence, from the above we can see that everyday life for the highly communication-apprehensive person can be restricted and threatening.

In this chapter, I will examine the possible impacts of communication avoidance in the social, educational, and organizational settings. These are contexts in which people are expected to communicate, and when they do not (usually negative), perceptions are formed.

Social Context

Since most social situations involve interacting on a dyadic or small group basis it is not surprising that the high and low communication-apprehensive persons differ in their behaviors in the social context. Generally, in this context the individual who avoids communication will withdraw from interaction and may even be stereotyped as the "wall flower." They will migrate to the recesses of a room in order to avoid interaction, and when approached by others they will avert their eyes, stare into their drink, and seem generally anxious or aloof and unfriendly. This type of behavior in a social setting does not encourage others to want to communicate with one, hence interaction may be terminated rather quickly.

On the other hand, the low communication apprehensive often is the "life of the party." The highly verbal person typically will involve themselves in far more social activities in general than do high communication apprehensives.

Dating

There is a striking difference between the high communication apprehensive and the low communication apprehensive in terms of dating. The research indicates that high and low communication apprehensives have an equal desire for a social relationship with a member of the opposite sex. However, low apprehensives report having over twice as many dates in a given time period as do high communication apprehensives. It appears that if a high communication apprehensive has a social relationship with a member of the opposite sex, it will tend to be an exclusive relationship. In other words, the high apprehensive will find someone and "hang onto them for dear life." On the other hand, the low communication apprehensive appears to "play the field" or take the attitude that "forget him/her; there are plenty more fish in the ocean."

The quiet individual may be devastated when they lose the "one and only" person that they have dated; whereas, the more verbal individual will go out to a bar or church meeting and find another. We might speculate that in some cases the high communication-apprehensive might be so distressed at losing the "one and only" they could even contemplate suicide. After all, the dating relationship is one of the most potent and essential relationships in a person's life. In the high apprehensive's case, it may even be more vital. The high apprehensive finds security through having someone to communicate for them in the dating relationship.

The dating relationship may be more difficult for the highly apprehensive male than for the highly apprehensive female. Our culture still says that the "man" must be the aggressor in the dating context and that the "woman" should be accepting and "submissive." Even though times are changing, they haven't changed much. The highly apprehensive male would appear to be nonaggressive and nondominant and could be misjudged and stereotyped as being a "wimp" or a "nerd" in the dating context. Of course, on the other hand, there is always the old cliché that "the quiet ones get the girls." However, in most cases, the inverse is probably true. Nonaggressive men in the dating context will be perceived negatively by men and women unless they have something else going for them, such as money, being a sports star, or the like.

How about the quiet woman in the dating relationship? Quietness may not be as devastating for the woman in the dating context as it is for the man. The quiet woman might be perceived as submissive by both males and females. However, if the quietness is not perceived as submissiveness, or the appropriate dating shyness, the female could be stereotyped by men as a "cold fish." When I was in college, there was a young woman who was very attractive and received dating requests from many men. The majority of them she refused because she was highly apprehensive. However, she did start dating one man on a somewhat regular basis, but she remained uncommunicative and this irrated the young man after awhile. In fact, on one date he told her she was so cold a telephone pole was more responsive. Needless to say, the relationship was ended and the highly apprehensive girl was devastated. In conclusion, this culture reinforces assertiveness and responsiveness in the dating context and only marginally tolerates the quiet person, whether female or male.

Marriage

The strong tendency to engage in exclusive relationships on the part of high communication apprehensives is also evident from their behavior with regard to marriage. In a study of college graduates ranging in age from 23 to 64, it was found that high communication apprehensives, over half of them, married within a year after completing their undergraduate degree. No similar pattern was found for low communication apprehensives.

Such behavioral patterns suggest that high communication apprehensives find it difficult to establish relationships and thus make a strong effort to maintain ones they can establish. But what are some possible consequences when a high communication apprehensive marries a low communication apprehensive? I know one couple, recently divorced, who fit this description. He was an extreme high verbal and she was an extreme low verbal. On several occasions throughout their marriage, he tried to get her to pursue a career; she said she couldn't because she didn't like talking with others. He would come home and find the heat and lights turned off because she forgot to pay the bills, and then was afraid to call the respective companies. More often than not, he and the children would have to answer the phone because she was afraid to talk on the phone. She would never go to the school to discuss the children's problems with the teachers, and rarely attended social functions when the children were involved. After several years of being married, both being highly dissatisfied with the relationship, they divorced. It only took him a few months to recover and find a dating partner; however, it took her over four years.

The above case may be the exception to the rule; however, I doubt it. I suspect marriages dissolve every year because of the differences in communication orientations. In addition, the shy partner might be more affected by divorce than the extroverted partner. Low communication apprehensives find it easier to reestablish social relationships and are not overly concerned that one may terminate — there will always be another.

Friendship

Since friendship also requires communication — and many times in-depth disclosive communication is expected — the communication avoider suffers in this context too. The communication avoidance behaviors of high apprehensives could lead to fewer friends, difficulty developing long-lasting friendships, and the tendency to find one or two friends and "hang on to them." The social context of friendship generally requires self-disclosure. The quiet person does not tend to be a high self-discloser, hence the development of long-lasting friends is difficult. This tendency to avoid communication could lead to an extremely lonely life.

Loneliness

Many researchers suggest that three areas of the antecedents of loneliness are the avoidance of communication, deficient communication skills, and being socially deficient. The individual who avoids communication may or may not be lonely, communication-skills deficient, and socially deficient; however, the research suggests that dyadic-interpersonal communication apprehension and shyness are associated with loneliness. This finding corresponds with the trend of CAs in terms of avoiding communication, difficulty in developing and maintaining relationships, and a general desire to withdraw from communication situations. Serious consideration should be given to understanding the lonely individual. For some, it may not present a problem; however, for others it could lead to extreme unhappiness and even suicide. Hence, the person who avoids communication and is uncomfortable with communication could also be extremely lonely, even in a crowd.

In conclusion, since most social contexts require and even demand communication, the person who is afraid to communicate is "left out in the cold." The highly communication-apprehensive person finds it extremely difficult to function in the social context.

Educational Context

The classroom is another major environment for communication. As such, it is not surprising that behaviors of quiet and talkative people in the classroom are substantially different.

To begin with, the high and low communication-apprehensive students vary greatly with regard to behavior. The quiet students rarely raise their hands or volunteer information or talk out in class. Some teachers may classify the quiet student as the "perfect student." The student who likes communication is active verbally, always has an answer, not necessarily the correct one, and often is perceived as a class distraction. In this section, we will examine these general communication tendencies and how they influence behaviors in specific educational situations.

Classes to Take or to Avoid

To begin with, high and low communication apprehensives make different decisions concerning what classes to take, when given free choice. Low communication apprehensives prefer classes with small enrollment where there is ample opportunity for students to interact with each other and with the instructor. High communication apprehensives, in contrast, tend to avoid small classes in favor of large, lecture-type classes in which most of the communication takes the form of the instructor talking to the students and the students simply listening and taking notes.

The students who select the large, mass-lecture class might be shortchanging themselves in terms of in-depth knowledge gain. They do not take the opportunity to interact with their peers and their instructor on a one-to-one basis. Nevertheless, if they were in smaller, interaction-oriented classes, their chances of success would be low because of the amount of interaction required. Thus, the quieter student should be allowed to opt for the larger, lecture-type classes.

Classroom Communication Orientation

What is expected, in terms of communication, in the class also influences people's choices of classes. Classes that require oral reports or speeches are avoided by high communication apprehensives, but are attractive to low communication apprehensives. Similarly, classes that base part of the final grade on "class participation" are attractive to low communication apprehensives, but are disliked by those with higher apprehension.

Once students are enrolled in a class, whether voluntarily or through a requirement, we might assume that the students will simply accept the requirements with regard to communication and try to do the best they can. Such an assumption is incorrect. High communication apprehensives often will drop a class with high communication requirements, even if it is a required course. For example, one study found that over 50% of the students with high communication apprehension dropped a required public speaking course during the first 3 weeks of the course, just before the first speech was due to be presented. Other studies have found that high communication apprehensives who remain in courses with high communication requirements are likely to be absent on days when they are scheduled for presentations. This is true not only at the college and high school levels but also at the elementary school level where "show and tell" or "book report" assignments are required. Young children often claim that they are unable to read so they can avoid having to read out loud to the class.

Low communication apprehensives are likely to engage in similar behaviors if there is little opportunity for communication in the course. Their attendance in lecture classes is likely to be low; they would rather get the necessary information by reading or talking to other students than by sitting through "boring" lectures. Similarly, research has indicated that low communication apprehensives do not like automated, individualized instruction where they are given objectives, reading or viewing assignments, and tests with no opportunity for interaction with a live teacher. They are likely to avoid or withdraw from the class, or, as an alternative if they must have the credit, complete the class in as short a time as is permitted.

Seating

Where a person chooses to sit in a classroom also reflects the person's level of communication apprehension. Low communication apprehensives tend to sit in the front and center of the traditional classroom. High communication apprehensives tend to sit along the sides and in the rear of the room. Most interaction in the typical classroom is focused on the center of the room in the first few rows. This is where the low apprehensive chooses to sit, and where the high communication apprehensive avoids sitting. In short, communication avoidance has a direct impact on student preferences for instructional systems and on student behaviors.

Small Group Discussion

The interaction in a small group discussion setting is relevant because so much classroom interaction takes place in the small setting. Numerous studies have replicated a consistent finding: People with high CA talk much less in the small group setting than do people with low CA. This is a classic example of withdrawal. In each study, people were unable to avoid being in the small group setting, and in each case those with high CA were found to be infrequent participants while those with low CA were found to participate extensively. To state the point simply, people who are apprehensive about talking in a small group setting tend not to, even when forced into such a setting.

Avoidance of communication in the small group setting is evidenced by individual's choices in seating within the group. In most seating arrangements, there are positions that are the focus of attention and positions that are relatively obscure. Research indicates that the individuals with low CA regularly choose the positions that are the focus of attention, while those with high CA regularly choose positions that are more obscure.

To illustrate this point, let us visualize a typical conference table with eight seats. The table is rectangular, with a seat at each end and three along each side. The most focal seats are the two at opposite ends. The next most focal are the two in the middle along the sides. The other four seats permit more obscurity. The research indicates that people with high CA will carefully avoid sitting in either of the end seats or the middle seats, while people with low CA will strive to obtain those seats. Sitting in obscure seats permits people with high CA to withdraw from communication more easily and be less likely to be addressed directly by others.

Several research studies have indicated that CA has an impact on the content of communication in the small group setting, most particularly on the content generated by people with high CA. Disruption of communication is a common impact. People with high CA have an abnormally high level of verbalized pauses and rhetorical interrogatives (such as "you know") in the small group setting. In addition when they talk, people with high CA tend to say things that are not relevant to the ongoing discussion. Probably most importantly, people with high CA tend to avoid expressing disagreement in the small group setting. When asked their opinion, they tend overwhelmingly to express agreement with the group, whether they actually are in agreement or not.

The small group setting seems not only to disrupt the communication of the person with high CA, but also to disrupt the thought processes of these individuals. When asked to brainstorm for ideas privately, people with high CA generate as many ideas as other people. However, when placed in a small group setting, these individuals generate far fewer ideas. In all likelihood, these individuals are thinking more about how to cope with the communication demands of the setting than they are about the problem being discussed.

In sum, the person with high CA tends not be a particularly useful member of a discussion group. They will avoid or withdraw from communication to the extent possible. If communication is thrust upon them, their communication probably will be disrupted, they will have less ideas to contribute, they may make comments that others will see as irrelevant, and they will tend to be submissive to the ideas of the group majority. On the other side of the coin, people with low CA typically will dominate the interaction of the group, generate numerous ideas, make relevant comments, and be quite willing to disagree with other group members.

In conclusion, since most educational contexts stress communication, it is not surprising that the quiet student is receiving the "short end of the stick." In most instances, our classrooms are set up in such a fashion that the quiet students' likelihood for success is decreased, whereas, the more verbal students' likelihood for success is increased.

Organizational Context

Effective communication is central to the efficient operation of an organization. Many organizations spend thousands of dollars each year to employ either consultants or regular staff to implement training programs to enhance the quality of communication within their systems. Much of this money, time, and effort is directed toward improvement of human communication skills. My concern with the person who avoids communicating in organizations stems from their basic behavioral response, which is the avoidance of and withdrawal from communication. In general, most organizations tend to reward high verbals and either ignore low verbals or dismiss them.

Occupational Choice

Given the strong tendency for high CAs to attempt avoidance of being forced to communicate, it might be expected that such people would select occupations that they perceive to have minimal communication requirements. As expected, high CAs express a strong preference for occupations where communication requirements are low, while people with lower CAs express a strong preference for occupations with high communication requirements.

At first blush, these tendencies may appear encouraging. After all, isn't it desirable that people be in positions compatible with their communication orientations? Yes and no. Yes, because these are the positions in which the person will feel most comfortable and be most likely to succeed. No, because with only a few exceptions, positions with higher communication requirements are also those that carry higher status in the society and provide greater economic return to the individual. Thus, as a result of their CA, it appears that high CAs tend to self-select themselves into occupational roles that insure them comparatively lower social status and lower economic standing. While this may be desirable for the organizations involved, whether or not it is good for the individuals is questionable.

Job Applicant Screening

Research in some organizations has discovered fewer high CAs in the system than would be expected on the basis of norms for the population as a whole. This suggests the possibility that high CAs are systematically excluded from being hired, or that for one reason or another they are more likely to leave the organization than are other people.

Studies suggest that more verbal job applicants are perceived as more task-attractive, more competent, in need of less training to do the job, and as having a greater likelihood for success. The reticent individual is perceived as being less competent, less task-attractive, projected to be less successful on the job, to require more training, to be less satisfied on the job, and to have more difficulty establishing good relationships with co-workers. As a result, the quiet person is less likely to be offered employment, or even an interview.

At present, we can only speculate about the fate of the high CA within the context of the employment interview. However, it appears that high CAs are discriminated against in the hiring process, possibly even when the available job is most compatible with the orientations of high CA.

Job Satisfaction

Virtually all occupations require some communication among peers and between peers and supervisors. The question arises, therefore, as to how well the high CA can adjust to this reality. If people are forced to do something they don't like (such as, communicate with others), it then follows that they will be less satisfied with their job than others. High CAs are significantly less satisfied than employees with lower CA, particularly with regard to satisfaction with their supervisor. It may be that supervisors provide more of a threat to the quieter individual than to others, since even communication from the supervisor that is intended to reward the high CA may be distasteful. In any event, the research suggests that high CAs are less likely to be happy in their work than are other people.

Employment Retention

As we noted previously, in some organizations fewer high CAs have been found than would be expected from population norms. In part, this may be a function of their never having been hired. However, if such people are employed, the organization is not likely to obtain the best efforts and input from these employees because of their reluctance to engage in the necessary communication required. In addition, their dissatisfaction is likely to contribute to a less positive overall organizational climate. In short, compared to other employees, high CAs are more costly to the organization. Not only are they likely to be less productive, but they are also more likely to leave or to be dismissed, and thus require an additional expenditure to train their replacements.

Advancement

Given that high CAs tend to retain employment for a shorter period than other employees, it would come as no surprise to find that few high CAs advance to top positions in organizations. Each advancement requires more administrative and/or supervisory activity and an accompanying increase in communication. Additionally, the cost of poor, absent, or ineffective communication becomes higher at each step in most organizations and increases the likelihood that the quiet person will fail and be removed from the position.

It appears that high CAs are well aware of both the low probability and lack of desirability for their advancement. High CAs, then, appear to be relegated to the lower levels of organizations through a tacit but usually unspoken agreement between them and their supervisors that that is where they belong.

In conclusion, the results of the research involving CA in organizations presents a bleak picture. For the quiet individual, prospects for employment, retention, and advancement are all significantly reduced. It is less likely that the person will develop good interpersonal relationships with employee peers. It is also less likely that the individual will be satisfied with whatever employment he or she does obtain.

Summary

From the implications that have been outlined in this chapter, we can draw brief profiles of the quiet person and the communication-oriented person: The communication-oriented person is successful in the social environment, establishing good relationships at school and work. The reticent individual is less successful in the social environment and has difficulty functioning and being successful in the educational and occupational environments.

10

Cross-Cultural Apprehension Research
A Summary of Pacific Basin Studies

DONALD W. KLOPF

A substantial amount of research has been completed regarding the nature and prevalence of oral communication (CA) in the United States (Beatty, Behnke, & McCallum, 1978). CA research is also underway in other cultures. Studies in Europe, Australia, and Asia have been reported among persons whose first language is English, and preliminary assessment of CA norms has been made of Puerto Ricans, primarily Spanish speaking (Fayer, McCroskey, & Richmond, 1982). McCann (1982) measured CA among foreign students enrolled in American university classes, while Pucel and Stocker (1982) observed CA stress among the Japanese.

Cross-cultural research in allied constructs is known. Zimbardo (1977) examined shyness in Israel and Japan as well as in American subcultures. Reticence in Korea was addresses by Elliot, Jensen, Scott, and McDonough (1982). General anxiety has been investigated cross-culturally in over 500 applications (Sharma, 1977).

CA research also has been completed involving populations in Australia, Japan, Korea, Micronesia, People's Republic of China, and the Philippines. A Taiwan study has begun. This CA research is comparative in nature and part of a preliminary study of the communication practices of Pacific Basin peoples. The preliminary study represents a familiarization phase in the cross-cultural research process. The results of the CA portion of this preparatory work are summarized here. Because cross-cultural research is unlike standard social science research (Starr & Wilson, 1977), the results should be viewed with circumspection. They may be tenuous at best. Nonetheless, they do suggest the extent and nature of CA in the Pacific.

Cross-cultural and monocultural research are different processes (Saral, 1977). Western-based researchers can approach potential subjects in their community, ask them questions, apply an experimental treatment, and accomplish whatever else is necessary to obtain the required data. They know the meaning of their procedures for they are members of the culture. With other cultures, the same group of researchers probably will not have the knowledge from which the investigation can be conducted (Brislin, Lonner, & Throndike, 1973).

Numerous factors affect intercultural research that would not bear on monocultural investigations. Among these are the affects of different societal variables from that being measured on questionnaire responses; the impact of paper-pencil testing, an extraordinary experience in many cultures; the translation of instruments into other languages; the selection of subjects based on easy access rather than on scientific interest; and the fatigue factor in testing that one culture's subjects can handle and another's may not (Campbell, 1969).

Use of questionnaires and other survey instruments, like the CA ones, cause problems. Western-based researchers may not know the meaning persons in other cultures will attach to questionnaires. Is the questionnaire a device to provide information to the tax collector, dreaded government agents, or friends of the ruling group? Researchers may not realize that different meanings from those intended are often assigned by foreign respondents to tests made for and standardized on Western samples. In some cultures, subjects respond positively to researchers by telling them what the subjects think the researchers want to hear, thus biasing the responses. In other cultures, subjects will give valid responses only to those researchers displaying an authoritarian attitude. Questionnaire items may be meaningful to persons in one culture, but strange or meaningless to those in another. Consequently, research procedures must account for the factors that might jeopardize the validity of the obtained data. Discovering problems is obligatory in cross-cultural research, and often as not the typical monocultural pilot study is not adequate, and requires more comprehensive preliminary research (Brislin et al., 1973). Hence, the extended exploratory study was conducted, the CA aspects of which are reported here.

Method

Subjects

Selected on an availability basis, the sample was composed of 219 Australians, 504 Japanese, 73 Koreans, 153 Micronesians, 184 Chinese from the People's Republic, and 312 Filipinos. The sample's characteristics were similar; the university students who took part were equally represented by males and females from multiple academic disciplines, 18 to 24 years of age, and possessing an English first or second language capability. In each culture, research collaborators chose the sample, the collaborators being of the same racial group, living in the same culture, and speaking the same vernacular as the respondents. A 397-person American sample from the University of Hawaii also participated for comparison purposes. The Hawaiian students were a mix of Caucasian, Chinese, Filipino, Japanese, and Korean-Americans.

CA Measurement

For the CA facet of the total project, the McCroskey (1970) Personal Report of Communication Apprehension (PRCA) was chosen for its proven reliability and validity (McCroskey, 1978) over other CA measures, particularly the Gilkinson (1942) Personal Report on Confidence as a Speaker and the Paul (1966) short form of Gilkinson's instrument.

Problems arise when instruments designed in one culture are administered to those in another (Hwang, 1973). The "emic-etic" distinction is a principal one (Berry, 1969). "Emic" refers to research that ferrets out monocultural principles of behavior, while "etic" refers to the search for pancultural principles. The PRCA was conceived to investigate CA in the United States, an emic type of research. Using it cross-culturally in an etic way presupposes that CA can be found in other countries and, if found, it can be understood by using the PRCA framework. Berry (1969) calls this the cardinal sin in cross-cultural research.

Another problem surfaces when different language versions of the same instrument are used (Brislin et al., 1973). Are the different versions functionally equivalent? If respondents to a different language version of an instrument perform poorly, the results may be taken as supporting a research finding, but they also may reflect a poor understanding of a badly translated instrument.

To prevent the emic-etic distinction and translation problems from occurring, various techniques have been developed. With the English-as-a-second-language respondents, two were tested in the research reported here: The Werner and Campbell (1970) back-translation method and the Prince and Mombour (1967) use of bilinguals system. The first starts with an English language instrument that can be translated. The PRCA proved to be such a device. Two bilinguals are then employed, one translating from the source to the target language (here, Japanese and Chinese), the second blindly translating back from the target to the source language.

The Prince and Mombour (1967) procedure seemed more appropriate for future research. It handles the translation problem and deals more completely with the emic-etic distinction. The procedure calls for a careful translation, which is tested on bilinguals (here, a Japanese sample). The bilinguals are randomly assigned to two groups. One group is asked the first half of the questions in English, the second half in the other language (Japanese). The other group follows a reversed order. Items eliciting discrepant response frequencies are translated again with further trial runs until comparable frequencies are obtained, and this was done with the PRCA.

Procedure

In-culture collaborators, interested in cross-cultural communication practices, were enlisted to complete the research process in their cultures. Each met the in-culture status requirements for conducting social science research (Berrien, 1970; Brislin et al., 1973). They were male, English-speaking natives, 40 or more years of age, married, and engaged in high status occupations, in this case, communication educators.

The collaborators in all but two cultures had to secure institutional or governmental approval for participating. Involving students and taking class time for research purposes are not universally accepted practices. Also, a modification in the total research project had to be made because a proposed data collection technique proved reprehensible in one culture.

Meetings between the principal researchers and the collaborators covered such items as the research topics, data collection procedures and data analysis methods. Since the research was to be transcultural, and, therefore, by nature is comparativist (Brislin et al., 1973), the collaborators as a group had to agree that CA deserved investigation.

All had to understand the CA construct and to consider the issues it raises. The collaborators familiarized themselves with the CA literature to understand the construct. Because the study compares CA across seven cultures, the collaborators had to determine whether CA holds the same degree of importance in each. To do so, the collaborators followed normal procedure (Berry, 1969) by reviewing in-culture literature and calling upon their first-hand knowledge of the speaking practices typical of their culture.

After the PRCA was administered in each culture, the completed instruments were returned to the principal researchers for scoring and analysis. The Tuccy T-Test Procedure (1975), an analysis method appropriate for independent samples of varied sizes, was chosen as the technique most suitable for data analysis. The results were examined by the collaborators as recommended by Lesser and Kandel (1968) in order to give their personal interpretations and these were analyzed by all for ethnocentric biases.

Results and Discussion

Table 10.1 reports the mean scores and standard deviations for the seven cultural groups. Additionally, the table shows the proportion of subjects in each sample falling into the High CA category. The High category includes those subjects scoring beyond one standard deviation above the mean (McCroskey, 1970).

Group comparisons were made, and these are explained next in a culture by culture discussion, following an alphabetical ordering of the countries involved.

Australians

The Australians were significantly less apprehensive than the Americans ($p < .01$) and Japanese ($p < .001$); significantly more apprehensive than the Koreans ($p < .001$) and Filipinos ($p < .05$); and not significantly different than the Micronesians and People's Republic Chinese. Other research reports comparing Australians with different American groups (Hansford & Hatlie, 1979; Klopf & Cambra, 1979; Crocker, Klopf, & Cambra, 1978) show no significant differences between the two.

Table 10.1 reveals the percentage of respondents who fall into the High CA category. The Australians with 22.4% rank fifth highest among the seven cultures analyzed.

TABLE 10.1
Mean and Standard Deviation PRCA Scores and High CA Percentages by Cultural Group

Culture	N	$\overline{X}$	SD	% High CA
American	397	63.34	12.48	33.5
Australian	219	60.37	12.94	22.4
Filipino	312	58.09	10.59	13.8
Japanese	504	65.90	10.72	35.9
Korean	73	52.78	10.59	2.8
Micronesian	153	60.78	13.35	22.8
People's Republic – Chinese	184	62.18	11.23	26.0

Crocker, Klopf, and Cambra (in press) studied the communication
style of Australian college students and found that they consider
themselves to be worthy communicators with a strong communicator
image. Those Australians perceived themselves to be animated as
speakers and nonverbally active, gesturing frequently and expressing
their feelings facially. They are friendly, relaxed, attentive, dramatic,
open, impression-leaving, and can take charge or oral encounters.
Crocker, Klopf, and Cambra (1979) noted that Australian college
students like to join groups, be a part of group activities, and be
controlled by group life.

Not much else is known about CA in Australia, including what
causes it. Klopf and Cambra (1980b) speculate that the causes differ
little from those suggested by American researchers — specifically,
heredity, modeling, reinforcement skill acquisition, and expectancy
learning (McCroskey & Richmond, 1980).

Japanese

The Japanese were significantly more apprehensive than all the other
groups: Americans ($p < .01$), Australians ($p < .001$), Koreans ($p < .001$), Micronesians ($p < .001$), People's Republic Chinese ($p < .001$),
and Filipinos ($p < .001$). These results are substantiated by other CA
research. Klopf, Cambra, and Ishii (1983) reviewed 8 years of CA
reports involving approximately 4500 Japanese university students and
business and professional persons. These people were compared to
various American and other foreign populations, and the results always
show the Japanese with a higher CA level. The High CA category noted

in Table 10.1 includes 35.9% of the Japanese, constituting the largest percentage among the seven cultures.

The research supports the observations made by many people about Japanese speaking. Yoshikawa (1977) believes that the Japanese place different values on speech from other cultures, and these differences may account for CA's high incidence. He claims that the Japanese value harmony and will avoid direct confrontation, being other-directed. In order to preserve harmony, openness and frankness are avoided, thus causing hesitancy or reticence. Morsbach (1976) and Doi (1973) note the stress on nonverbal communication among the Japanese and less emphasis on the oral aspects of communicating. Lebra (1976) believes that the Japanese experience communicational frustration because of the culturally shared mistrust of words and the alleged ineffectiveness of verbal communication. Direct communication, she says, is often considered undesirable or inappropriate. Rogers and Izutsu (1980), on the other hand, contend that the Japanese have been incorrectly labeled inarticulate and nonverbal. They claim that many Japanese see constant verbal communication as unnecessary, a talkative person being considered a "show-off" or insincere. Thus, the Japanese are not taught to speak out at every opportunity. Regardless, reserved and restricted communicative behavior, both verbal and nonverbal, is practiced in Japanese society. The strong belief in the meaning implied in the saying, "all evil comes from the mouth," causes the typical Japanese to unconsciously control the natural flow of their inner feelings. Dynamic communicative behavior is indecent and ever shameful to the Japanese, except for professional people such as actors, singers, and politicians (Klopf & Ishii, 1983).

Koreans

The Koreans were significantly less apprehensive ($p < .001$) than all of the other groups, and had the fewest in the High CA category. However, the Korean sample size was small as compared to the others. Nevertheless, the literature lends credence to the results, portraying the Koreans as orally assertive people. Cha, Choi, and Suh (1976) picture the Koreans as outgoing, talkative people who are relatively active, pleasant, industrious, friendly, and fast. McQuerrey (1975) characterizes them as aggressive, conspicuous, and more temperamental than expected of Orientals. Oliver (1944) believes that several hundred years of a strong village government system that fostered the individual expression of opinion partially accounts for their oral expressiveness.

Lee (1978) feels that critical and selective patriotism is a reason for their oral fluency. Park, Cambra, and Klopf (1979) found Koreans to be more dominant and talkative than Americans, Australians, and Japanese. Their talk tends to be task-centered, and less inclined toward matters that enhance group relations. Park (1979) sees the Koreans as enjoying conversation, following a prose-oriented communication pattern. Instead of going directly to the point, Koreans tend to take up long descriptive accounts about a person or an event in subjective terms.

Micronesians

The Micronesians were significantly less apprehensive than the Americans ($p < .05$) and the Japanese ($p < .001$), significantly more apprehensive than the Koreans ($p < .001$) and the Filipinos ($p < .05$), and not significantly different from the Australians and Chinese. About 22% were High CAs as Table 10.1 reveals. With regard to the Americans, research by Bruneau, Cambra, and Klopf (1980) compared this Micronesian group with an American population composed of students from places other than Hawaii. In this instance, the Micronesians were not significantly different from the more representative American group.

The Micronesian respondents were a mix of Chamorros, Chinese, Filipinos, Palauans, Caucasians, Trukians, and Koreans, who in the Micronesian setting project a positive communicator image. As a group, they find it easy to talk with others and perceive themselves to be friendly, dramatic, animated, and impression-leaving. They appear to themselves as being interested in others, generally demonstrating goodwill in communication situations. Their speaking, they believe, is picturesque, tending toward the exaggerated, being active nonverbally. People will remember a typical Micronesian, they feel, after engaging one in a conversation (Mordeno, Cambra, & Klopf, 1980a, 1980b).

People's Republic Chinese

With 26% in the High CA category, the Chinese were significantly less apprehensive than the Japanese ($p < .001$), significantly more than the Koreans ($p < .001$), and not significantly different from the other groups. Klopf and Cambra (1980) compared this Chinese sample to Americans elsewhere and also uncovered no significant difference.

A cursory review of the communication literature in America finds little written about the oral communication practices of the billions of people living in the People's Republic of China. In other academic fields, such as business, history, linguistics, psychology, and sociology, journal articles about China touch on facets of oral communication, albeit indirectly, referring to a communication practice while discussing a concern more akin to the particular field. Books on China also make passing references to oral communication, but none examine oral communication per se.

The literature on the People's Republic refers to a series of campaigns conducted during the period of the Great Leap Forward in order to alter aspects of Chinese life and eliminate problems of various sorts. About 1958, a *perpetuum mobile* of campaigns swept the countryside, dealing with disparate sorts of problems. The campaign against the Four Evils, for instance, was directed to the elimination of flies, mosquitoes, sparrows, and rats. The campaign to "Offer Your Heart to the Party" was an attempt to instill in the people a desire to support the present and forget the past. One of the more important campaigns was the campaign against individualism and the "Five Vices" — timidity, vanity, luxury, bureaucratism, and egocentrism. Apparently timidity was a serious enough problem that a campaign had to be launched to eradicate it and to encourage the people to speak up (Goldman, 1969).

However, evidence in the literature neither confirms or denies the need to campaign nationally against the people's failure to speak up. For instance, Eberhard (1971), in the late 1950s and early 1960s studied Chinese regional stereotypes and discovered that talking too much was a pronounced characteristic of the people in at least one province and existent among the citizens in others. The stereotypes, he claimed had been stable for several thousand years, and he believed they constituted an excellent means of assessing the people's character. He also pointed out that the regional differences are great in China, and what is true of one is by no means true of the others.

Barnett (1969) described the group indoctrination practices of the Chinese — practices born during the revolution's early stages and apparently still in effect, if the Rogers (1979) report is accurate. These practices are termed *hsueh-hsi*, or "to learn and practice," and involve group discussions among all of the people. Millions gather in groups of a half-dozen to a dozen people in factories, shops, schools, and offices each day to discuss the ideology and policies of the Communist regime. Under pressure to speak, group members readily talk about the Party and express the Party line. However, many people apparently are reticent about voicing their true feelings at these meetings on whatever the discussion topic is. They fear punishment if they do. So they freely expouse the Party doctrine, but are reluctant to discuss their personal feelings and beliefs with the others.

Char, Tseng, Lum, and Hsu (1980) suggest that many young Chinese are as vocal and outspoken as Caucasians. They can be open and free with their thoughts and feelings, but they usually avoid expressing their inner feelings, thoughts, and problems, especially with strangers and particularly if the feelings are negative.

Alter, Cambra, and Klopf (1980) report that the Chinese belong to groups representing the family, immediate and larger neighborhood, factory, and commune — groups that rarely change membership. Because of group stability, they feel comfortable with the other members and talk much, but rarely express their inner feelings.

Filipinos

The Filipinos were significantly less apprehensive than all of the groups but the Koreans: Americans ($p < .001$), Australians ($p < .05$), Japanese ($p < .001$), Micronesians ($p < .05$), and Chinese ($p < .001$). They were significantly more apprehensive than the Koreans ($p < .001$). Mordeno, Cambra, and Klopf (1980b) compared the Filipino group to Americans elsewhere, and this American sample proved to be significantly more apprehensive.

CA is not as serious a problem in the Philippines as in most of the other countries studied. Table 10.1 shows only 13.8% in the High CA category, lower than all groups but the Koreans. Certain cultural influences may be the reason. Typically, the Filipino child grows up in a large network of relationships — kin and social. Maturation is not comparable to independence; it means, instead, forming an expanding and satisfying series of dependency relationships with others. The result is that Filipinos seek the company of others, preferring to do things in groups or through groups rather than by themselves (Alcantra, 1975). They value the company of others and cannot stand being alone for long periods. Acceptance by others, therefore, is a vital factor in a Filipino's behavior and group harmony is encouraged (Golis, 1979). Family and social relationships are maintained by communication, principally oral, and the Filipino child growing up in a strong group environment learns to interact orally in order to be accepted and in harmony with the others. The fear of speaking usually does not find fertile fields for development in such surroundings.

Mordeno, Cambra, and Klopf (1980a) studied Filipino oral communication styles, and the results indicate that Filipinos think of themselves as friendly, dramatic, relaxed, open, animated, and impression-leaving. They hold a good communicator image of themselves. Ponce (1980) thinks they behave like Americans in conversation situations, and Forman (1980) stresses the family desire to be literate, with emphasis placed on communication skills.

Americans

The Americans represented by University of Hawaii students were significantly more apprehensive than the Australians ($p < .01$), Koreans ($p < .001$), Micronesians ($p < .05$), and Filipinos ($p < .001$). The Chinese were not significantly different. Only the Japanese were more apprehensive ($p < .01$), and only the Japanese had a higher percentage of respondents in the High CA category as Table 10.1 reports. This American population undoubtedly is not representative of populations elsewhere in the United States; it was chosen for convenience purposes.

Studies suggest that a large percentage of Hawaii students have a high degree of oral communication apprehension. Meredith (1964) found that Japanese-American college students exhibit a significantly higher anxiety level than their Caucasian counterparts in Hawaii. About 32% of Hawaii's population is of Japanese ancestry and about 20% is Caucasian. Matsumoto, Meredith, and Masuda (1970) compared Honolulu Japanese-Americans with those in Seattle on a number of factors. They reported a significant difference between the two groups on anxiety-related factors, with the Hawaii group having a higher incidence. Ishii, Cambra, and Klopf (1978) indicated that 48% of the University of Hawaii students enrolled in speech and human development classes perceive themselves as high apprehensives. Admittedly, the problem in Hawaii is multicausal, and several classes of variables are responsible, especially those sociocultural and educational in nature. Sociocultural influences include economic status and locality of the family's residence, peer-group expectations, and ethnic backgrounds. Certainly, island dialect plays a vital role (Meredith, 1964).

As a consequence of various language patterns and the remoteness of Hawaii from the mainland United States. Hawaii developed its own characteristic speech, island dialect (or "pidgin"). Over time, the dialect became a common language, permitting easy communication across the diverse social, cultural, and linguistic lines (Aspinwall, 1960). It carried, unfortunately, the stigma of a lower-class status, partially because it became the mode of communication between the "workers" (the "bosses" used standard English), and partially because it had no literature, a limited vocabulary, and restricted forms of expression (Lind, 1960).

Considerable pressure was exerted, principally by the schools, to speak general American and drop the use of dialect. At the same time, peer-group expectations and social control placed severe demands on the students to conform to island dialect speech patterns. The conflict between schools and society has been identified as a cause of the high anxiety (Meredith, 1964).

For the largest segment of the population, the Japanese-American, a cultural influence compounded the problem. "Silence is golden" in Japan, and the children are trained from early childhood not to talk much (Klopf, Ishii, & Cambra, 1978). This motherland-Japanese characteristic came with the Japanese immigrants to Hawaii, and its impact remains strong (Meredith, 1964).

Conclusions

The CA research reported here constitutes part of an exploratory phase of a study of Pacific Basin communication practices. This research was completed for the purpose of identifying possible problems in methodology, so the results should be viewed as tentative. In addition to the caveats normally associated with monocultural research, those characteristic of cross-cultural research bear on the CA results and the preliminary conclusions noted next.

First, The PRCA seems usable with English-speaking subjects who are not Americans — for instance, the Australians, Filipinos, and Micronesians sampled in this project, as well as bilingual, nonnative speakers of English, like the Chinese, Japanese, and Koreans who participated. Back-translation and bilingual usage appear to be helpful procedures for overcoming translation problems, should the PRCA be used with non-English speakers. By closely following the bilingual usage procedure and by employing native collaborators, other cross-cultural research problems for the most part can be dealt with satisfactorily.

Second, CA appears to be a Pacific Basin problem, and it is a North American one. Among the Pacific cultures sampled, only in Korea does the incidence seem minor. That may be reflective, however, of the small Korean sample, although the literature suggests that Koreans like talking. In the other countries, there is little doubt that CA represents a problem to considerable numbers of college students, and an obvious serious one both for the multiethnic University of Hawaii and Japanese college students.

PART IV

REMEDIATION

11

Systematic Desensitization

GUSTAV FRIEDRICH and BLAINE GOSS

The first reports of systematic desensitization (SD) as a treatment procedure were presented by Wolpe in the early 1950s. In his most definitive work (*Psychotherapy by Reciprocal Inhibition*), Wolpe (1958) reported that of 210 clients he had treated, 90% were either cured or much improved after a mean of 31 interviews (success, for him, meant that the original problem was at no greater than 20% of its original intensity as measured by client ratings). Wople contrasted his success rate with a success rate for other forms of therapy — primarily psychoanalytic — of approximately 60%.

The promise of SD as a treatment technique produced a flood of published case histories. Paul and Bernstein (1976) note that selective reviews of the literature prior to 1971 revealed "over 150 separate reports on the work of hundreds of therapists with thousands of clients." Representative of such reports are those of Hain, Butcher, and Stevenson (1966) — a 78% improvement for 27 treated patients — and Lazarus (Paul, 1969) — a 85% success rate for 220 clients.

These early reports stimulated numerous experimental research investigations in the 1960s. In 1976, Kazdin and Wilcoxon were able to report that a "cursory count" of controlled outcome studies published in but five journals from 1970 through 1974 yielded a total of 74 studies. They summarized the results of those studies in this fashion:

In 55% (N = 41) of these studies, systematic desensitization was more effective than the control condition(s) used in the particular study. Results from an additional 20% (N = 15) of the studies suggest that systematic desensitization was effective but that one of the major components (relaxation, graded exposure, pairing) is not critical to its success. Another 14% (N = 10) of the studies found that systematic desensitization was effective but was no better than other procedures or was only effective under conditions that maximized client expectancy for change. Only 11% (N = 8) of the studies indicated that systematic desensitization was not at least as effective as other therapies; in two studies none of the groups improved, but in six studies other procedures were more effective than systematic desensitization. (1976, p. 730)

The difficulties successfully treated by SD vary widely — including, for example, fear of heights, driving, a variety of animals, insects, classroom examinations, flying, water, going to school, rejection by another, authority figures, injections, crowds, physical injury, death, sexual disorders, insomnia, speech disorders, anger, sleepwalking, nightmares, motion sickness, racial prejudice, alcoholism, childbirth fear, and a variety of communication dysfunctions.

One of the earliest experimental investigations was a classic study by Paul (1966). Using subjects screened from 710 students registered in an introductory speech class, he discovered that SD was more effective at reducing speech anxiety than either insight-oriented treatment or an attention-placebo condition. In a follow-up study, Paul and Shannon (1966) discovered that a group SD treatment equaled or excelled the results obtained via individual SD treatments on all measures employed. A two-year follow-up (Paul, 1968) revealed maintenance of improvement with some indications of additional improvement in other areas of behavior.

The success of SD in treating communication dysfunctions was not lost on the communication discipline. In 1970, McCroskey, Ralph, and Barrick reported a study conducted at Michigan State during the winter term of 1968. They found a significant treatment effect for SD regardless of whether the trainer was a professional or a subprofessional. Two years later, McCroskey (1972) reported a study conducted at Illinois State and then provided guidelines for others who wished to implement large-scale programs of SD for reducing communication apprehension.

Hoffman and Sprague (1982) recently reported the results of a ten-item survey sent to 1628 institutions in the spring of 1980. With 847 institutions responding (52.4% of those contacted), the authors identified 58 institutions that operate a special treatment program or curriculum for communicatively apprehensive students. Six of these programs, however, are operated outside of the communication department — by counseling or student services on campus. Thus, 52 (or 6.1%) of the responding departments offer a special treatment program. In terms of treatment methods and procedures, these programs utilize one of three treatment methods:

systematic desensitization, rhetoritherapy, or a combination of a number of treatment methods. The majority of programs (54.7%) utilize a combination of treatment methods. The data reveal that no particular combination of treatment methods is preferred. Twenty-two of the twenty-four combination programs utilized some or all of the following treatment methods: systematic desensitization, goal setting, cognitive restructuring, skills training, modeling, and role playing. One program utilized self-hypnosis and skills training, while another program utilized group counseling, systematic desensitization, and skills training. The second most popular treatment method is systematic desensitization, utilized by 33.3% of the respondents. Rhetoritherapy is used by 9.5% of the respondents. (Hoffman & Sprague, 1982, pp. 187-188)

While Hoffman and Sprague do not provide data on the specific number of combination programs which include SD as one of the methods, it appears safe to conclude that well over half of all treatment programs use SD as at least one component of the program. Thus the purpose of this chapter is to (1) describe standard procedures that define SD as a treatment method for dealing with communication dysfunctions, (2) identify factors that, when varied, can influence the effectiveness of SD, and (3) discuss competing theoretical explanations of the factors that explain SD's success.

SD Procedures

As developed by Wolpe, SD refers to a treatment package that systematically includes (1) training in deep muscle relaxation, (2) construction of hierarchies of anxiety-eliciting stimuli, and (3) the graduated pairing, through imagery, of anxiety-eliciting stimuli with the relaxed state. Within each of these components many variations are possible. These nuances in procedures become important to the extent that they influence treatment outcome.

Relaxation Training

The method used most frequently is a much-abbreviated version of Jacobson's (1938) progressive muscle relaxation training. With this technique, the client is taught to relax by successively tensing and releasing gross muscle groups throughout the body on instruction from the trainer. A common sequence involves (1) hands, (2) biceps and triceps, (3) shoulders, (4) neck, (5) mouth, (6) tongue (extended and retracted), (7) tongue (mouth roof and floor), (8) eyes and forehead, (9) breathing, (10) back, (11) midsection, (12) thighs, (13) stomach, (14) calves and feet, and (15) toes. After the completion of the last tension-relaxation cycle, many therapists have the client engage in cue-controlled relaxation — a procedure whereby clients focus on breathing while verbalizing a cue such as "calm," "relax," or "let go" as they exhale. This procedure produces an even deeper state of relaxation.

While there are variations in the timing of both the tension and relaxation phases, a common range is 5-10 seconds for tensing a muscle group and 10-15 seconds for relaxation. The total procedure typically takes 30-40 minutes.

While variations of the above procedures, or some close approximation, are those used most commonly, Hillenberg and Collins (1982) identified 26 distinct approaches to relaxation training in their review of the empirical literature from 1970 to 1979. In addition, relaxation can also be induced chemically (via drugs) or through biofeedback.

Both Wolpe's theory and the early research reports (Yates, 1970) suggested that relaxation is a necessary and important component of SD. More recent work has conditioned that conclusion. Yates (1975), for example, cites 16 studies that suggest that relaxation procedures do not add to the effectiveness of SD as a treatment method.

Anxiety Hierarchy

In order to desensitize a person, a relevant hierarchy of anxiety-provoking situations needs to be constructed. This usually entails interviewing the subject to discover those situations that are perceived to be noxious. Once the list of noxious situations is compiled, they are ordered from least anxiety producing to most anxiety producing. Paul and Bernstein (1976) stress the importance of the clarity and order of the items. For instance, they recommend that the hierarchy items be written operationally so that they can be visualized easily. Second, they warn users that the items should be arranged and presented in ascending order of difficulty. Carelessness in constructing a hierarchy may cause generalization problems later. Thus Paul and Bernstein (1976) write that "to the extent that interitem steps are inappropriately large or items do not accurately represent the client's particular anxiety dimension(s), the degree of effectiveness of anxiety reduction in the *real* fear-stimulus situation is reduced" (p. 66).

While the total number of hierarchy items depends on the severity and breadth of the problem, most hierarchies are within a 10- to 15-

item range. Illustrative of such a hierarchy is one used in Paul's 1966 study:

(0)   Lying in bed in room just before going to sleep — describe room.
(1)   Reading about speeches alone in room (one to two weeks before).
(2)   Discussing coming speech a week before (in class or after).
(3)   In audience while another gives speech (week before presentation).
(4)   Writing speech in study area (room, library).
(5)   Practicing speech alone in room (or in front of roommate).
(6)   Getting dressed the morning of speech.
(7)   Activities just prior to leaving for speech (eating, practice).
(8)   Walking over to room on day of speech.
(9)   Entering room on day of speech.
(10) Waiting while another person gives speech on day of presentation.
(11) Walking up before the audience.
(12) Presenting speech before the audience (see faces, etc.).

Recent research shows that the rules for constructing a hierarchy can be more flexible than earlier believed. For instance, one hierarchy can be used with a number of different people experiencing similar problems in dissimilar fashion. Thus group hierarchies can be employed successfully instead of tailoring the hierarchy to meet the ordering needs of each individual in the group (McCroskey, 1972; Goss, Thompson, & Olds, 1978). There is also evidence to suggest that the order of presentation of items need not be ascending. Krapfl and Nawas (1970) found that the items could be presented in either ascending order, descending order, or randomly without seriously changing the results of the treatment. In addition, Goldfried and Goldfried (1977) discovered SD to be equally effective for reducing speech anxiety with either a speech anxiety relevant or a speech anxiety irrelevant hierarchy. As Yates (1975) concludes, "on the whole . . . it seems that neither individualized hierarchies nor any special way of presenting the hierarchies are critical to the success of desensitization" (p. 158). As with relaxation, then, a carefully constructed hierarchy is part of the theory of SD, but not necessarily a practical requirement for successful usage of the method.

Desensitization Proper

Subjects in SD are induced into a state of physical relaxation (usually by a much briefer method than that used in initial training) and then presented anxiety-provoking stimuli they are requested to imagine (e.g., "You are talking with a friend"). If subjects feel any tension, they are asked to forget that imagined event and go back to relaxing. After the subjects are relaxed, the trainer resubmits the anxiety-provoking stimulus. If the subjects do not report any tension, they are told to go back to relaxing while the trainer prepares to offer another stimulus item. Thus the sequence is relax, imagine, stop imagining, relax.

In order to present SD effectively, the subjects should be seated or reclined in a comfortable position, using either soft furniture or pillows. The room should be dimly lit and the temperature should be sufficiently warm to prevent chills while subjects are in an inactive state. Before beginning the relaxation procedures, the subjects should be told how to signal when they feel tension. Often this means raising the right index finger in a way that the trainer can see. When subjects are ready, the relaxation exercises begin. After completing the relaxation procedures — and being assured that the subjects are awake — the trainer proceeds through the hierarchy. One at a time, each item on the hierarchy is presented. A common goal is to accomplish a 15-second and a 30-second trial without any subject reporting tension. When all the items have been completed successfully, the training is finished. Depending on the number of items in the hierarchy, more than one session is usually required and the norm is four or five sessions.

Mediating Factors

Having described standard SD procedures and some common variations, we turn now to some additional factors that potentially mediate the impact of SD as a treatment method. Our discussion focuses first on variations in SD delivery and then on trainee characteristics. Where possible our discussion features 52 controlled outcome studies that have focused on communication dysfunctions and that have been published in the journal literature (Bander, Steinke, Allen, & Moser, 1975; Bloom & Craighead, 1974; Calef & MacLean, 1970; Curran, 1975; Curran & Gilbert, 1975; DiLoreto, 1971; Fremouw & Harmatz, 1975; Fremouw & Zitter, 1978; Gatchel, Hatch, Maynard, Turns, & Taunton-Blackwood, 1979; Gatchel, Hatch, Watson, Smith, & Gaas, 1977; Goldfried & Goldfried, 1977; Goldfried & Trier, 1974; Goss et al., 1978; Gurman, 1973; Hemme & Boor, 1976; Jaremko & Wenrich, 1973; Johnson, Tyler, Thompson, & Jones, 1971; Kanter & Goldfried, 1979; Karst & Trexler, 1970; Kirsch & Henry, 1979; Kirsch, Wolpin, & Knutson, 1975; Kondas, 1967; Lohr & McManus, 1975;

Maleski, 1971; Malkiewich & Merluzzi, 1980; Marshall, Presse, & Andrews, 1976; Marshall, Stoian, & Andrews, 1977; Marzillier, Lambert, & Kellett, 1976; McCroskey, 1972; McCroskey et al., 1970; Meichenbaum, Gilmore & Fedoravicius, 1971; Mitchell & Orr, 1974; Myers, 1974; Mylar & Clement, 1972; Orr, 1978; Orr & Mitchell, 1976; Orr, Mitchell, & Hall, 1975; Paul, 1966, 1967, 1968; Paul & Shannon, 1966; Russell & Wise, 1976; Sherman, Mulac, & McCann, 1974; Slutsky & Allen, 1978; Thorpe, 1975; Trussell, 1978; Weissberg, 1975, 1977; Weissberg & Lamb, 1977; Woy & Efran, 1972; Wright, 1976; Zenmore, 1975).

SD Variations

In addition to the variations in relaxation training and hierarchy usage identified earlier, additional variations in delivery system have been studied empirically. Among the more significant are the following:

SD in Groups. Since Paul and Shannon's (1966) initial demonstration of the equivalency of individual and group methods for treating speech anxiety, most uses of SD with communication dysfunctions have been administered in groups. Rimm and Masters (1979) summarize numerous studies that support such a practice.

Automated SD. Several studies (Kirsch & Henry, 1979; Lohr & McManus, 1975; Marshall et al., 1976, 1977) suggest that automated desensitization (the presentation of instructions to the trainee in some sort of mechanical fashion — most commonly a tape recorder) may be as effective as live desensitization.

Massed SD. Yates (1975) reviews five studies that suggest that marathon sessions are equally as effective as carefully spaced sessions.

In Vivo Hierarchy. Gurman (1973) and Kirsch et al. (1975) successfully used live (in vivo) rather than imaginary presentation of hierarchies. The latter authors discovered that flooding (beginning with the delivery of a difficult speech) was slightly more effective than talking and giving speeches in increasing order of difficulty.

Vicarious SD. Weissberg (1977) discovered no significant differences between being treated by SD (performance-based treatment) and seeing a videotape of others being treated via SD (vicarious treatment). Performance-based treatment was, however, slightly more effective.

Trainer Variations. In addition to focusing on characteristics of SD as a method, researchers have also focused on characteristics of trainers who use SD. While both McCrosky (1972) and Lohr and McManus (1975) discovered that the sex of the trainer is irrelevant, Franks and

Wilson (1975, p. 71) suggest that in both live and automated (tape-recorded) desensitization, a warm therapist ("soft, melodic, and pleasant voice") achieves significantly superior results over a cold therapist ("harsh, impersonal, and businesslike voice"). Several studies (e.g., Mccroskey et al., 1970; Russell & Wise, 1976) suggest that paraprofessionals (including undergraduate peers) can be trained to administer SD as effectively as professionals. Fremouw and Harmatz (1975), using subjects in an undergraduate public speaking class at the University of Massachusetts, trained speech-anxious subjects to act as behavior therapists for other speech-anxious subjects. They discovered that both the helpers and the helpees reduced their speech anxiety on both behavioral and self-report measures; this improvement was still present at a three-month followup.

Expectancy Instructions. Starting in the early 1970s, researchers began to explore the role played by subject expectancy. Maleski (1971), hypothesizing that the effectiveness of SD depends in part on the subject's awareness of the rationale for the method, studied three versions of SD (SD alone, SD plus suggestion, and SD plus awareness). Although his hypothesis was not supported, he discovered that the awareness manipulation was unsuccessful. Woy and Efram (1972), and a replication of their study by Hemme and Boor (1976), compared high expectancy SD (subjects were provided with evidence on the effectiveness of SD) with neutral expectancy (subjects were administered a standard version of SD). The data from these studies suggest a slight expectancy-set manipulation effect on self-reports of subjective perceptions of anxiety, but no effect on overt behavioral indices. Goldfried and Trier (1974) contrasted two rationales for the effectiveness of relaxation for treating public speaking anxiety and discovered a slight advantage for the rationale that subjects were learning an active coping skill as opposed to the rationale that relaxation would automatically reduce their anxiety. Slutsky and Allen (1978) contrasted SD with a placebo ("T Scope" therapy) under two instructional sets: a therapeutic procedure versus a laboratory study of fear. While SD was effective in both conditions, the placebo worked only when subjects were provided with the therapeutic rationale. Rather than manipulating expectancy, Kirsch and Henry (1979) assessed the perceived credibility of their treatments. They discovered that positive changes in physiological manifestations of anxiety were present for all of their treatment conditions *if* subjects rated the treatment rationale as highly credible. In a related study Blom and Craighead (1974) assessed the impact of a location manipulation (in a speech anxiety clinic versus in a nonverbal communication laboratory) and two instructional cues (researchers were testing the nature of fear versus testing the simulated effects of relaxation training) on experienced anxiety. They discovered that subjects exhibited greater anxiety in the speech anxiety clinic; that they showed and reported more anxiety with the fear testing cue; and that the highest fear was produced by the combination of a fear-testing rationale in a speech anxiety clinic. They also discovered that the impact of location was less potent than the impact of instructional cue. By way of summary, then, how an instructor introduces SD may influence a student's expectations of treatment effectiveness, which will, in turn, influence the effectiveness of SD as a treatment method.

Client Characteristics

Two major categories of client variables mediate the effectiveness of SD as a treatment method: personal characteristics and the nature of the problem.

Personal Characteristics. Few studies of SD as a method for treating communication dysfunctions have focused on the individual characteristics of the subjects and those that have not been especially informative. For example, McCroskey (1972) reports that SD is slightly more effective for working with males, while Lohr and McManus (1975) report the opposite. DiLoreto (1971) discovered that SD works equally well for both introverts and extroverts.

Treatment research working with other problems has produced more useful generalizations, Rimm and Masters (1979), for example, suggest that SD is less effective for individuals who

(1)   are high in arousability (as measured by spontaneous fluctuations in the electrical conductance of the skin or galvanic skin response);

(2)   are unable to create images or scenes;

(3)   can clearly imagine scenes that ought to be frightening to them but do not experience the expected emotional response (this may occur, according to Wolpe, in as many as one individual in ten); and

(4)   are unable to relax via deep muscle relaxation or some practical alternative.

Nature of the Problem. Perhaps more important than individual characteristics as mediating variables is the nature of the problem to be treated. A number of studies have contrasted SD with cognitive and/or skills approaches to treating situation-specific versus generalized communication dysfunctions (Curran, 1975; Curran & Gilbert, 1975; DiLoreto, 1971; Johnson et al., 1971; Kanter & Goldfried, 1979; Marshall et al., 1977; Marziller et al., 1976; Meichenbaum et al., 1971; Sherman et al., 1974; Thorpe, 1975; Trussell, 1978; Weissberg & Lamb, 1977; Wright, 1976.) The pattern of the results from these studies suggest that SD works best when the nature of the problem is situation-specific (e.g., public speaking as opposed to a more generalized dysfunction) and when the problem does not reflect a major skills deficit. When dealing with generalized dysfunctions, cognitive procedures may be more effective. Kanter and Goldfried (1979, p. 409) speculate that "individual's anxiety reactions that are generalized to many social situations are symbolically mediated and therefore best approached by a cognitively oriented intervention strategy." For situations involving an actual skills deficit, communication skills training is likely to be more effective than SD.

Implied in the above generalization is the suggestion that a particular communication dysfunction may have multiple causes. A failure to use appropriate organizational principles while making a public presentation, for example, may be the result of one of the following:

(1)   skill-deficit: the individual either lost or never had the requisite communication skills in his or her repertoire;

(2)   response-inhibition: the individual has the skills but is inhibited from using it because of a conditioned anxiety response;

(3)   cognitive-distortion: the individual has the skills but because of faulty perceptions, among other things, does not know whether or how to apply them in this particular situation;

(4)   rational-choice: the individual has the skill but choses not to exercise them for perfectly valid reasons (fatigue, lack of concern, etc.).

While SD is likely to be effective for communication dysfunctions resulting from response-inhibition, it is less likely to be useful for situations that evolve from a skill-deficit, cognitive-distortion, and/or rational-choice.

Theories of Desensitization

No matter which variation a program takes, nearly all of them are based on the assumption that communication apprehension is not a natural state. In other words, communication apprehension is learned through negative experiences. The act of speaking is not, in itself, a negative act. But if people directly experience or observe that speaking can lead to embarrassment or other forms of psychological discomfort, they will develop avoidance patterns. Thus a college student who has learned that speaking in public may cause discomfort will postpone enrolling in a speech class until it is absolutely necessary. These avoidance patterns, over time, become habits. By continually avoiding certain communication situations people reinforce their feelings that these situations are noxious. Communication apprehension thus becomes a vicious cycle — and a difficult one to break.

Etiology of Communication Apprehension

How do people learn that public speaking and other forms of communication are to be avoided? Where do they pick up these feelings? According to Daly and Friedrich (1981), the problem can be traced to experiences at home and at school. The more your communication attempts are positively reinforced at home, the less likely it is that you will have high levels of communication apprehension. Encouragement is the key to minimizing the development of communication apprehension. It was also found that the more students were corrected for "inappropriate" speech in grade school, the more communication apprehension they would develop. This effect was not as strong in high school, suggesting that levels of communication apprehension are established during the early years of schooling. Altogether these results suggest that communication apprehension has its beginnings early in life through negative experiences while interacting with others.

Reciprocal Inhibition, Habituation, or What?

There is little doubt that communication apprehension is learned and that it is a behavioral problem than can be treated successfully by SD. But what is it about SD that makes it work? There are numerous explanations of SD, but the most popular ones focus on reciprocal inhibition, habituation, and coping strategies.

Wolpe (1958) claims that SD is an operationalization of the principle of reciprocal inhibition. Thus when relaxation is superimposed over the anxiety response, it inhibits the anxiety response. By enforcing relaxation during the presentation of anxiety-producing cues, the originally learned S-R linkage between communication and anxiety is weakened. As Wolpe (1958) writes:

> If a response antagonistic to anxiety can be made to occur in the presence of anxiety-evoking stimuli so that it is accompanied by a complete or partial suppression of the anxiety responses, the bond between these stimuli and the anxiety response will be weakened. (p. 71)

Since one cannot be tensed and relaxed simultaneously, repeated trials that impose relaxation on anxiety should cause the anxiety reaction to dissipate and be replaced by the relaxation response. This change occurs at both the neurological and behavioral levels. SD, then, is a counterconditioning procedure in which subjects learn a new response to formerly anxiety-producing communication situations; and the new response they learn is relaxation.

Another possible explanation of SD is habituation. Watts (1979) defines habituation as the "waning of a response to a stimulus that occurs when the stimulus is repeatedly presented." (p. 627). By repeating the anxiety cues enough times, the subjects become accustomed to them and experience a decrease in their anxiety response rate. The relaxation part of SD is not for response substitution purposes but to lower the arousal level of the subjects so that habituation can be speeded up. The key to SD, according to the habituation explanation, is the repetitious presentation of the anxiety-provoking situations. In contrast to reciprocal inhibition, no new response is learned; rather, the old one simply goes away. In this sense, then, SD is not a counterconditioning technique, but rather a deconditioning technique in which the subjects return to a neutral state that may or may not be relaxed.

Still another possible explanation for why SD works comes from a coping hypothesis. Recent trends in cognitive restructuring techniques (used in addition to desensitization) assume that if subjects think differently about communication situations, this will facilitate more positive attitudes about them (Meichenbaum, 1977). Consequently, by teaching people how to relax and how to replace negative self-statements ("I will forget part of my speech") with positive self-statements ("I have done this before and it came out just fine"), the person's level of apprehension should decrease because they are more in control of their responses. Even if cognitive restructuring modifications are not included in SD therapy, the subjects will learn to relax and to know the difference between tension and relaxation. Such learning at least makes them aware of their responses and they can develop their own coping strategies when they feel uptight (i.e., they can use self-induced relaxation by going through some of the muscle exercises before they speak).

It would be nice at this point to take a bold stand in favor of one explanation over another. As with any controversy between scholars, however, it is difficult to know which explanation of SD is correct. One thing is clear. SD works, and it doesn't seem to matter a great deal how it is conducted. The differences in theory do no necessarily manifest themselves in practice.

Conclusions

Having described standard SD procedures, some of the variables that influence its effectiveness, and theoretical explanations for its success, we conclude this essay with three suggestions for future research.

First, scholars need to give higher priority to conceptualizing and assessing the nature and causes of communication dysfunctions. Effective treatment requires not only a specification of the precise nature of the dysfunction and of the situations in which it occurs but also an identification of the probable source of that dysfunction. It does little good, for example, to reduce individuals' anxieties about public speaking if they still lack the basic skills necessary to be an effective public speaker. Thus until we are able to distinguish response-inhibition from skill-deficit, cognitive-distortion, and/or rational-choice explanations, it is not possible to know whether to prescribe SD, cognitive restructuring, skills training, and/or motivational sessions as the treatment of choice.

Second, treatment research needs to expand its focus beyond the formal speaking context. While some of the 50 controlled outcome studies focused on less formal settings (e.g., dating behavior, classroom participation), by far the majority have focused on the domain of public speaking. The need to expand this focus is suggested by Schlenker and Leary's (1982) distinction between two broad classes of social anxiety: interaction anxiety (e.g., shyness, reticence, and dating anxiety, which occur in contingent interactions where people must continually be responsive to the actions of others) and audience anxiety (e.g., communication apprehension, stage fright, and speech anxiety, which occur in noncontingent interactions where people are performing some preplanned material before others). Schlenker and Leary argue that compared with contingent interactions (interaction anxiety), noncontingent ones (audience anxiety):

(a) usually focus the attention of a larger number of people on the actor (e.g., as in a play or a class lecture), (b) are often more important, since they usually occur less frequently and often involve some sort of formal evaluation (e.g., a play will be reviewed, a class speech will be graded), (c) must be planned more thoroughly in advance (e.g., composing the speech or memorizing the lines), (d) provide people with greater structure and less ambiguity during the performance, (e) require somewhat different social skills (e.g., require less "ad lib" ability during the performance), and (f) provide people with different sorts of options for controlling how they participate (e.g., it is usually not practical for a person in a non-contingent interaction to withdraw from the stage, fade into a corner, remain silent, or so on, even though he or she might want to; these options and others exist in contingent interactions). (p. 663)

Third, researchers need to monitor and report procedural differences in treatment delivery. In a rare study that reported doing so, Maleski (1971) discovered that trainers supposedly using a standardized form of SD differed significantly in terms of (a) amount of time devoted to discussion and to relaxation training, (b) number of items presented per session and length of item exposure, and (c) length of intertrial interval. Equally important, he determined that these variations made a difference. The most successful trainer "devoted more time to discussion and less time to relaxation training, presented items two to four times longer (and more variably), and presented the shortest intertrial intervals" (p. 446). Hillenberg and Collin's (1981) review of relaxation training research published from 1970 to 1979 provides additional evidence of both the rarity of and need for reporting procedural variations. They discovered that discriminating the degree of similarity and difference between the 26 distinct approaches they identified was difficult for several reasons:

First, studies vary with respect to the degree to which procedural formats are clearly stated. Factors such as the content of each session, rationale presented to Ss, muscle groups employed and the use of tension/release instructions are often not specified. Second, several studies . . . indicated that they utilized a modified version of a commonly referenced procedure without describing those changes made. In addition, when less commonly referenced procedures were employed, there were not specific explanations as to how these procedures differed from more common approaches.

As guides for future research, the above three suggestions must, of course, be supplemented by those of Glaser (1981), Page (1980), and the authors of other chapters in this book. Such research can only enhance the utility of SD as an already proven treatment approach for coping with a variety of communication dysfunctions.

12

Social Skills Training as a Mode of Treatment for Social Communication Problems

LYNNE KELLY

A number of researchers have examined the effectiveness of skills training as a mode of treatment for a variety of social communication and anxiety problems, such as dating anxiety (Christensen, Arkowitz, & Anderson, 1975; Curran, 1975, 1977; Curran & Gilbert, 1975; Curran, Gilbert, & Little, 1976; MacDonald, Lindquist, Kramer, McGrath, & Rhyne, 1975; McGovern, Arkowitz, & Gilmore, 1975; Twentyman & McFall, 1975), unassertiveness (Eisler, Hersen, Miller, & Blanchard, 1975; Hersen, Eisler, Miller, Johnson, & Pinkston, 1973; Kazdin, 1974; McFall & Lillesand, 1971; McFall & Marston, 1970; Wolfe & Fodor, 1977), and public speaking and social communication difficulties (Domenig, 1978; Fremouw & Harmatz, 1975; Fremouw & Zitter, 1978; McKinney, 1980; Metzger, 1974; Oerkvitz, 1975; Weissberg & Lamb, 1977; Zolten & Mino, 1981). The primary assumption underlying skills training is that at least part of these problems is due to social skills or communication skills deficits. If individuals who experience these difficulties can be taught more effective performance, their problem will be alleviated or diminished.

This chapter examines training as it is used for the three categories of problems listed above: dating anxiety, unassertiveness, and public speaking and social communication difficulties. First, the nature of these problems will be elaborated. Then, the research that has been conducted to test the effectiveness of skills training as a mode of treatment for the three types of problems will be reviewed systematically. The chapter will conclude with a discussion of future directions that research needs to take and suggestions for improving the quality of skills training research.

The Nature of the Problems

Before discussing the various forms that skills training can take and its effectiveness as a treatment, it is necessary to elaborate on the specific nature of the three categories of social communication and anxiety problems. Nearly all researchers who concern themselves with dating or heterosexual social anxiety conceptualize it as a tripartite problem (Bander, Steinke, Allen, & Mosher, 1975; Christensen et al., 1975; Curran, 1977; Twentyman & McFall, 1975). The problem is seen as consisting of a conditioned anxiety component, skills deficits, and faulty cognitive-evaluative appraisal (Curran, 1977).

The anxiety component of the problem of dating anxiety "is a result of classical conditioning episodes in which the previously neutral cues of heterosexual interactions are associated with aversive stimuli" (Curran, 1977, p. 141). Some researchers argue, however, that the anxiety component of dating anxiety is not classically conditioned, but rather is reactive (MacDonald et al., 1975). In this model, the anxiety experienced by the individual is a reaction to an inadequate behavioral repertoire rather than the result of conditioning. Regardless of the source of anxiety, however, researchers generally conceptualize hetero-sexual-social anxiety as having a substantial anxiety component.

A second component of dating anxiety is the skills deficit. Individuals may have learned inappropriate behaviors or may never have learned appropriate ones (Curran, 1977). As Curran (1977, p. 143) states: "Consequently, given this inadequate repertoire the individual does not handle the demands of the situation appropriately and experiences an aversive situation that elicits anxiety." For some researchers, then, in addition to the conditioned anxiety, the individual experiences anxiety as a direct result of inadequate social skills (Curran, 1977; MacDonald et al., 1975).

The final component of dating anxiety revolves around faulty cognitive-evaluative appraisal. As Curran (1977, p. 141) notes: "This faulty appraisal may be the result of unrealistic criteria, misperceptions regarding performance, negative self-evaluation, and insufficient self-reinforcement." A more narrow view of the same component is offered by Bander et al. (1975, p. 259) who claim that this component consists of "misconceptions and inappropriate fears concerning dating and the opposite sex." There is some empirical evidence for the cognitive component of the problem. A study by Clark and Arkowitz (1975) found that high anxious males underestimated the positive aspects of their performance and overestimated the negative aspects, whereas low anxious males *overestimated the positive* aspects of their performance.

We would expect skills training to be an effective mode of treatment in addressing the skills deficit component of dating anxiety and perhaps the reactive anxiety. However, there is no reason to assume that it is effective in alleviating the conditioned anxiety or the faulty cognitive-evaluative appraisal. This is not to say that it is a weak mode of treatment, only that it is designed to tackle one aspect of a multidimensional problem.

There is not as much agreement among researchers who conceptualize unassertiveness as to what the nature of the problem is. In several studies on the effectiveness of skills training on assertiveness, no definition of assertive behavior was offered (Eisler et al., 1975; Kazdin, 1974; McFall & Martson, 1970; Wolfe & Fodor, 1977). Some researchers accept the definition of Alberti and Emmons (1970) that assertiveness has to do with the ability to stand up for one's rights (Galassi, Delo, Galassi, & Bastien, 1974; Hersen et al., 1973). Although McFall and Lillesand (1971) specified that they were concerned with the ability to refuse unreasonable requests, they did not clarify how they conceptualized assertive behavior. Overall, the researchers cited thus far seem to have a fairly narrow view of assertiveness that tends to overemphasize the expression of negative affect and the ability to contradict others (Lazarus, 1973).

Broader conceptualizations of assertiveness have been offered by Lazarus (1973) and Adler (1977). Lazarus (1973, p. 697) claims that assertiveness "may be divided into four separate and specific response patterns." Those response patterns include "the ability to say 'no'; the ability to ask for favors or to make requests; the ability to express positive and negative feelings; the ability to initiate, continue, and terminate general conversations" (Lazarus, 1973, p. 697). For Adler (1977, p. 6) "assertiveness is the ability to communicate the full range of your thoughts and emotions with confidence and skill." Adler (1977) makes it clear that he presumes assertiveness to be a skill, that one needs to have a wide behavioral repertoire, that the expressed emotions and thoughts can be positive or negative, that to have confidence means to have courage rather than a lack of fear, and that assertion is not aggression.

Underlying all of these definitions of assertiveness, regardless of whether those definitions are broad or narrow, is the assumption that assertion is a skill that can be learned. None of these researchers hints that he or she believes a lack of assertiveness to be a personality problem. Thus, it makes sense that these researchers advocate skills training as the preferred treatment for unassertiveness.

The third category of problems concerns public speaking and more general social communication difficulties. In the research on public speaking anxiety, researchers have generally refrained from conceptualizing and have moved directly to operationalizing. Thus we can only infer from the operationalization procedures how these researchers conceptualized the problem of public speaking anxiety. Weissberg and Lamb (1977) were concerned only with the outward manifestations of public speaking anxiety and the participant's subjective experience of that anxiety. Thus, in their conceptualization of public speaking anxiety, it seems to be a problem of internal anxiety (whether conditioned or reactive cannot be inferred) that produces behavioral disruptions. A similar conceptualization is offered by Fremouw and Zitter (1978) and Fremouw and Harmatz (1975). Pilkonis (1977) presents a broader conceptualization of public speaking problems. Anxiety about or difficulty with public speaking can be the result of internal anxiety-producing behavioral disruptions or behavioral disruptions due to lack of skill. None of the researchers cited specifies his or her conceptualization of public speaking problems, however, although in many cases they appear to be talking about a concept identical to Clevenger's (1959) concept of stage fright. In a review of the research on stage fright, Clevenger (1959, P. 135) pointed out a problem he saw with that research: "The measuring instrument in a stage fright experiment is not only the measurement of stage fright, it is the definition as well." This same problem occurs in the research on public speaking anxiety. It seems that researchers ought to clarify their conceptualizations of the problem. Not only might this lead to better research, but it could lead to better skills training programs for individuals with public speaking anxiety or ineffectiveness.

Those who have been concerned with more general social communication problems have tended to be more precise about their conceptualizations of the problems and the requisite skills. Argyle (1981) delineates several components of social competence: (1) the ability to perceive others accurately; (2) the ability to take the role of the other; (3) the ability to communicate one's attitudes and emotions nonverbally; (4) the ability to provide others with clear reinforcement and rewards; (5) the ability to plan goals and modify behavior as necessary while pursuing those goals; (6) the ability to send signals that accurately present one's role, status, and other aspects of identity; (7) the ability to analyze situations and their rules in order to adapt behavior; and (8) the ability to make utterances that fit into the orderly sequence of interaction. Social incompetence could, then, be due to inadequacies in one or more of the eight skill areas.

Another general social communication problem, "reticence" has been developed by Phillips (1977, 1980, 1981). The problem is conceptualized as avoidance of and ineffectiveness in a variety of communication situations due to inadequate social and communication skills. The types of skills delineated as necessary for competent communication performance are actually quite similar to those offered by Argyle (1981). According to Phillips and his colleagues, individuals designated as "reticent" can have problems in (1) identifying situations in which communication could make a difference; (2) defining their communications goals; (3) analysis of persons and situations; (4) selecting ideas and putting them in a logical sequence; (5) choosing appropriate words to express the ideas; (6) speaking clearly enough to be understood and with appropriate nonverbal communication: and (7) accurately perceiving the level of success achieved and making adaptations in communication in the case of failure to achieve goals (Cohen, 1980; Kelly, 1980; Phillips & Sokoloff, 1979).

The general social communication problem referred to by Zimbardo (1977) as "shyness" is conceptualized as "an attribute which spans a wide behavioral-emotional continuum" (Zimbardo, Pilkonis, & Norwood, 1975, p. 70). A shy person may lack adequate social skills, fear negative evaluation, lack self-confidence, have low self-esteem, or experience anxiety, or may have any combination of these problems. As in the case of reticence, the problem of shyness produces avoidance of communication situations.

Finally, one could have a social communication problem if one lacked the social skills delineated by J. Kelly (1982), who claims that social skills (1) are behaviors that elicit reinforcement from the environment, including the facilitation of relationship development, the occurrence of nonsocial reinforcement, and the prevention of the loss of current reinforcement; and (2) include the ability to perform effectively in a variety of situations by adapting to the unique and normative characteristics of situations.

Overall, each of the problems discussed, dating anxiety, unassertiveness, and public speaking and social communication problems, is viewed as having a skills deficit component. In much of the research, however, even when the problem is broadly conceptualized, it tends to be rather narrowly operationalized. One needs to keep this in mind while reading the following review of research on the effectiveness of skills training. It may be that skills research can be demonstrated to be effective in alleviating these problems only when the behaviors or perceptions that serve as the dependent variables are unidimensional or fairly minute. Future research on skills training of more complex behaviors may reveal inadequacies in skills training as a mode of treatment of these types of problems.

Research on the Effectiveness of Skills Training

Skills Training for Heterosexual-Social Anxiety

Skills training programs for dating anxiety have followed one of two approaches: the response-practice approach or the response-acquisition approach (Curran, 1977). The assumption of the response-practice approach is that individuals have the necessary social skills and simply need to practice in order to employ those skills more effectively. The response-acquisition approach, on the other hand, presumes that individuals have inadequate behavioral repertoires which produce anxiety (Kanfer & Phillips, 1970) and avoidance (Curran & Gilbert, 1975). To alleviate dating anxiety, one needs to help these individuals develop their social skills.

Studies that have focused on practice dating have found some support for the effectiveness of practice, although they exhibit a number of methodological deficiencies (Curran, 1977). The earliest study, done by Martinson and Zerface (1970), found that participants in the practice dating treatment reported significantly less dating fear and significantly greater dating frequency than participants in a counseling program and a control group. Research by Christensen and Arkowitz (1974) examined the effectiveness of practice dating and found that participants who were in the practice dating group reported a significant decrease in social anxiety and a significant increase in frequency of dating and skill on actual dates. Dating skill was measured through the feedback reports of the dating partners of the participants in the study. Christensen et al. (1975) compared the effectiveness of practice dating plus feedback from the dating partner with practice dating alone and a control group. The results of this study indicated that the two practice dating groups did significantly better than the control group on a variety of self-report and behavioral measures, but the addition of feedback to practice dating did not lead to significant improvements. In fact, what these researchers found is that the dating partner feedback "encouraged some Ss while it made others anxious" (Christensen et al., 1975, p. 330).

Thus it would appear that practice dating can be an effective form of skills training for the alleviation of heterosexual-society anxiety. Recall that this approach presumes that individuals with the problem have the requisite social skills and simply need to practice them. It seems likely that there probably are persons who possess adequate skills but who are inexperienced in exercising those skills. Furthermore, there are undoubtedly persons who possess inadequate social skills for whom practice might do very little and might even lead to further anxiety and avoidance. Among the methodological weaknesses of these studies that Curran (1977) points out is poor screening of subjects. Those persons utilized in the experiments may not have had sufficiently severe problems to be considered minimal daters (Curran, 1977). In light of this and other methodological weaknesses such as reliance on assessment instruments with face validity only, inadequate control groups, and poor follow-up procedures (Curran, 1977), we should accept the conclusions of this research only tentatively. If the subjects indeed cannot be considered to have a dating anxiety problem, then we cannot conclude that practice dating is an effective form of skills training for individuals who have more severe problems. Perhaps those with more severe problems belong in the category of those who do not possess the necessary social skills and for whom practice dating might be of questionable value.

Research utilizing the response-acquisition approach also generally provides empirical support for the effectiveness of skills training as a treatment for dating anxiety. A variety of different types of skills training have been examined in these studies, including discussion groups, behavioral rehearsal, feedback, modeling, therapist reinforcement, coaching, and sensitivity training. In many of the studies, the researchers would compare the effectiveness of several different forms of skills training in order to determine which types produced the greatest positive change in the participants.

McGovern et al. (1975) compared the effectiveness of three behavioral training programs for college-age men who experienced dating anziety. The three treatment conditions were as follows: (1) readings from a social interaction manual, discussion with female trainers: (2) readings from a social interaction manual, discussion with female trainers, behavioral rehearsal, and feedback in the laboratory environment; and (3) all of the conditions of the second treatment group plus behavioral rehearsal in natural environments outside of the laboratory.

These researchers found that all three treatment procedures were effective in reducing self-reported anxiety and in increasing skill level (although self-report procedures were used to measure changes in skill levels). There were no significant differences among the three treatment conditions, thus providing no evidence that the natural environment behavioral rehearsal training was more effective than laboratory-based rehearsal. What is most surprising about these results is that the discussion group condition was as effective as the behavioral rehearsal conditions. If this finding can be continually replicated, then skills training programs could be simplified to include only discussions groups without sacrificing effectiveness. This finding, however, remains to be replicated.

MacDonald et al. (1975) examined the effects of behavioral rehearsal, behavioral rehearsal plus assignments, and a placebo control that actually consisted of relaxation therapy. Behavior rehearsal consisted of the giving of instructions, role playing, and feedback. The results of the study indicated significant improvements for both behavioral rehearsal groups in terms of reduced anxiety and increased skill as measured by behavioral assessments. No significant improvements were seen for the control group.

A study that compared the effectiveness of two reeducative behavioral therapies and a sensitivity training program in reducing dating anxiety was conducted by Bander et al. (1975). Participants were placed in the following groups: (1) reeducative therapy, which consisted of instructions, role playing, feedback, and outside assignments; (2) reeducative therapy plus systematic desensitization; (3) microlab, a type of sensitivity training; and (4) control group. The results indicated that both reeducative therapy groups improved on self-report measures, but not on behavioral measures. Systematic desensitization did not appear to add to the effectiveness of the skills training program, nor was the sensitivity training program effective.

Similar results regarding the ineffectiveness of sensitivity training in reducing dating anxiety have been reported by Curran et al. (1976). They compared a behavior replication program, which consisted of information, modeling, behavioral rehearsal, coaching, video and group feedback, and in vivo assignments, with sensitivity training. The behavior replication treatment was found to produce significant improvements as measured by self-reports and behavioral indices, whereas sensitivity training did not. There were no significant differences between the two treatments on a measure of general social anxiety, however. The behavioral training program appears to have addressed only anxiety experienced in the specific situation of a dating interaction as opposed to more general anxiety.

Curran (1975) compared the effects of systematic desensitization and behavior replication on heterosexual-society anxiety. He found that both treatments led to significant improvements as measured by self-report and behavioral assessments of dating anxiety. This is in contrast to Bander et al. (1975), who found that the addition of systematic desensitization to a behavioral training program did not produce increased improvements. However, a study by Curran and Gilbert (1975) found further evidence in support of systematic desensitization as a treatment of dating anxiety. In addition, they found that a skills training program also produced decreases in self-reported and behavioral indices of dating anxiety, and that there were no significant differences between the skills training and the systematic desensitization treatments. Both treatments were associated with increases in dating frequency at a 6-month follow-up. Thus the research regarding the effectiveness of systematic desensitization as a treatment for dating anxiety has produced inconsistent results. Further replication seems to be warranted at this time.

A final study by Twentyman and McFall (1975) examined the effectiveness of behavior replication training on heterosexual-social anxiety in college males. The treatment program consisted of instruction, behavior rehearsal, modeling, coaching, feedback, and replication. When compared with participants in a control group, participants in the treatment program showed significant improvements on self-report, autonomic, and overt behavioral measures.

In summary, all of the studies that can be categorized as following the response-acquisition model provide evidence that skills training can be an effective means of decreasing dating anxiety. The difficulty in trying to generalize from these results is that the studies are difficult to compare. The actual content of the treatment programs differed from study to study, as did many of the pre- and posttreatment assessment procedures. A very useful next step in this line of research would be a series of studies that standardized both the treatment conditions and the assessment procedures so that cross-study comparisons could be more valuable.

Skills Training for Unassertiveness

A number of researchers have been concerned with the potential of skills training in reducing unassertive behavior. As in the case of dating anxiety, generally speaking, skills training has been found to reduce unassertiveness, although these studies tend to focus on minute behaviors (Glaser, 1981) and the expression of negative feelings rather than other types of assertive behavior (Lazarus, 1973). These limitations need to be kept in mind as one examines the results of skills training on unassertiveness.

A study by McFall and Marston (1970) compared the effectiveness of two forms of behavior rehearsal with a placebo treatment and a control group. In the one behavior rehearsal group performance feedback was given, whereas in the other group it was not. The placebo control group was exposed to explorations of the problem in the form of a group discussion led by two therapists. Two weeks after the experiment, participants were telephoned by the experimenter, who posed as a magazine salesman. This follow-up procedure was designed to obtain a measure of the participants' assertiveness outside of the laboratory. Results of the study showed that while there were no significant differences between the two types of behavior rehearsal treatments, both treatments led to improvements in assertiveness as measured by self-reports and behavioral and autonomic indices. In addition, the follow-up telephone assessment provided some evidence that the improvements transferred outside of the laboratory.

McFall and Lillesand (1971) compared the effects of two types of behavior rehearsal on unassertiveness, specifically on the ability to refuse unreasonable requests. One group was assigned to the treatment condition of overt behavior rehearsal with modeling and coaching, another group received similar treatment but rehearsal was covert, and the third group acted as a placebo control group. On general measures of unassertiveness, no differences were found between the control group and the treatment groups. However, on specific measures, both self-report and behavioral, only subjects in the two behavior rehearsal treatment groups showed significant improvements in their ability to refuse unreasonable requests. Results also suggested that the covert rehearsal procedure tended to be more effective than the overt rehearsal treatment, although results did not achieve statistical significance. A telephone follow-up procedure similar to that used in the McFall and Marston (1970) study did not reveal clear-cut differences among groups, thus calling into question the transfer of participants' improvements in assertiveness.

Another study that examined the effects of covert modeling was conducted by Kazdin (1974), although he did not compare it to overt modeling. Participants were assigned to one of four treatment conditions: (1) covert modeling plus reinforcement; (2) covert modeling; (3) no model; and (4) delayed treatment control. Subjects were presented with scenes requiring assertive behavior. In the no-model condition, subjects simply imagined a person in scenes where assertive behavior would be appropriate. In the covert modeling condition, subjects imagined a person in the scenes, and imagined the person behaving assertively. In the covert modeling with reinforcement condition, subjects imagined a person in the scenes, imagined the person behaving assertively, and imagined favorable consequences resulting from the model's assertiveness. The results of the study indicated significant improvements in assertive behavior for participants in both modeling groups as measured by self-reports and behavioral indices. There were few differences between the modeling and modeling plus reinforcement groups; those in the reinforcement group showed greater improvement at the time of follow-up. However, the follow-up phone call assessment did not discriminate subjects in the various groups, causing Kazdin (1974 p. 250) to conclude: "The present study provides no evidence for generalization of behavior change *outside* of the treatment setting."

The effects of practice, modeling, and instructions on assertiveness were examined by Hersen et al. (1973). Participants were divided into five groups: (1) practice-control; (2) test-retest; (3) instructions; (4) modeling; and (5) modeling plus instructions. Unlike the Kazdin (1974) study, subjects in this study viewed videotaped models demonstrating assertive responses. The results of the study indicated that in general modeling plus instructions was the most effective treatment, followed by modeling and then instructions. Specifically, modeling plus instructions was most effective in producing changes on the variables of duration of reply, affect, and overall assertiveness. Instructions was most effective in producing changes in loudness, and modeling produced the greatest change in compliance content. Modeling plus instructions and modeling seemed to be about equally effective in changing requests for new behavior, while modeling plus instructions and instructions seemed to bring about the greatest changes in duration of looking. It should be noted, however, that the sample used in the study consisted of hospitalized psychiatric patients, making it impossible to generalize the results to more general populations.

Wolfe and Fodor (1977) compared the effectiveness of behavior therapy, behavior/cognitive therapy, and consciousness raising in treating unassertiveness problems in women. Women in the behavioral treatment condition saw videotaped models, role played assertive behaviors, and received therapist and group feedback. Those in the behavioral/cognitive treatment condition had identical behavioral therapy as those in the behavioral group, plus there was an effort to identify and dispel irrational self-statements of the participants that could sustain their unassertiveness problem. The third treatment group experienced a group discussion consciousness-raising session. There was also a waiting list control group in the study. The results indicated that those in the behavior therapy and behavior/cognitive therapy improved significantly on behavioral and self-report measures of assertiveness. There were no significant differences between the two treatments except that only in the behavioral/cognitive treatment condition did participants show a significant decease on a measure of situational anxiety. The consciousness-raising treatment was effective on only one dependent measure, the subjective experience of benefit reported by the participants.

Thus there is some evidence to suggest that skills training can be an effective means for treating problems of unassertiveness. As in the case of skills training for dating anxiety, the content of the skills training programs that researchers have examined has varied greatly. As Glaser (1981, p. 335) notes: "It must now be empirically determined which operations are most effective for specific populations and communication context." We do not know, for instance, whether modeling, instructions, or behavioral rehearsal are equally effective types of skills training or under what conditions one may be more effective than the rest. There is some evidence that covert rehearsal is superior to overt rehearsal (McFall & Lillesland, 1971), but this finding has to be replicated. In most of the studies reported here, judges would rate the level of assertiveness in the participants' responses, not taking into account situational determinants of assertiveness (Eisler et al., 1975). Eisler et al. (1975 p. 338) found that "in situations requiring assertive expression an individual's behavior is functionally related to the social context of the interpersonal interaction." The difficulty with this is that skills training programs may teach people assertive skills without teaching them audience and situation analysis skills so that they know when assertive behavior is appropriate. If the research does not emphasize this, it is unlikely that the skills training programs will.

A final weakness of skills training as a treatment for unassertiveness is that in most studies it was not shown to transfer outside of the laboratory. There are a number of possible explanations for this lack of transfer. It may be that the skills training is so specific to the situation used in the studies that the participants do not leave the laboratory with heuristic principles or general skills. For example, perhaps participants see models engaging in assertive behavior and understand that what they are seeing is assertiveness, but they do not learn when assertiveness is appropriate or what the behavioral components of assertiveness are. Another possibility is that the follow-up procedures used to test carryover of treatment are inadequate (Kazdin, 1974). Future research ought to utilize a variety of follow-up procedures or employ more realistic techniques. In many of the studies reported here, the follow-up telephone call was made by the experimenter, who posed as a person soliciting volunteers to work for some charitable cause, such as at the hospital. It is unlikely that individuals are confronted with this kind of request very often, and thus may not know how to respond to it, even if they have improved their assertive behavior in general.

Skills Training for Public Speaking and Social Communication Problems

Research on the effectiveness of skills training as a treatment for public speaking difficulties has been extremely limited, and so it is not possible at this time to draw any definitive conclusions from it. Not only has the quantity of research been limited, but researchers have employed very limited conceptualizations of public speaking in their studies. Generally, they have focused only on whether or not skills training leads to decreases in self-reported and outward manifestations of anxiety. Clearly there is more to public speaking effectiveness, and we need to examine the effects of skills training on other behavioral components of public speaking.

Weissberg and Lamb (1977) compared the effectiveness of three modes of treatment on speech anxiety: (1) systematic desensitization; (2) cognitive modification plus desensitization; and (3) speech preparation, which involved outlining, practicing aloud, and practicing eye contact. Results indicated that all three treatments were effective in reducing self-reported anxiety, but only the cognitive modification and speech preparation treatments were effective in reducing behavioral manifestations of anxiety. Systematic desensitization and cognitive modification were most effective in reducing general anxiety levels.

Fremouw and Zitter (1978) also compared the effectiveness of speech preparation or skills training and cognitive modification-relaxation. The skills training program consisted of modeling, behavioral rehearsal, and feedback via videotape. The public speaking behaviors focused on in the training were voice rate, voice volume, voice inflection, body stance, eye contact, gestures, and speech organization. Their results indicated that both treatments were effective in reducing overall anxiety as rated by observers and outward manifestations of anxiety as measured by the Behavioral Checklist. On a self-report measure of speech anxiety, participants in the skills training group reported a greater decrease in anxiety than those in the cognitive modification-relaxation group. Neither treatment was effective in decreasing performance anxiety in social and communication situations other than public speaking.

A study by Fremouw and Harmatz (1975) looked at the effects of speech-anxious participant training other speech-anxious participants. The training consisted of relaxation therapy and skills training of posture, gestures, and speech organization through discussion and rehearsal with feedback. Compared to a control group, subjects improved significantly on measures of speech anxiety and a measure of more general social anxiety.

Zolten and Mino (1981) examined the effects of a specific program of oral reading on the reduction of public speaking problems. Although subject responses were generally very favorable to the program, the study lacked the necessary controls and specific dependent measures. A replication of the study was done by Mino (1982). She selected volunteers from a public speaking course and a special course designed for those with social and public speaking problems. About half of the subjects were given the oral reading treatment program, and all subjects were trained in public speaking in their classes. When the speeches were rated by trained judges, there were no significant differences between those who have been trained and those who had not, although the self-reports of those who had undergone the oral reading training were very positive. Although these studies would suggest that on objective measures, oral reading training does not appear to be effective in alleviating public speaking problems, the subjective experience of the subjects is so positive that is might warrant using this kind of training. However, it is possible that any kind of special training might have produced similar results.

Overall, research on skills training for public speaking problems has focused too narrowly on the reduction of anxiety. Although it seems clear that skills training does produce reductions in speech anxiety, it is unlikely that just because an individual feels less anxious and is observed to be less anxious that he or she is an effective public speaker. Skills training must focus on other behavioral components of public speaking that are related to effective performance. Furthermore, both systematic desensitization and cognitive modifications appear to achieve similar results in terms of reducing anxiety, but it is difficult to see how these two treatment modes could produce change in regard to speech organization, effective use of visual and verbal aids, persuasiveness, and so forth. The strength of skills training may be in its potential for producing broader behavioral changes, not just reductions in anxiety that can be achieved by other treatments.

Some researchers have focused on the effectiveness of skills training on more general problems of social communication. In the field of speech communication, the first skills training program to be tested was that proposed by Phillips at the Pennsylvania State University (Phillips 1977, 1982; Phillips & Metzger, 1973). The program designed to alleviate the problem of reticence, combines instruction, goal setting, behavioral rehearsal, in vivo assignments, and feedback. Students select problem areas, set increasingly difficult communication goals, engage in classroom discussion, practice behaviors, and attempt to complete the goals outside of the classroom.

Several studies have been conducted to examine the effectiveness of this skills training program. The earliest study (Metzger, 1974) looked at the effects of the program during instruction and up to one year later. The study compared evaluations of improvement made by the trainer, the students, and outside observers who viewed the communication behavior of the students during several videotaped interviews that were conducted prior to the training, at two separate points during training, and six months or later after training was completed. On the basis of all three modes of evaluation, subjects generally were rated as noticeably or adequately improved, although a few were rated minimally improved.

A second longitudinal study (Oerkvitz, 1975) studied student perceptions of their improvement one year or more after completion of the program. Of the 154 subjects who responded to the questionnaire, 75% said that they had improved. 17% reported that they had not, and a number of them gave mixed responses. Overall, 80% said that they continued to use one or more of the skills they had been taught in one or more communication contexts.

Domenig (1978) also examined self-reports of individuals who had undergone this particular skills training program immediately upon completion of the program. Participants in the study rated their performance in a variety of communication situations as more competent after receiving treatment.

Finally, McKinney (1980) employed four self-report scales to assess the degree of change reported by students who had undergone the program and compared their scores with those obtained from students in regular public speaking and group discussion classes. Students in the special reticence program reported significant decreases in anxiety and avoidance behavior on virtually all items concerned with social interaction, class participation, group discussion, and interviewing, and on eight of thirteen public performance items. Students in the regular courses did not report significant improvements.

All of these studies provide evidence for the effectiveness of the skills training program developed by Phillips as a treatment for reticence. As other authors have noted, however, these studies have generally lacked sufficient methodological rigor, such as the use of control groups, and their results must be accepted tentatively (Glaser, 1981; Page, 1980).

The effectiveness of other types of skills training programs on social communication problems has also been examined. J. Kelly (1982) reports that conversational skills training programs have been employed with psychiatric patients, mentally retarded persons, adolescents, and college students. The studies that he describes tend to be case studies, thus making it inappropriate to draw any general conclusions. For instance, he reports a study by Urey, Laughlin, and Kelly (1979) in which conversational skills training was employed with two male psychiatric patients. Training consisted of instruction, modeling, and behavioral rehearsal with videotaped feedback. Follow-up procedures at one and six months included videotaping of conversations of the subjects with novel partners. Results indicated improvement in both subjects at the two follow-up points.

Kelly, Furman, Phillips, Hathorn, and Wilson (1979) tested conversational skills training on two mentally retarded adolescents. The training was designed to increase the frequency of particular behaviors, including self-disclosing statements, conversational questions, and social invitations. The training program consisted of instruction, modeling, and coaching, and was found to be effective in increasing the frequency of the target behaviors.

These and other studies reported in J. Kelly(1982) demonstrate the effectiveness of conversational skills training with psychiatric patients and mentally retarded persons. Unfortunately, because of the small sample sizes and the nature of the samples used, conclusions about the effectiveness of these types of skills training programs in alleviating social communication problems in more general populations cannot be drawn. Future research should test the effects of these types of conversational training on other populations.

In summary, skills training appears to be an effective mode of treatment for social communication problems such as reticence and related problems. However, more methodologically rigorous research is needed. In addition, various types of skills training for social communication problems need to be tested as well as what types of training are effective for what specific types of problems. The labels "social communication problem" and "reticence" are quite broad and could refer to a wide range of problems. The same is true of shyness, another social communication problem. Perhaps a more precise typology of social communication problems can be developed and then various types of social skills training can be tested to determine which are most effective for which kinds of problems.

Conclusions and Suggestions for Future Research

Skills training has been utilized to alleviate problems of heterosexual-social anxiety, unassertiveness, and public speaking and social communication problems. Research on the effectiveness of social skills training has indicated that a variety of types of social skills programs seem to be capable of alleviating all of these problems. At this point in time, that is about the most precise conclusions that one can draw from a review of the skills training literature. The inability to be more specific in drawing conclusions stems from a number of methodological problems apparent in the skills training research, some of which have been noted by other researchers (Curran, 1977; Glaser, 1981). The following suggestions for future research on the effectiveness of skills training identify some of those methodological weaknesses and suggest ways to overcome them.

Clarification of Conceptualizations of Problems. For the problems of unassertiveness and public speaking difficulties in particular, researchers need to clarify their conceptualizations of the problems. In none of the studies reported here on public speaking problems did researchers offer a definition of the problem. One was forced to infer what the nature of the problem was presumed to be on the basis of the operationalization of it. If researchers do not know what the components of the problem are, how can they adequately test the effects of skills training in reducing problems?

Improved Screening of Subjects. As Glaser (1981) and Curran (1977) point out, in much of the research on skills training, subjects for research are poorly screened. Thus those selected for study may not have the problem or have it to such a minimal extent that one cannot generalize research results to populations with more severe problems.

Use of Standardized Treatment Conditions and Assessment Procedures. One of the major difficulties in trying to draw any general conclusions from the research on the effectiveness of skills training is that the actual content of the types of skills training examined and the pre- and postassessment procedures vary widely. Thus, for instance, the technique of modeling in one study may be the presentation of videotaped models; in another, the models may be live; in yet another, the models may be imagined or described. Is it possible to compare these studies and conclude that modeling is an effective type of skills training? It might be possible if modeling were the only component of the skills training examined in each of the studies; however, it is usually coupled with one or more other types of skills training. Different studies, then, examine different combinations of types of skills training, making it impossible to compare studies. What is needed is greater standardization of the content of skills training programs *for the purposes of research.* I am not advocating that at this time we need greater standardization of actual skills training programs; we do not have the empirical evidence to support one standard skills training program as more effective than others.

Improved Follow-Up Assessment Procedures. As Glaser (1981) notes, skills training effects research often employs limited follow-up procedures. If skills training programs cannot be found to be effective in producing long-term changes, then perhaps the content of those programs needs revision. We do not know at this point if skills training produces long-term effects because in most studies follow-up procedures are not utilized. The exception is the assertiveness training research, in which the follow-up procedure usually involved a telephone call to the subjects up to six months after treatment. The caller would ask the subject to buy magazines or volunteer at a church or hospital, and the assertiveness of the subject's response would be rated. In nearly all studies, the follow-up assessment failed to discriminate subjects and thus provided no evidence of long-term effects. However, the adequacy of this procedure has been questioned (Kazdin, 1974). Researchers need to use a variety of follow-up assessment procedures.

Evaluation of the Interaction Between Treatment Procedures and Subject Characteristics (Glaser, 1981). There is to date no evidence regarding whether certain types of skills training are more effective with certain types of problems. More precise typologies of the problems are needed in order to facilitate the testing of various kinds of skills training procedures. Persons with a specific kind of assertiveness problem, for instance, may benefit more from a particular technique of skills training than from other techniques.

Broader Operationalization of the Problem. Most of the problems discussed here are rather broadly conceptualized, such as dating anxiety, assertiveness (by some researchers), reticence, shyness, and other social communication problems. However, in the research on these problems often the problems were operationalized very narrowly. For instance, conversation skill was operationalized in one study as the frequency of self-disclosing statement, conversational questions, and social invitations (Kelly et al. 1979). If the effects of skills training on these problems is examined only in regard to very limited behaviors, we cannot conclude that skills training is effective in alleviating the problems. We need to discover if skills training is capable of improving more complex skills of social interaction, such as situational analysis and adaptation. If skills training is not capable of this, it is unlikely that we will find evidence of its long-term effectiveness.

Overall, skills training seems to be a very valuable mode of treatment for a variety of social communication problems, as is evidenced by the research presented here. Some methodological modifications in the research should produce new findings that will greatly enhance skills training programs, and thus the social skills of many individuals.

13

Cognitive-Behavioral Therapies for Modification of Communication Apprehension

WILLIAM J. FREMOUW

While the measurement of interpersonal communication problems and study of the impact of these problems has produced significant advances during the last decade, progress on the modification of these significant problems is gradually following these other advances. As summarized in this volume, a diversity of perspectives, definitions, and measurement procedures exist for communication problems. Similarly, alternative approaches for the modification of communication avoidance are also available. This chapter summarizes the historical development, theoretical assumptions, and treatment approaches available for cognitively oriented modification procedures for communication avoidance. Because little direct research is available specifically on the cognitive modification of communication apprehension, reticence, or shyness, this chapter relies on the research about modification of all types of performance anxiety. Communication avoidance is assumed to be a type of performance anxiety in which the person experiences anxiety when anticipating or engaging in communication with other people.

Historical Development

The cognitive modification of communication problems is based on Schachter's (1964) formulation of anxiety as a two-dimensional construct, incorporating both physiological and cognitive responses. His series of studies conclude that anxiety states are an interaction between cognitive and physiological responses in the following manner: (a) given a state of physiological arousal and no immediate explanation for it, individuals will label the state in terms of the cognitions available; (b) given a state of physiological arousal and an appropriate explanation, individuals will label their feelings in terms of the explanation provided; and (c) given a cognitive state, individuals will label it emotional only to the extent that physiological arousal is experienced.

Within the specific area of anxiety research, Borkovec (1976) also has focused on the interaction of physiological and cognitive responses. Borkovec conceptualizes anxiety as a shorthand term for a complex and variable pattern of behaviors. His definition of anxiety includes cognitive arousal, physiological arousal, and both overt manifestations of arousal and observable avoidance behavior. Thus, this conceptualization of anxiety necessitates the multiple measurement of three separate but interacting response channels; the cognitive, behavioral (motor), and physiological domains. The preceding chapters summarize modification approaches that primarily focus on these latter two dimensions.

Rational-Emotive Therapy

Several treatments have been developed to change the cognitive channel of anxiety that would affect communication problems. The procedures are labeled cognitive-behavioral treatments because they are based on the assumption that cognitive factors such as irrational beliefs, or expectations, directly mediate change in the other physiological and motoric response channels of anxiety. Initial strategies for cognitive-behavioral intervention are based on Ellis' (1962) seminal writing on rational-emotive therapy (RET). Ellis' approach focuses on the underlying beliefs-premises that contribute to a subject's thinking and maladaptive behaviors. He identified eleven irrational beliefs as underlying all emotional problems. Among the most common irrational beliefs are (a) everyone must love me all the time or I am a bad person; (b) I must be competent or successful in all situations or I am a bad person; and (c) when life is not the way I want, it is awful and upsetting.

The first goal of RET is to identify the irrational themes leading to avoidance of communication. The therapist then challenges, questions, and logically analyzes these themes with the person and attempts to replace them with more rational ones. For example, if the therapist found that a person was operating under the theme "everyone must love me," the therapist might induce the person to replace this irrational theme with the following self-statement:

> Although I would prefer most people to like me, it is impossible to please everyone all the time. Therefore, I will not try to focus on others when I am talking, but on what I want to say.

Thus, the strategy of the therapist using RET is to assist the person in the logical reinterpretation of irrational themes, and then to provide general philosophies designed to assist the person in coping with communication situations. Research on the effectiveness of RET compared to control or placebo conditions have been encouraging.

In the earliest study, Ellis (1957) compared his effectiveness during three periods of professional practice; psychoanalytic, directed psychoanalytic, and rational-emotive. Although methodologically weak, this study demonstrated RET's clear superiority to the other two treatments as measured by percentage of cases judged to have improved. Research by Karst and Trexler (1970) and Trexler and Karst (1972) with public speaking anxiety confirmed the effectiveness of RET as compared to waiting list and attention-placebo conditions.

Cognitive Restructuring

An alternative cognitive therapy to RET is Meichenbaum's cognitive restructuring procedure (Meichenbaum, 1976). Meichenbaum gives less emphasis to the logical analysis of irrational beliefs than RET. He argues that it is not the incidence of irrational beliefs that distinguishes normal and abnormal populations; rather, that people differ in the coping response they make to their irrational thoughts. Meichenbaum's self-control procedure is conceptualized as a 3-stage process. The first step involves teaching clients to become good observers of their thoughts, feelings, and behavior. The second stage involves the process of self-observation becoming the occasion for the emitting of adaptive cognitions and behaviors. The third stage, which determines the generalization of treatment effects, is concerned with practice altering the content of individual's internal dialogues. Problem situations are role played so that clients can practice using coping statements before, during, and after the situations.

Based on a more detailed description by Fremouw and Scott (1979), the following summarizes the major steps in cognitive restructuring for treatment of communication apprehension:

Step 1: Introduction

The first step is to provide anxious subjects with a thorough rationale and purpose for the training. The trainer explains that communication apprehension is a *learned reaction* and a *set of behaviors* that most people can modify by spending a few hours in the process of learning new skills. Apprehension can be reduced if people become aware of the negative self-statements they make in communication situations, and then learn coping statements that will refocus their attention in such situations.

Step 2: Identifying Negative Self-Statements

Following the introduction, the subjects are taught to identify specific negative self-statements or thoughts that inhibit communication, such as "I'll sound stupid; I don't have anything to say; Everyone is watching me." To help subjects identify these negative self-statements, the trainer provides many examples and then asks each person to identify three or four personal negative self-statements. These statements are then listed and rationally discussed in terms of how each statement affects their communication and social behaviors. Common logical errors such as overgeneralizations — "I *never* speak well" — or self-fulfilling prophecies — "I won't be liked" — are discussed.

Step 3: Learning Coping Statements

Once subjects learn to identify negative self-statements, they are taught to substitute them with more adaptive coping statements. The trainer divides communication situations into temporal phases – before, during, and after — that require different coping strategies. The trainer then teaches subjects to generate coping statements that can be used throughout the communication event; for example, "It's only a small group of students like me;" "Speak slowly;" "So far, so good; continue to speak slowly and ask questions."

Step 4: Practice

Once coping statements are defined and understood, training time is devoted to the active rehearsal of coping statements through role playing. Specifically, clients form groups and are asked to discuss topics of increasing controversy as they practice using coping statements. In addition, each person completes a diary that contains both stressful situations and the coping statements the person utilized during these situations. Practice sessions continue for at least three hours and culminate when each subject reports the ability to use coping statements during the week.

Cognitive restructuring has been compared to other treatments and has been proven effective for many communication problems. In the treatment of speech anxiety, Meichenbaum, Gilmore, and Fedoravicius (1971) found "insight" therapy to be just as effective as desensitization, as assessed by cognitive, behavioral, and self-report measures. "Insight" therapy as described by Meichenbaum et at., resembles RET, the goal being to increase the awareness of self-verbalizations without any specific training in emitting coping statements. Fremouw and Zitter (1978) compared skills training to combination of cognitive restructuring and relaxation for speech anxiety, and found both treatment groups improved as measured by subjective and behavioral measures. Elder, Edelstein, and Fremouw (1981) directly compared response acquisition (skills training) and cognitive restructuring on the enhancement of social competence and the alleviation of social anxiety. Results indicated that both treatments were superior to attention placebo, and that each treatment tended to impact its primary target-dependent measures. That is, response acquisition training led to greater increases in behavioral and self-reported social skills, while cognitive restructuring led to greater reductions in self-reported and behavioral anxiety.

In a related area, Glass, Gottman, and Shmurak (1976) compared cognitive self-statement modification, response acquisition training, and a combination of the two treatments, for dating-anxious males. They reported cognitive self-statement training subjects showed significantly better performance in novel role-play situations, made significantly more phone calls, and made significantly better impressions on the women than subjects in the other groups. Kanter and Goldfried (1979) compared the effectiveness of rational (cognitive) restructuring and desensitization in reducing social anxiety. Though behavioral and physiological measures did not differentiate between treatments, self-report data indicated rational restructuring was significantly more effective than desensitization in reducing state anxiety, trait anxiety, and irrational beliefs. Thus, for a variety of performance anxiety deficits, cognitive restructuring has been shown to be superior to waiting list control and attention placebo groups, and at least equal to comparative treatments.

Component Analyses of Cognitive Treatments

To understand the therapeutic process underlying cognitive behavior treatment, research has been conducted to evaluate the relative contributions of insight into irrational negative self-statements, and learning coping statements. In the first component analysis of cognitive restructuring, Wine (1970) reported that test-anxious subjects who learned coping statements significantly improved, compared to subjects in a "insight" group that only concentrated on the examination of negative self-statements. Based on these results, Meichenbaum (1973) warned that just insight into negative self-statements without learning coping statements may increase anxiety. Thorpe, Amatu, Blakey, and Burns (1976) reexamined the role of insight into negative self-statements and the use of general coping statements for treatment of speech anxiety. Based on an RET form of cognitive restructuring, they compared (a) general insight — discussion of Ellis's eleven irrational ideas; (b) specific insight — discussion of the 4 irrational ideas most relevant to public speaking; (c) instructional rehearsal — instruction and rehearsal of four general coping statements that relate to the common irrational ideas; and (d) insight plus rehearsal — a combination of specific insight and instructional procedures. The general and specific insight groups improved significantly more on the self-report measures than did the rehearsal or combination groups, but none of the treatments produced significant improvement on behavioral measures. Based on this data, Thorpe (1976) concluded that insight into maladaptive self-statements contributes more to cognitive restructuring than the use of coping statements.

To clarify these results, Glogower, Fremouw, and McCroskey (1978) also conducted a component analysis of cognitive restructuring. The study assessed the contribution of the following components of cognitive restructuring: (a) extinction, (b) insight into negative self-statements, (c) knowledge and rehearsal of coping statements, and (d) a combination of insight into negative self-statements followed by learning and rehearsal of coping statements. Communication-apprehensive college subjects were divided among the four treatment groups and a waiting list control group. On both self-report and behavioral measures, the coping statement group improved more than the negative self-statement or extinction groups. The combination of the components produced the largest improvement at posttreatment and at a 6-week follow-up.

These results suggest that while all of the components produce some improvement, the coping statement component is of primary importance to cognitive restructuring. This finding supports Wine's (1970) conclusion that coping statements are the major therapeutic component in cognitive restructuring, and directly contradict the conclusion of Thorpe et al. (1976).

Summary

Rational-Emotive Therapy and Cognitive Restructuring are approaches to modify the cognitive dimension of communication avoidance problems. The previously cited research demonstrates the well-established results that cognitive modification techniques produce significant improvements for many types of communication problems, including public speaking anxiety (Fremouw & Zitter, 1978), communication apprehension (Glogower et al., 1978) and dating anxiety (Glass et al., 1976). While the major therapeutic component of cognitive modification procedures appear to be the learning of coping statements (Glogower et al., 1978), additional research is continuing on the refinement of these procedures to further enhance their effectiveness for anxiety treatments. Modification of communication apprehension, shyness, and reticence will benefit from more application of these cognitive therapy procedures.

PART V

IMPLICATIONS

14

An Analysis of Research on the Social Anxieties

THEODORE CLEVENGER, Jr.

The last fifteen years have witnessed an unprecedented explosion of research into what might be called the social anxieties. An impressive mass of findings has accumulated on communication apprehension, shyness, reticence, performance anxiety, and related concerns. Old assumptions, conceptualizations, and theoretic frameworks are challenged by this new knowledge. There is growing awareness of parallel trends and cross-linkages among heretofore separate research programs and schools of thought. A feeling is in the air that major breakthroughs may be just around the corner. The field is ready for a new synthesis.

This book offers much of the raw material for such a synthesis, and goes some way toward it. Collectively, the preceding chapters represent a watershed. No one reading them in the present context can continue to think about social anxieties in quite the same way as before. Our horizons have been expanded too far into too many directions, calling for new maps of the territory that are more comprehensive, detailed, and accurate.

The present chapter will analyze the broadened perspective offered by the foregoing chapters, not with the purpose of summarizing their content, but with an eye to the basic formulations they imply. We will look not only *at* the research, but also *under* it to discern the parameters within which a new synthesis must be built. We will organize the analysis around three central themes: (1) terminology and definition, (2) basic classifying principles, and (3) areas of conceptual underdevelopment.

Terminology and Definition

To begin with, just what is the phenomenon in question? In recent times, more studies have been published under the rubric of "communication apprehension" than any other (McCroskey, chapter 1), but alongside these are other studies of apparently related phenomena called reticence (Phillips, Chapter 2), social reticence (Jones & Russell, 1982), social anxiety, shyness (Buss, Chapter 3), audience anxiety (Daly & Buss, Chapter 4), quietness (Richmond, Chapter 9), unwillingness to communicate (Burgoon, 1976), predisposition toward verbal behavior (Mortensen, Arntson, & Lustig, 1977), social-communicative anxiety (Daly & Stafford, Chapter 8), communication avoidance (Fremouw, Chapter 13), and dispositional speech anxiety (Daly & Buss, Chapter 4). Kelly (Chapter 12) links this body of research to such phenomena as dating anxiety and unassertiveness.

Daly and Stafford claim that "while the constructs associated with each of these labels differ in emphasis, the general thrust of all is the differing proclivity of people to participate and enjoy, or avoid and fear, social interaction." They coin the term "social communicative anxiety" to refer to "this disposition," but throughout most of the chapter, use the less specific label of "the anxiety." In some ways, this nonspecific terminology is most appropriate of all, for none of the available terms fully captures the variety of related phenomena.

Each of the terms by which we refer to the anxiety focuses on a different set of variables. Some of the differences are obvious, while others are subtle, as in the distinction between unwillingness to communicate and reticence. Some of the differences are situational, as in the interaction anxiety-audience anxiety distinction, but other concepts are cross-situational, such as predisposition toward verbal behavior. At this point in time, the field presents the confusing appearance of a large and expanding glossary of overlapping and intersecting terms with no generally accepted principles of classification.

To this point, the casual proliferation of terms could be accepted with equanimity. Each school of thought has developed its own research program with little immediate need to consider its conceptual relationship to others. For example, what we now know about communication apprehension, reticence, and social anxiety is truly impressive in spite of the fact that each research program has developed largely "in house," with only incidental reference to the work of the others. However, the preceding chapters make it abundantly clear that the era of innocent disregard must come to an end. There are so many important isomorphisms, as well as significant distinctions that it has become inefficient for programs to proceed without regard to their conceptual positioning vis-à-vis other programs and the field as a whole.

The solution to this problem is not to impose conceptual-methodological orthodoxy on the entire field of research, if indeed that could be done. Individual research programs will, as in the past, continue to define problems, invent terminology, and devise instruments as they deem appropriate, and the resultant variety will enhance the field. The solution to our present confusion is to locate basic principles of classification that allow us to place each concept and research finding in meaningful context with the rest.

The first step in building a viable classification system is to recognize that it cannot be developed deductively from any presently imaginable definition, because we are dealing with not one phenomenon having many subvarieties, but with many distinct phenomena that share certain properties among themselves in varying degrees. For that reason, I have chosen the plural term "social anxieties" to refer to this research area. While this usage shares some meaning with the "social anxiety" of Buss (Chapter 3) and Schlenker and Leary (1982), it is conceptually broader and, in contrast with each of the more specific terms used to refer to the phenomena reviewed here, it shall remain for the time being consciously undefined.

At first glance, the decision to leave a central term undefined may seem irresponsible, but in this instance it represents the ultimately responsible course of action. Each of the terms used to refer to the social anxieties can make a reasonable claim to coherence. In those cases where a body of research findings have accumulated, the evidence suggests that each term enjoys some measure of construct or predictive validity. Yet there is no one property that all of these concepts share. Any classification scheme robust enough to comprehend essentially all of the extant research, and sufficiently hueristic to guide future research and theory construction, must grow out of the research, not be imposed upon it. In the absence of universal common properties, a traditional "conceptual definition" of the term "social anxieties" is not available.

At this point, two questions may arise: (1) Can a term that cannot be defined in the usual way possibly refer to anything in the real world? and (2) if we can't define it in the usual way, why bother with it?

Wittgenstein answered the first question when he pointed out that terms like "game" have empirical referents yet defy traditional definition. Of the concepts referred to by such terms, he says,

> And the result of this examination is: we see a complicated network of similarities overlapping and criss-crossing: sometimes overall similarities, sometimes similarities of detail . . . as in spinning a thread its strength does not reside in the fact that some one fibre runs through its whole length, but in the overlapping of many fibres (Wittgenstein, 1955).

The contents of the preceding chapters suggest that the term "social anxieties" represents just such a concept. Even so, the term cannot be defined in the usual scientific way; why use it in developing a conceptual framework for classifying scientific work? The term is necessary because it brings together under a single referent an extended family of studies whose members share among themselves in varying degree certain similarities and distinctions. A relationship discovered in one branch of the field may be applicable to others; a distinction shown to be critical in one branch may aid analysis in others. Parallel findings across many branches may lead to fundamental theoretical syntheses. Inexplicable contradictions between branches may lead to break-throughs in concepts or methods. In point of fact, much of this sort of cross-fertilization and interdisciplinary synthesis has already occurred in the study of social anxieties, as the preceding chapters testify. Thus, the term simply recognizes a de facto state of affairs within the field. It is a useful way of holding together diverse yet related streams of research and theory development.

The term "social anxieties" is not to be construed as a substitute for any of the more specific terms employed in extant theory and research, but rather as an umbrella concept covering, but not holding, all of them. Each of the existing terms, along with others that undoubtedly will be coined in the future, should be understood as retaining its own integrity. Their conceptual definitions are vital to the success of the individual research projects growing out of them.

Given this usage of the term "social anxieties," the classification system for its referents becomes the real definition of the term, for it reflects the set of variables that aggregate and segregate the various concepts and research findings to which the term refers. The validity of the concept will be judged by the extent to which it facilitates an organized understanding of the extant literature and promotes economy of effort in research and theory construction.

Fundamental Classification Principles

Two principles of behavioral classification are fundamental to understanding research and theory in the social anxieties. To the extent that these distinctions are blurred or ignored, the literature becomes contradictory and confusing, and forward theoretical progress is stalled. The first of these is the state-trait distinction. The second is the separation of response systems into three domains: cognitive, behavioral, and physiological.

The State-Trait Distinction

Spielberger (1966) was the first to explicate clearly the distinction between personality traits and momentary states. The trait is a predisposition or general response tendency; it describes how a person feels, thinks, behaves, or responds characteristically or in general across time and across situations. As McCroskey explains in Chapter 1, the trait is a characteristic predisposition. Individuals differ in trait anxiety: some are inclined to become more anxious, more often and in more different situations than are others. A person high in CA is characteristically predisposed to react with substantial elevations in anxiety level when confronted with almost any communication situation. One who is low in CA usually will react with much less anxiety in most communication situations. The PRCA is designed to measure individual differences in this trait (McCroskey, Chapter 1).

Some find it perplexing that PRCA scores do not predict with any accuracy the anxiety experienced by a given individual on a given occasion. Although PRCA scores predict transient anxiety in communication situations better than it could be predicted by drawing lots or flipping coins, the accuracy of prediction is not much better (Hewes & Haight, 1980). But this finding is not at all mysterious in light of the state-trait distinction. While trait measures assess predisposition, state measures assess momentary condition. I may have high CA (trait), but for any number of reasons it may fail to manifest itself on a given occasion (state). Buss makes a distinction between shyness as a characteristic predisposition or trait and "transient shyness" — a state (Chapter 3). To assert that trait should predict state without fail is to assume a rigid response system, rarely justified in the human species.

McCroskey describes communication behavior as the product of at least two interacting factors: characteristic predispositions of the individual and situational constraints on behavior at a given time. As the constraints vary, we may expect variance in the expression of the trait in the momentary state of the individual (Chapter 1).

Prior to Spielberger's formulation, much confusion was introduced into earlier research on stage fright by failing to note the state-trait distinction. Trait measures were inappropriately employed to assess state without awareness of the distinction. Cognitive measures of trait were correlated to observational measures of state, and the resultant low correlations used to demonstrate no relationship between self-report and observational measures. Though much abated, the problem persists to the present day. Whenever a researcher assumes that a general trait measure (such as the PVB) should predict behavior on a specific occasion (such as verbal output in an experimental setting), the trait-state distinction has been violated and a disappointing or misleading result can be obtained.

One distortion of the state-trait distinction is the assumption that trait is situation-invariant, leading to what McCroskey calls a "false dichotomy" between state and trait (Chapter 1). Between general trait and momentary state, he sees a hierarchy of situational constraints constituting a sort of continuum. As his development of the PRCA-24 indicates, individuals vary not just in general trait but in situational trait as well. One may be relatively high in trait CA for a given class of situations (say, public speaking), but low in trait CA for another class of situations (say, dyadic interaction). Thus, trait is not homogeneous but is situation-dependent.

Bridging the gap between trait and state are what Daly and Buss call "the transitory causes of audience anxiety" (Chapter 4). Given a measure of one's general communication anxiety trait, it is possible to predict anxiety on the occasion of a particular communication transaction a little better than we could predict it by chance alone. With a situational trait measure for the specific type of communication transaction, it should be possible to predict significantly better. Given a knowledge of relevant situational factors as they affect the communicator, we also should be able to predict the individual's anxiety with better-than-chance success. But with a trait measure and knowledge of relevant situational factors together, it should be possible to predict the level of anxiety with much improved accuracy. We must always be aware of the fact that trait alone is a fallible predictor of one's momentary anxiety state, which is also much affected by various factors of the specific occasion. And in referring to the social anxieties, we must always be clear as to whether we have in mind the general or situational trait or the momentary state.

Three Response Domains

In 1959, I proposed that the distinction among cognitive, behavioral, and physiological measures be maintained, but that we devote significant research effort toward studying the interactions among them (Clevenger, 1959). The research evidence accumulated since that time reinforces both parts of that injunction.

Most of the formulations reviewed in previous chapters recognize a distinction among the three types of anxiety response. McCroskey (Chapter 1) notes it explicitly as essential to his concept of communication apprehension. Phillips (Chapter 2) speaks of signs of apprehension, effects of adrenalin flow, and personal reports in defining his concept of reticence. Buss (Chapter 3) defines shyness as including all three components. Kelly says that virtually all researchers on dating or heterosexual social anxiety conceptualize it as incorporating the components of conditioned anxiety, skills deficit, and faulty cognitive-evaluative appraisal (Chapter 12). The latter formulation, though not perfectly isomorphic, reflects at least partial recognition of the distinction.

Of course, the three response systems are by no means isolated from one another, and to my knowledge no one has ever suggested they were. In some sense, each does "measure" what we mean by the term "anxiety," and they must be interrelated by some dynamic. But if they are all in the same parade, it is obvious that each is marching to a different drummer. Study after study shows that stimulus conditions and purported therapies generally affect these three response systems in different ways (Fremouw, Chapter 13).

The evidence is clear now that the roots of the distinction lie not merely in differing approaches to measurement, but in different response *domains*, a term that serves well for this classification. The area within a domain is governed by an organized set of laws that differ from the laws of other domains. At the same time, there are interactions across boundaries that are for the most part governed by an additional set of laws. Each domain may be viewed as an open subsystem interfacing with the others in the context of a larger system, which we call anxiety response.

At this stage of development, we know something about how each subsystem works, but little about their interfaces with one another. The little understood implication of this situation is that we cannot claim to know a great deal about anxiety in the global sense. We understand a good deal about the social anxieties as cognitions, much less about the social anxieties as physiological response, and less yet about the social anxieties as overt behavior. We are just learning how we might come to know more about the interrelationships among the three subsystems.

Research and theory development would be much enhanced if researchers would consistently honor the distinctions among the three response domains, for the results of empirical research make no sense without them. To take just one example, the effects of alternate therapies differ among domains. Cognitive therapies reduce cognitive anxiety response, but have little or no effect on overt behavior. Relaxation therapies reduce physiological anxiety response, but have a less predictable effect on cognitions or behaviors. Behavior modification and overt behavioral skills training affect behavioral anxiety response, but seem to have little effect on either physiological or cognitive responses. For the most part, notable effects of short-term therapies on more than one response system have been achieved only by combination or hybrid approaches in which it could be inferred that each component of the therapy reduced anxiety response within its respective target domain.

With this considerable mass of research data in hand, it makes no sense to claim that this or that therapy reduces a particular social anxiety; it does or doesn't, depending on which response domain one has in mind. If one does not have in mind any particular response domain, then any such claim is at best empirically ambiguous and at worst nonsensically vague.

Most researchers and theorists do have in mind a particular response domain or domains, if only implicitly. McCroskey is quite explicit in defining "communication apprehension" as cognitive response (Chapter 1). He even goes so far as to claim that behavioral-observational and physiological measures are invalid measures of CA. He is unquestionably correct in this for neither behavioral nor physiological assessment is a valid approach to *measuring* cognitions, whether we are concerned with state or trait. Under certain conditions, physiology of behavior may be used to *infer* cognitions, a fascinating detective game, but is no substitute for direct measurement when that is available.

Phillips consciously treats reticence as a behavioral problem with cognitive foundations and works across the interface. His students learn skills that modify their overt behaviors, but this is done in conjunction with cognitive modifications. He specifically rules out any concern with physiological anxiety response (along with the affective component of self-report). A full theoretical development of Phillips' approach would explain how cognitions and behaviors influence one another and how one might change without changes in the other.

Buss defines shyness in the most comprehensive terms of all: "Shyness is inferred whenever behavioral inhibition or disorganization, somatic reactions or cognitive disruption occurs in a social context" (Chapter 3). In short, shyness is defined operationally as an anxiety response in *any* of the three domains. As so defined, its understanding presents the full challenge of the three-domains problem. Within the class of social contexts contemplated, a fully explicated theory of shyness must account for cognitive, behavioral, and physiological responses, as well as their mutual influences and discrepancies.

As the preceding examples illustrate, theorists may define a particular social anxiety as they choose with respect to response domain; any one, two, or all three of the available choices, as suits the demands of their theoretic or therapeutic formulation. The more response domains they include within their definition, the greater and more complex will be the research demands of that theory. The less explicit they are about which domains are referenced, the more confusing are the resultant research findings likely to be.

A Six-Way Classification

Combining the state-trait distinction with the three response domains generates a six-way classification of behaviors for the social anxieties: (1) cognitive trait, (2) cognitive state, (3) overt behavioral trait, (4) overt behavioral state, (5) physiological trait, and (6) physiological state. At present, (3) and (5) represent essentially empty sets, but they are not null. Authors of preceding chapters have pointed to the difficulty of assessing trait in the behavioral or physiological domains (McCroskey, Chapter 5; Beatty, Chapter 6; Mulac & Weimann, Chapter 7), but the work of Epstein (1979) suggests that the problem is not insurmountable (see Daly & Stafford, Chapter 8).

A classification of social anxiety responses based on the state-trait distinction and response domain allows investigators to focus on the observable phenomena with which theories and research efforts are directly concerned. This facilitates both the transition from theory to research and the feedback of research results to theory construction. To the extent that these important distinctions are ignored, research results will appear equivocal and theory development will be confounded.

Situational Classifications

This analysis will not attempt to create a classification or situational factors basic to understanding the social anxieties, though Daly and Buss may have made a significant start toward that goal (Chapter 4). It is instructive that some of the social anxieties discussed in preceding chapters are defined in part by situational variables. Shyness and audience anxiety are differentiated on the size of the listener group (Buss, Chapter 3). Dating anxiety is distinguished on the basis of dyadic interaction genre, and, unassertiveness may be defined in terms of perceived conflict (Kelly, Chapter 12). It appears that such situational variables make a difference in the expression of anxiety responses.

It it not surprising that situation variables enter into the study of the social anxieties at all levels, from conceptualization of a syndrome, through analysis of its dynamics, to design of treatment. The social anxieties view anxiety itself not as an ambient condition but one that is elicited by social situations. As the situations vary, so may the response; any situational difference one notices has the potential to exacerbate or ameliorate the anxiety response.

Klopf's review of cross-cultural differences in communication apprehension strongly suggests that cultural differences incorporate situational variables that have significant impact on the social anxieties (Chapter 10). Beyond mere differences in mean apprehension level from one cultural group to another, Klopf has identified specific social-communicative forms and values within cultures, which appear capable of raising or lowering the CA level within an entire population.

When an appropriate classification of situational factors is found, it probably will include two kinds of variables: those concerned with the structure of the social context and those associated with transient developments within that context. Dating and public speaking, for example, represent significant, identifiable social structures. Such structures present the possibility of situation-specific anxiety traits: simply participating in structured social interactions of a certain identifiable type may elicit anxiety without regard to anything that actually happens on the particular occasion. On the other hand, variables such as breach of privacy, identified by Buss as a cause of transient shyness, may occur in any social situation (Chapter 3).

Taken together, state-trait, response domain, and the two classes of situational variables fit into a familiar pattern in the analysis of communication transactions. Several communication models growing out of the combination of behaviorist and symbolic-interactionist approaches postulate a communicator with modifiable internal response tendencies (traits) acting through a variety of response systems (response domains) in response to stimulus complexes (transient features of the occasion) within the constraints of a known social context (social structures). (See, for example, Clevenger & Matthews, 1971). Possibly, the research and theory in social anxieties has taken on this shape because most psychologists and communication scholars implicitly accept some such model for the basic structure of human communication.

Opportunities for Conceptual Development

Several authors of preceding chapters have asserted, and most of the others have implied, that conceptual development must receive a high priority as a foundation for future research (Friedrich & Goss, Chapter 11; Kelly, Chapter 12; Fremouw, Chapter 3). While opportunities for conceptual development are numerous, this analysis points to five areas of conceptual underdevelopment that appear especially critical to advancing our understanding of social anxieties. Their characterization as underdeveloped is justified by virtue of their having remained unexplored or unresolved in spite of their obvious relationship to one or more of the problems touched by this volume. These conceptual problems deal with (1) the internal structure of each response domain, (2) interactions among the three domains, (3) the relationship of social anxieties to introversion (4) the relationship of social anxieties to productive activation, and (5) etiology and individual differences.

Internal Structure of Response Domains

Our earlier discussion of response domain might be misconstrued to imply that anxiety response within any domain is homogeneous and undifferentiated. In fact, all available evidence points to a rich and highly differentiated structure within each of them. Mulac and Weimann (Chapter 7) point to studies going back almost a quarter century, showing that observer-perceived speech anxiety has an interpretable factor structure (Clevenger & King, 1961). Improvements in earlier methodology and instrumentation led to the development of the TBC (Paul, 1966) and BASA (Mulac & Sherman, (1974), which reveal more demonstrably reliable and, in the case of BASA, more highly differentiated, yet generally compatible, factor structure. It is not improbable that the BASA scores for observed rigidity, inhibition, disfluency, and agitation relate to other variables in separate ways. Nor is it unlikely that distinct therapies would affect each factor differently.

Working with a variety of self-report and behavioral instruments, Sallinen-Kuparinen and I have observed a rich factor structure in each domain. Early analysis of the data points to a striking observation. Our factor structures display a remarkable tendency for positive-affect items to load heavily on different factors than negative-affect items. This finding echoes an earlier result by McCroskey (1978) that was regarded at the time as measurement artifact. It also parallels Burgoon's (1976) findings in developing the unwillingness-to-communicate scale, which contains two independent factors labeled "communication apprehension" and "communication rewards."

This positive versus negative factor clustering should be explored more closely, for it does not square with the notion that response is unidimensionally ordered along a continuum from positive to negative. The data suggest that positive and negative responses may exist side by side within the same response domain.

Indeed, this is precisely what Mulac and Weimann claim regarding observed anxiety behavior: "Anxiety and relaxation can been seen as separate dimensions of social behavior. Perceived relaxation is probably not caused by the mere absence of anxiety-related behaviors" (Chapter 7). Kelly quotes Adler (1977) to the effect that to have confidence means to have courage rather than a lack of fear (Chapter 12). When Buss administered an instrument having both shyness and sociability items, each set of questions emerged on its own factor (Chapter 3). Had sociability and shyness been opposite ends of the same continuum, they would have emerged on the same factor(s).

All of this evidence suggests that polarity of affect is not an incidental methodological issue in the construction of social anxiety measures, but that it may go to the root of the matter. Positive may not be the mere absence of negative, nor does negative invariably drive out positive where the social anxieties are concerned. The algebraic sum of positive and negative affects may conceal important data.

This sampling of issues is enough to indicate that research into the structure of the various response domains old potential for significant conceptual development in a wide variety of social anxieties.

Interactions Among Response Domains

For twenty years, Schachter and Singer's (1962) attributional approach to the relationship between physiological and cognitive anxiety states represented the only cogent explication of the relationships of any one of the three response domains to the others. Its influence has been noted in this volume (Beatty, Chapter 6; Fremouw, Chapter 13). More recently, Beatty and Behnke (1980) incorporated the CA trait into the paradigm. These conceptualizations represent an excellent beginning, and they should become springboards for exploring the dynamics of the relationship among all three domains.

One avenue available for such conceptual development is the relationships among factors across domains. In the Sallinen-Kuparinen study mentioned above, there was a second striking feature of the factor structures of observed and self-reported anxiety state. Although each domain displayed some factors not present in the other, some of the factors had similar or closely related content in both domains. If confirmed, this finding suggests the possibility that where gross cross-domain correlations prove uninformative, selected factor correlations may help unlock the relationship.

Relation of Social Anxieties to Introversion

By my count, the word "introversion" appears in the first thirteen chapters of this volume only three times. This is remarkable because of the formulations presented here border on or appear to overlap with the concept of introversion.

Phillips (Chapter 2) defines reticence in terms entirely compatible with introversion. The "predisposition to verbal behavior" (Mortensen et al., 1977) must surely by an aspect of introversion if either term carries the usual meaning. Unwillingness to communicate (Burgoon, 1976) or communication avoidance (Fremouw, Chapter 13) is the introvert's distinguishing mark, along with unassertiveness (Kelly, Chapter 12) and quietness (Richmond, Chapter 9).

Daly and Stafford define social-communicative anxiety as the differing proclivity of people to participate and enjoy or avoid and fear social interaction (Chapter 8), which some schools of personality psychology would accept as a fair definition of introversion. Yet, in citing over 100 separate findings regarding "personality correlates," not one of those studies dealt with the relationship between social anxiety and introversion. It was interesting that many of the traits associated with social anxiety are also associated with the introversion syndrome: lack of assertiveness, venturesomeness, tendency to be outgoing, surgency, social orientation, tendency to self-disclosure, social responsiveness, and argumentativeness. Also, high CAs are low in self-esteem, sometimes found to correlate with introversion.

Conceptually, the relationship between introversion and the social anxieties may run deep. McCroskey defines CA as "an individual's level of fear or anxiety associated with either real or anticipated communication with another person or persons," but some of the items on the PRCA are virtually identical with questions on various tests of introversion (Chapter 1). Buss defines shyness as "discomfort, inhibition, and awkwardness in social situations, especially with people who are not familiar." According to this definition, introverts would certainly be shy; and several of his questions are similar to items on standardized tests of introversion (Chapter 3).

Conceptual clarity would be enhanced by explicating the relationship between introversion and each of the social anxieties. To the extent that we are calling the same thing by two different names, it would be useful to know it. Where introversion can be separated conceptually from the social anxieties, it should be done and the relationship between the two explored.

One major advantage to be gained from examining the introversion-social anxieties interface is that there exists a substantial literature on introversion, which might enhance our understanding of the social anxieties. This could be especially instructive as regards the positive values of introversion.

Because most writing about the social anxieties is done by people with a professional academic interest in some kind of communication training, the field is subject to an extravert bias. We find it natural to assume that seeking opportunities to communicate and responding positively to communication demands is valuable, while the contrasting behaviors are somehow lacking. That is precisely how extraverts think (Kiersey & Bates, 1978). Even those among us who are themselves moderately introverted are socialized to extravert values by the nature of the field. There is no force at work within the field to call to our attention the fact that extraversion may not always be preferable to introversion, which may lead to unqualified claims that are generally but not invariably true.

For example, Richmond says that quiet persons are more costly to an organization than less quiet ones. They are less productive and more likely to quit or be fired, so additional expense is required to train their replacements (Chapter 9). This statement is undoubtedly true of many positions, especially sales or first-line management. But it probably is not true for many other positions in a complex organization. Would the average employer benefit from hiring a loquacious accountant, computer programer, or financial analyst? There are many situations in which the propensity to verbalize is anything but helpful. In those situations, introverts do better than extraverts, but communication scholars and teachers tend to forget that.

A Jungian approach to the concept of introversion holds that introversion and extraversion, though identifiable individual predispositions, are at root functions rather than traits (Jung, 1923). The predisposition is a preference for one function over the other, and most people can and do exercise both functions to some degree. The most mature individuals can alternate introversion with extraversion, according to the demands of the situation (Myers, 1962).

Concepts like the above place a different light on some assumptions underlying our notions about the social anxieties. Analysis of those assumptions and formulations in light of the introversion-extraversion literature could extend the range and flexibility of our theories.

Relation to Facilitative Activation

Most authors make a distinction between facilitative activation and disruptive social anxiety. Whether intended or not, the sharp boundary created by this disjunction leads to the notion that the two processes are qualitatively dissimilar. For example, Daly and Buss distinguish anxiety from excitement in that the latter involves no sense of discomfort or other negative experience (Chapter 4). McCroskey notes that considerable research indicates that people experiencing anxiety and those who report feelings of exhilaration can have similar arousal levels (Chapter 5). To distinguish the two states on the basis of cognitive attributions is consistent with Schachter's paradigm (Schachter & Singer, 1962), but may not go far enough.

That further analysis and research into this question may be needed is underscored by Daly and Buss' example. They liken exhilaration versus to anxiety) to "the same anticipatory excitement that runners experience just before a race." That anticipatory experience can be painful indeed and is the object of much research in sports psychology (Landers, 1980; Morgan, 1970; Weinberg, 1977).

The notion that some level of activation is necessary for satisfactory performance in social, performance, or competitive situations is older than the organized literature in these fields and was present in the earliest books on music, sports, and public speaking. According to this model, disruptive anxiety is seen as too much of a good thing.

In studying the social anxieties, we have paid great attention to those with too much and almost no attention to those with too little. McCroskey seems to be alone in his interest in those whose CA might be regarded as abnormally low (Chapter 1). My own experience watching heart rate records during student speeches suggests that the extreme low-reactive presents a dull and lifeless image. Some of the best professional speakers with whom I have worked display heart rates like those of a pilot landing a jet on the deck of an aircraft carrier; their heart rates repeatedly rise to levels 50% to 60% above resting rates throughout the course of a 20-minute speech. They are generally inclined to attribute their performance vitality to a high level of activation coupled with an anxious concern for their effectiveness. The immediately foregoing observations must be taken with appropriate caveats, for they are not backed by carefully controlled and refereed research publications. They are not offered to support any particular conclusions, but to suggest that sometimes what appears to be an anxiety response may in fact facilitate rather than disrupt communication behavior. Neither published findings nor the everyday experience of teachers and coaches squares with the notion that activation is harmful only when coupled with cognitive distress or that cognitive distress is invariably harmful with or without activation.

In focusing attention almost exclusively on serious and disruptive social anxiety problems, we have neglected the borderline between normal and abnormal processes, thus foregoing a potential wealth of information about the gradations by which normal, facilitative response systems shade into patterns of negative experience and problem behavior.

Etiology and Individual Differences

Beatty and Behnke (1980) have shown how communication apprehension may over time grow to problem proportions. Friedrich and Goss make a similar case for communication avoidance (Chapter 11). While these and a handful of related formulations outline a dynamic process whereby a social anxiety trait may become established, they have not yet been extended to comprehend the interaction of the process with individual differences. A comprehensive theory of etiology will require that this additional step be taken, and such a theory is vital to enhanced effectiveness in therapy and training.

Individual differences in inheritance, personality, and life experience may be central to understanding the sources of social anxiety in the individual case. Of course, understanding would be much improved by developing a detailed conceptualization of the problem. Kelly notes that

> the label "social communication problems" and even "reticence" is quite broad and could refer to a wide range of problems. The same is true of shyness, another social communication problem. Perhaps a more precise typology of social communication problems can be developed and then various types of social skills training can be tested to determine which are more effective for which kind of problems (Chapter 12).

Without doubt, if we are to understand the sources of a problem, we must know as specifically as possible what the problem is.

Classifying the problem is the first step, but Friedrich and Goss note that a particular communication dysfunction may have multiple causes (Chapter 11). The recognition of a possible genetic component may be essential. Daly and Stafford (Chapter 8), McCroskey (Chapter 1), and Buss (Chapter 3) all note the evidence for genetic predispositions toward the social anxieties, but they do so reluctantly. Daly and Stafford sum up the viewpoint of communication researchers and psychologists in these terms:

> Although some genetic contribution exists, its role is probably minimal in the entire scheme of events contributing to an individual's level of anxiety. The three remaining components, reinforcements, skills, and models contribute much more (Chapter 8).

We have recently come through a period of absolute rejection among behavioral scientists and social thinkers of any possible relationship between human behavior and genetic inheritance. The frozen position of Western science on this question is just beginning to thaw. Yet, breeders of animals that must interface with humans, such as dogs and horses, have never been able to ignore the inheritance of individual behavioral predispositions among the species with which they work. Most greyhounds will chase game (or a lure) with virtually no training, but learn to retrieve only with great difficulty or not at all. Most retrievers perform just the opposite. Most terriers are aggressive and pugnacious, regardless of training or environment; most hounds are not. Comparative biology and the rule of parsimony suggest the hypothesis that humans may inherit some predisposition toward social anxieties. It will require much research to ascertain just how pervasive or prepotent such inherited tendencies may be.

In the meantime, research needs to push forward on other individual factors that may evoke or interact with the social anxiety responses. Buss notes that remediation must respond to different sources of the problem (Chapter 3), and Kelly suggests that more attention should be given to the interaction between treatment procedures and subject characteristics (Chapter 12). This seems like excellent advice in light of Fremouw's conclusion that each therapy tends to impact its own primary target-dependent measures (Chapter 13).

Conclusion

This volume marks the end of an age of innocence as regards theory and research in the social anxieties. This diverse yet complexly interrelated set of phenomena can now be seen to constitute a meaningful cluster of theoretic formulations and research findings. It is inefficient for research and treatment-training programs to proceed without positioning themselves with respect to the field as a whole. Research and theory development in each of the communication anxieties will profit greatly from examining the work of the others.

Within the broad context of the social anxieties, clearcut conceptual definitions of each syndrome are critical to further advancement. To facilitate such definition, a classification system is proposed based on three factors: the state-trait distinction; the distinction among cognitive, physiological, and behavioral response domains; and distinctions based on situational variables, both structural-cultural and transient. Maintenance of these distinctions will facilitate clearer understanding of extant research as well, and lead to more productive future research and theory construction.

Within the broad parameters of such a classification system, conceptual development stands as the leading challenge of social anxiety theory and research. Five areas of underdevelopment are identified: research and theory construction are especially needed regarding the internal structure of each response domain; interactions among the domains; the relationship of social anxieties to introversion; relationship to productive activation; and etiology and individual differences.

15

Some (Moderately) Apprehensive Thoughts on Avoiding Communication

GERALD R. MILLER

As the editors of this volume indicate in the Preface, I have made no scholarly contributions to the area addressed in this volume. Nevertheless, I accepted their invitation to write a brief response without hesitation, primarily because of two long-standing, firmly held beliefs: First, I believe it is socially and scientifically vital for students of communication to understand as much as possible about the factors influencing people's communicative attitudes and practices; second, I believe that teachers of communication have a responsibility to help students in overcoming their fears about communicating and to assist students in developing more positive perceptions of communicative activities. Stated succinctly, our classes should produce students who are more confident about reaching out symbolically to others, rather than withdrawing from them.

My commitment to these beliefs does not stem from detached perusal of books and articles about communication apprehension, reticence, and shyness; nor even from sympathetic observation of students suffering painfully from these social maladies. Instead, it is rooted in my own personal agonies as a communicatively anxious youngster. Though my present friends and acquaintances will probably find it hard to believe, I entered high school with a deep-seated reluctance about communicating orally with others. Early social activities, particularly dates, were marked by long periods of uneasy silence, and my few ventures into conversation were accompanied by considerable fear and anxiety. In the idiom of mid-1940s, middle American, Iowa society, I was a "bashful child," and this condition caused me a great deal of personal and social consternation.

My communicative travails did not exempt me from the required ninth-grade speech course at Muscatine High School. Even though I dreaded the moment of my first speech, a communicative metamorphosis began when I opened my mouth and started speaking. What I talked about has long since faded from memory, but I still recall that, for some inexplicable reason, I perceived that my classmates reacted favorably to my efforts. These positive experiences in freshman speech had a profound impact on my life: I became active in debate and other forensic activities; I embarked on a profession that required me to spend a fair amount of my time communicating with students and other audiences; and eventually, as a result of my success with such audiences, I became more comfortable in my interpersonal transactions. To this day, however, I am typically more at ease talking with 100 strangers in a classroom or an auditorium than conversing with a single stranger in my office or living room.

Not surprisingly, I have frequently reflected on my own experiences as a communicator. What caused my childhood fears of communication? My father was a gregarious, outgoing person who, to borrow a midwestern cliche, "never met a stranger." By contrast, my mother was withdrawn and reticent. She talked only when it was absolutely necessary, usually resorting to adages and cliches. Most of my home involvement in oral communication consisted of listening to my father. I was never encouraged to express my ideas or feelings, though on those rare occasions when I did, I cannot recall being ridiculed or punished save for one vividly imprinted instance when I corrected my father's erroneous recounting of an event. Moreover, though I was loath to talk, I read and wrote voraciously, so much that my father often complained about my tendency to avoid or desert chores in favor of "sticking my nose in a book." While all these events doubtless helped to shape my youthful aversion to oral communication, they have never seemed to fit together into any coherent explanatory mosaic.

Just as I have mused about basic causes of my problem, I have often pondered why my symbolic ventures in freshman speech had such a salutary effect on my future communicative behaviors. Certainly, my case is the exception rather than the rule; few students with a lengthy history of communication apprehension respond positively to their initial ventures into public speaking. Granted, it is tempting and comfortable to invoke labels such as "positive peer reinforcement" (a strategy I resorted to in my earlier account of the situation) to "explain" my perceived smashing success, but such a verbal translation trick really explains nothing. Since I cannot remember the words and acts that prompted this perceived positive response by my audience, I am still puzzled as to why I sat down after my first speech feeling more positive and confident, whereas most students with my fears and anxieties react in an entirely opposite way.

The preceding exercise in self-disclosure was not undertaken because of any optimistic belief that the reader is curious about the details of my ordinary childhood. Rather I, have recounted my personal communicative history in some detail for two reasons: First, to illustrate why I believe the issues addressed by contributors to this volume are of utmost significance; second, and of greater import, to demonstrate how my own personal experiences with communication apprehension mirror and relate to many of the more general conceptual and empirical matters discussed in these chapters. Because of both its personal relevance and its broad scientific and social import, I have read the entire volume with interest. Notwithstanding the kind image of omniscience conferred on me by the editors, I am most assuredly incapable of telling anyone "what it all means." Still, the insightful presentations of the various contributors have stimulated a number of thoughts and questions, and my remaining remarks will identify and elaborate briefly those that strike me as most important.

Labeling and Conceptualization

The first four chapters of the book conceptually explicate four constructs: *communication apprehension, reticence, shyness*, and *audience anxiety*. These chapters do not exhaust the inventory of potentially relevant terms — for example, a chapter on unwillingness to communicate (Burgoon, 1976) could surely have been included. Although each of the authors explicates his or her construct crisply and thoughtfully, there is relatively little discussion of similarities and differences among the four terms. In Chapter 8, Daly and Stafford duly note this surplus of terminological riches, asserting that the study of the relative enjoyment versus avoidance of social interaction has been characterized by each investigator's apparent need to create a new construct and a new assessment instrument. Moreover, not wishing to be perceived as scholarly deviants by their colleagues, Daly and Stafford proceed to mint yet another conceptual coin, *social-communicative anxiety*.

This proliferation of constructs perpetuates scientific confusion, rather than promoting scientific understanding. Daly and Stafford themselves provide strong support for my contention, stating:

> There is considerable evidence that, by and large, the many different constructs within this area tap a single, broader disposition. The average intercorrelation among the various constructs is relatively high. . . . Further, when findings based upon different operationalizations are compared virtually no major inconsistencies emerge. In no case do different constructs make diametrically opposed predictions. Differences between varying operationalizations are always ones of magnitude rather than direction; one construct might propose a strong positive relationship while its conceptual cousin suggests only a moderate one.

The typical imprecision of ordinary language, plus the value for stylistic variety widely espoused in speech and English classes, permits and even encourages the everyday conversational use of a multitude of terms such as "shy," "bashful," "apprehensive," "scared," and "anxious" to characterize people who have a hard time communicating with others. Indeed, among Toastmasters and Rotarians, to describe the plight of someone whose hands are trembling and legs are shaking with such antiseptic terms as "social-communicative anxiety" or "communication apprehension" may provoke a few disapproving or bewildered glances from the describer's peers. But the norms and values of scientific discourse differ sharply from those of everyday conversation. Precision and parsimony are the scientific order of the day, not stylistic vividness and a flare for neologism. Thus the communication scientist who proposes a new construct assumes the burden of demonstrating that construct's independence from others currently residing in the community's scientific literature. Furthermore, to anticipate a possible rebuttal, when two or more similar-appearing constructs pop up in the literature virtually simultaneosuly, it is the task of the coiners of these constructs, as well as their like-minded colleagues, to reach a rational conclusion concerning their relative scientific utility. To do otherwise, in the words of one contributor to this volume, would be to sacrifice sound scientific scholarship on the altar of "commitment to scholia" (Phillips, 1981 p. 361).

Given the capabilities and credentials of the contributors, I am disappointed that none has revealed much of an appetite for tackling this issue; in fact, save for scattered, brief comments, the problem is never acknowledged nor its implications explored. Lest my disappointment strike the reader as an excessively harsh indictment, I am quick to grant the failure to explore the multiple construct problem does not negate the informative value of the volume's contents. Indeed, I suspect that most contributors view the major objective of the book as a state-of-the-art summary of conceptual, methodological, and empirical work dealing with communication avoidance, regardless of the problems associated with it. Though I have no major quarrel with this objective, I remain convinced that the volume would be more useful and provocative if it commenced adjudicating the conceptual foundations that should undergird both the present research edifice and subsequent additions that will be built.

A second conceptual issue concerns the need for a careful, holistic explication of the complex process associated with avoidance of communication. As amply documented by the chapters on conceptualization and measurement, three aspects of this process have been addressed by students of communicative avoidance: people's self-reports of their feelings about communicating, autonomic arousal accompanying anticipation of or participation in communication, and communicators' overt behaviors while interacting with others. Although it sometimes may be scientifically and socially useful to center on one of these aspects at the expense of the others, a satisfactory conceptualization of communication avoidance probably requires some attention to possible relationships among the three variables.

One conceivable causal path can be plotted as follows: A communicator perceives some anxiety and apprehensiveness about communicating. This awareness translates into certain autonomic changes — heart rate and blood pressure increase, skin conductivity changes markedly, and so on. Finally, as a result of these autonomic changes, a disruption of certain overt behaviors such as speech fluency, paralinguistic cues, and bodily activity occurs. In short, the process moves from self-awareness of apprehension, to physiological arousal, to disrupted, less effective communicative behavior — a sequence that reinforces the individual's tendency to avoid future symbolic contacts.

A second scenario reverses the first two steps of the preceding path. The communicator experiences heightened autonomic arousal. Because a number of situational cues point in this direction, the cause of this arousal is labeled "communicative anxiety." Once again, arousal and self-awareness culminate in disruptions of ongoing message behaviors. Thus the process moves from arousal, to emotional labeling, to changes in behavior.

A final sequential path originates with communicative behavior. Because of certain features of message production and/or transmission, the communicator perceives unfavorable audience responses. This negative assessment produces autonomic arousal, which may, in turn, exacerbate the behavioral problem. These aversive features motivate withdrawal and future avoidance. When queried about her or his feelings about communication, the communicator infers the answer from prior behavior (Bem, 1965, 1972); that is, "I must not like to communicate because I'm always avoiding it." Such a causal path is consistent with discussion in several of the chapters concerning the impact of early communicative activities (or, more precisely, the *consequences* associated with such activities) on subsequent attitudes and feelings about communicating.

The three previously outlined alternatives all focus on sequential relationships, in the language of equation modeling, they are viewed recursively. It strikes me as more likely that the relationships are reciprocal, or nonrecursive, that the values of some or all of the three variables are affected reciprocally and relatively simultaneously by the values of the others: A (autonomic arousal) causes B (behavioral disruption), and B causes A. This conceptual stance seems particularly relevant to material in this volume dealing with the relative merits of attitudinal modification versus skills training. As a first step, discussion of this issue could be sharpened by a more detailed explication of the construct of *communicative skills.* The construct embraces a large bag of differing behaviors, some of which may be related reciprocally to autonomic arousal and others of which may not. Stated differently, behaviors such as marshaling evidence and reasoning cogently may be relatively independent of arousal, though my continuing commitment to a Hull-Spence view of motivation (Brown, 1961) makes me skeptical about this possibility. Conversely, experimental and clinical evidence leave little doubt about the relationship between arousal and such behaviors as fluency, rate of speech, and various bodily activities. Furthermore, these motivational and behavioral variables appear to be reciprocally related: Changes in the values of the motivational variables affect the values of the behavioral variables, *and* changes in the values of the behavioral variables affect the values of the motivational variables. Thus, though McCroskey's (Chapter 1) free-throwing analogy is ingenious, things are often not this simple; development of a better breed of free-throw shooters may depend on concomitant attention to both attitudes and skills, as well as the structuring of situations that permit the reciprocal influence of both classes of variables to operate.

The chapters in this volume certainly are not bereft of concern for these relational issues; nevertheless, I feel they have been conceptually shortchanged by the authors. It should be emphasized that any of the proposed relational schemes, as well as other unmentioned alternatives, may prove to be theoretically and socially valuable. Indeed, particular schemes may be appropriate for some educational objectives but not for others. My interest lies not in some elusive, futile quest for the *one* superior conceptual model of the process of communicative avoidance, but rather in assuring that the conceptual forest is not lost in a flourishing clump of terminological seedlings.

Relationship with Other Variables

Three chapters examine the relationship of communicative avoidance to other variables. Most reported relationships concern correlates and consequences of communication apprehension, with few specific linkages to antecedent variables being identified. Rather than reiterating many of these findings, it seems more useful to consider the scientific and social import of the various types of relationships summarized by Daly and Stafford, Richmond, and Klopf.

One type of relationship represents little more than a validation check of the communication apprehension, reticence, and shyness measures. It is not surprising to discover that people who score high on these measures talk less than low scorers, prefer classes and occupations requiring little interaction on their part, tend to occupy peripheral seating positions in groups, and usually receive lower grades for assignments in communication courses. In a similar vein, it would be discouraging for proponents of the various avoidance measures if highly apprehensive persons did not score lower on dominance than low apprehensive individuals, were not less argumentative and less assertive, and were not more fearful of negative evaluation. To a large extent, the underlying conceptual logic of the various communicative avoidance constructs mandates these relationships. Indeed, many of the above-mentioned variables are neither conceptually nor ostensively independent from the avoidance constructs, leading to the conclusion that the relational propositions suffer from analyticity — that is that the two variables stated in the proposition share considerable identity, or overlapping meaning. Though such validity checks constitute an important step in developing and refining constructs, their substantive import should not be exaggerated.

A second type of relationship documents the fact that individuals who avoid communication are professionally disadvantaged. As Richmond indicates, highly apprehensive people are less likely to be hired, retained, and advanced than their low-apprehensive counterparts. In terms of one of the standard "American dreams" — economic success and status enhancement — the professional cards are stacked against communicatively apprehensive individuals. Just as mathematics, science, and business educators seek to ensure a fairer deal for students when they enter the professional arena, teachers of communication should assist students in developing communicative attitudes and behaviors that increase the likelihood of success.

A third, closely related type of relationship provides evidence that apprehensive people face serious social handicaps, particularly in their efforts to initiate relationships and to maintain satisfying contacts with strangers and casual acquaintances. As several of the contributors indicate, the negative impact of apprehension has not as yet been convincingly demonstrated for firmly established, more intimate relationships. When attempting to assess this area, other potentially relevant variables come into play. For instance, Richmond paints a bleak picture of the matrimonial prospects for partners who differ sharply in avoidance of communication. Though her analysis may be accurate for many couples, research dealing with need complementarity (Winch, 1958) suggests that the combination of a high and a low apprehensive mate could result in a good marital fit. But regardless of what future research reveals about the influence of communication apprehension on established relationships, its debilitating effects on relational formation and maintenance of casual acquaintanceships is a cause for serious concern.

A fourth type of relationship underscores relatively dismal self-conceptions of highly apprehensive individuals. Not only does such negative view foster personal dissatisfaction, it exacerbates the problem faced in forming relationships. Indeed, personal acceptance and social facility are inextricably bound together and exert a strong reciprocal effect: Improvement in self-concept enhances the likelihood of successful initiation and maintenance of relationships, and heightened relational success produces an additional positive increment in self-concept.

The four types of relationships discussed above focus primarily on the consequences or outcomes of avoiding communication. As mentioned earlier, there is a dearth of information about the antecedents or determinants of avoidance. If genetics plays a role, as prior research hints, the possibility of affecting hereditary change by external intervention hinges on future developments in genetic engineering. To the extent that environmental causes can be identified, however, some thoughtful social engineering can take place, possibly resulting in fewer elementary, secondary, and college students who arrive at communication classes as explosive bundles of communicative anxiety.

At least three promising research approaches are capable of providing clues about the environmental genesis of avoidance. Laboratory and field experiments can be used to study the influence of manipulated or naturally occurring events on communicative attitudes and practices. Intensive case studies of persons suffering from lengthy bouts with communicative apprehension may well uncover some of the key experiences leading to their present plight. Finally, cross-cultural research that borrows from and extends the work reported in this volume by Klopf can potentially reveal cultural regularities associated with high versus low incidence of communicative avoidance. Klopf's present chapter understandably centers on the first step of compiling comparative statistics regarding the frequency of avoidance among residents of various Pacific Basin societies. Though considerable speculation and a smattering of data are offered to explain differences among these Pacific societies, the paucity of systematic research is apparent. Should such research eventually reveal cultural features associated with a relatively low frequency of communicative avoidance, at least some of these features might be adaptable to other societies where the problem is more acute. Admittedly, this a complex, "iffy" proposition, but it is promising enough to warrant investigation.

Treatment Goals and Procedures

My opening autobiographical tale underscores my personal and professional commitment to the goal of helping individuals afflicted with the social curse of avoidance of communication. The three chapters devoted to treatment describe useful approaches to the possible achievement of this goal. Rather than nitpicking them, I will content myself with two general caveats about the treatment issue.

The first caveat concerns the identification of a primary treatment goal. Stated differently, it concerns the question: What is the most important class of behaviors to be modified? Should treatment focus on people's perceptions of communication, their physiological responses to communicative events, or their overt verbal and nonverbal message behaviors?

Since I have argued that these three variables domains are related, the causal issues involved in answering this question are thorny ones. From a social perspective, however, the sought-for end seems transparently clear: *The primary treatment goal should be modification of the overt behaviors that provide inferential grounds for labeling a person "communicatively apprehensive."* The justification for this caveat is contained in its articulation. Seldom in everyday discourse can we access another's self-feeling reports about communication, nor can we monitor physiological responses such as heart rate, blood pressure, or skin conductance. What is invariably scrutinized is the *way* the individual communicates with others; these ongoing message behaviors trigger our assessments of relative enjoyment of, versus apprehension about, communicating. People are described as "shy" or "anxious" because they seldom speak, communicate in halting tones, and avoid eye contact; people are described as "assertive" or "relaxed" because they speak frequently, communicate in confident tones, and return our gaze. Thus the proof of the treatment pudding lies in the eventual emergence of more functional, socially approved communicative behavior, even though this objective may be furthered by altering self-feeling states and/or autonomic arousal.

My second caveat rests on my conviction that it is futile to hope for treatment progress within the evaluative confines of the typical communication classroom. People are apprehensive and avoidance oriented at least partially because of a history of unrewarding experiences with communication. The classroom environment, with its emphasis on grades as primary reinforcers, fosters continued perceived failure on the part of apprehensive students. Long ago, our colleagues in speech pathology and audiology realized that stuttering and sibilant /s/ sounds are not items for grading but rather problems for clinical remediation. Severe cases of communicative avoidance are also clinical problems: *Treatment of communication apprehension should be carried out in environments shorn of the evaluative stresses of the classroom.* Failure to heed this caveat virtually ensures that the well-intentioned efforts of communication educators will amount to naught in the treatment of communicative avoidance, or worse, will be counterproductive.

To conclude with a stale but appropriate accolade, this is a book whose time has come. Its pages document the progress made in studying communicative avoidance; its omissions underscore important theoretical, methodological, and research questions as yet unanswered. Though my thoughts about the chapters are far from exhausted, two considerations compel me to draw finis. I am nearing the page limits suggested by the editors, but, more important, this assignment is tardy, and should I tarry much longer, Editor Daly may invite me to take a Writing Apprehension Test. This prospect is sufficiently foreboding to ensure my prompt avoidance of further communication.

APPENDIX

A Bibliography of Related Research and Theory

STEVEN K. PAYNE and VIRGINIA P. RICHMOND

This bibliography includes the references cited in the articles comprising this book as well as a number of other entries related to communication avoidance. The literature in communication, psychology, and related areas was surveyed to obtain references related to communication apprehension, reticence, shyness, and other constructs believed central to communication apprehension. Originally, this bibliography was completed as a separate unit in this book. For space reasons, the reference lists for each of the chapters were incorporated into the bibliography.

The primary criterion for inclusion in this bibliography, aside from the presence of a citation in this book, was the degree to which the reference was related to at least one of the constructs in this area. Many sources with passing reference to communication apprehension or shyness, for example, were omitted. Similarly, many articles related to treatment methodologies, such as systematic desensitization and cognitive modification, did not focus on communication and hence were omitted.

Our goal was to generate as complete a bibliography as possible of articles, books, and papers directly related to communication avoidance. Since relatedness is a relative concept, many references fell into a grey area. Thus some entrees included may be seen as less related than some that were omitted, particularly by an author of one we chose to omit. We used our best judgment and must live with the product. We do wish to stress, however, that inclusion or exclusion was not based on a judgment of the quality of work reported, only on its relevance to the main area of concern. Thus while inclusion does not indicate an evaluative endorsement, neither does exclusion suggest a negative evaluation. Further, a very limited amount of materials cited, while relevant to a particular chapter in this book, will not be of direct relevance to the topic of communication avoidance.

We believe this is the most complete bibliography available in this area through early 1983. We trust it will be useful to scholars and students concerned with the general area of communication avoidance.

Adams R. L. A study of the effects of a group counseling program on self perceived speech anxiety. Thesis, University of Kansas, 1968.

Adams, W.C. Beatty, M.J. & Behnke, R.R. Social facilitation and social desirability. *Psychological reports*, 1980, 47, 1297-1298.

Adler, Ronald B. *Confidence in communication: A guide to assertive and social skills.* New York: Holt, Rinehart & Winston, 1977.

Adler, Ronald R. Integrating reticence management into the basic communication curriculum. *Communication Education*, 1980, 29, 215-221.

Ainsworth, S. H. A study of fear, nervousness, and anxiety in the public speaking situation. Dissertation, Northwestern University, 1949.

Akin Clifford, Kunzman, Glen G. A group desensitization approach to public speaking anxiety. *Canadian Counsellor*, 1974, 8, 106-111.

Alameda County School Department. *The reticent child in the classroom: oral communication concepts and activities.* Hayward, CA: Author, 1969, 94554.

Alcantara, R. R. *American sub-cultures.* Honolulu: University of Hawaii Open Program, 1975.

Allen, Jerry L., Andriate, Gregory S. Cuzick, Richard D. A comparison of communication apprehension in basic studies and non-basic studies students. Paper presented at the Eastern Communication Association, Hartford, 1982.

Alter, Jason, Cambra, Ronald, & Klopf, Donald. The educational impact of communication apprehension: An exploratory study in the People's Republic of China. *Waiyn Jiaouzue Yu Yenjiu,* 1980, 3, 45-51.

Alter, Jason, Cambra, Ronald, & Klopf, Donald. Data on the oral communication practices of the Chinese. Paper presented at the Communication Association of the Pacific — Japan Conference, June 14-15, Kobe. 1980.

Alter, Jason, Cambra, Ronald, & Klopf, Donald. The interpersonal needs of students in the People's Republic of China as compared to those elsewhere. *Indian Journal of Applied Linguistics,* 1980, 6, 94-101.

Amator, P. P, & Ostermeier, T. H. The effect of audience feedback on the beginning public speaker. *Speech Teacher,* 1966, 16, 56-60.

Ambler, Robert S. The speech anxiety program at UTK: A training program for students with high speaking anxiety. Paper presented at the Speech Communication Association convention, Louisville, 1982.

Ambler, Robert S, & Holt, Jr. J. B, Speech anxiety training: Alternative to systematic desensitization. Paper presented at the Central States Speech Communication Association, Chicago, 1976. American Psychiatric Association. *Diagnostic and Statistical Manual of Mental Disorders* (3rd ed). Washington, DC: APA, 1980.

Andersen, Janis F. The relationship between teacher and immediacy and student learning. Dissertation, West Virginia University, 1978.

Andersen, Janis F. Perceptions of immediacy and communicator style as altered by communication apprehension level. Paper presented at the Western Communication Association convention, Los Angeles, 1979.

Andersen, Janis F. The relationship among interpersonal touching, interpersonal smiling, communication apprehension, and verbal output in children, grades 1-5. Paper presented at the Eastern Communication Association convention, Philadelphia, 1979.

Andersen, Janis F., Andersen, Peter A. & Garrison, John P. "Singing apprehension and talking apprehension: The development of two constructs. Paper presented at the Western Speech Communication Association convention, San Francisco, 1976.

Andersen, Peter A. The relationship between body type and communication avoidance. Paper presented at the Eastern Communication Association convention, Boston, 1978.

Andersen, Peter A., & Singleton, G. W. The relationship between body type and communication-avoidance. Paper presented at the Eastern Communication Association convention, Boston, March 1978.

Andersen, Peter A., Andersen, Janis F., & Garrison, John P. Singing apprehension and talking apprehension: The development of two constructs. *Sign Language Studies,* 1978, 19, 155-186.

Andersen Peter A., & Coussoule, Alexandra R. The perceptual world of the communication apprehensive: The effects of communication apprehension and interpersonal gaze on interpersonal perception. *Communication Quarterly*, 1980, 28, 44-54.

Andersen Peter A., & Leibowitz, Kenneth. The development and nature of the construct of touch avoidance. *Environmental Psychology and Nonverbal Behavior,* 1978, 3, 89-102.

Andersen, Peter A., & Singleton, George W. The relationship between body type and communication avoidance. Paper presented at the Eastern Communication Association convention, Boston, 1978.

Anderson, Ruth. A curriculum for the reticent minority university student. Paper presented at the Southern Speech Association convention, Birmingham, Alabama, 0000.

Andriate, Gregory S. Teacher communication and student learning: The effects of perceived solidarity with instructor and student anxiety proneness on three learning outcomes. Paper presented at the international Communication Association convention, Boston, 1982.

Andriate, Gregory S. Teacher communication and student learning: The effects of perceived solidarity with instructor and student anxiety proneness on three learning outcomes., In Michael Burgoon (ed.), *Communication yearbook 6.* Beverly Hills, CA: Sage, 1982.

Apple, W., Streeter L. A., and Krauss, R. M. Effects of pitch and speech rate on personal attributions. *Journal of Personality and Social Psychology*, 1977, 35, 443-449.

Argyle, M. *Social Interaction.* Chicago: Aldine, 1969.

Argyle, M. The contribution of social interaction research to social skills training. In J. D. Wine & M. D. Smye (Eds.), *Social competence.* New York: The Guilford Press, 1981.

Argyle, Michael, Trower Peter E. & Bryant, Bridget M. Explorations in the treatment of personality disorders and neuroses by social skills training. *British Journal of Medical Psychology*, 1974, 47, 63-72.

Arnold, Bill R., & Parrott, Ross. Job interviewing: Stress-management and interpersonal-skills training for welfare rehabilitation clients. *Rehabilitation Counseling Bulletin*, 1978, 22, 44-52.

Arnold, M. B. Stress and emotion. In M. H. Appley & R. Trumbull (Eds.), *Psychological stress.* New York: Appleton-Century-Crofts, 1967.

Arkin, R. M., Appelman, A. J., & Burger, J. M. Social anxiety, self-presentation, and the self-serving bias in causal attribution. *Journal of Personality and Social Psychology*, 1980, 38, 23-35.

Arnston, P., Mortenson, D., & Lustig, M. Predispositions toward verbal behavior in task oriented interaction. *Human Communication Research*, 1980, 6, 239-252.

Ashem, B. The treatment of a disaster phobia by systematic desensitization. *Behavior Research and Therapy*, 1963, 1, 81-84.

Asher, Fred M. The ancillary effects of group assertion training on the level of self-perceived risk-taking, degree of trait anxiety and selected manifest needs. Dissertation, East Texas State University, 1979.

Aspinwall, D. B. Languages in Hawaii. *P.M.L.A.*, 1960, 75, 7.

Axtell Bryan, & Cole, Charles W. Repression-sensitization mode and verbal avoidance. *Journal of Personality and Social Psychology*, 1971, 18, 133-37.

Baade, Roberta C. A study of the effects of metaphoric thinking on communication apprehension and ideation output in small groups. Paper presented at the Western Speech Communication Association convention, San Jose, February 1981.

Baker, Eldon E. An experimental study of speech disturbance for the Measurement of stage fright in the basic speech course. *Southern Speech Journal*, 1964, 29, 232-243.

Baldwin, John H., McCroskey, James C. & Knutson, Thomas J. Communication apprehension in the pharmacy student. *American Journal of Pharmaceutical Education*, 1979, 43, 91-93.

Baldwin, Sandra F. Communication anxiety and personality. Dissertation, Florida State University, 1976.

Bander, K. W., Steinke, G. V., Allen, G. J., & Moser, D. L. Evaluation of three dating specific treatment approaches for heterosexual dating anxiety. *Journal of Consulting and Clinical Psychology*, 1975, 43, 259-266.

Bandura, Albert. Self-efficacy: Toward a unifying theory of behavior of behavior change. *Psychological Review*, 1977, 84, 191-215.

Bandura, Albert, Blanchard, E. B., & Ritter, B. The relative efficacy of desensitization and modeling approaches for inducing behavioral, affective, and attitudinal change. *Journal of Personality and Social Psychology*, 1969, 13, 173-199.

Barker, Larry L., Cegala, Donald J., Kibler, Robert J., & Washlers, K. J. Hypnosis and the reduction of speech anxiety. Paper presented at the Speech Communication Association convention, New Orleans, December 1970.

Barker, Larry L., Cegala, Donald J., Kibler, Robert J., & Wahlers, Kathy J. Hypnosis and the reduction of speech anxiety. *Central States Speech Journal*, 1972, 23, 28-35.

Barnes, Richard E. Interpersonal communication approaches to reducing speech anxiety. Paper presented at the Central States Speech Association convention, Chicago, 1976.

Barnes, Richard E. Communication anxiety, a psychotherapeutic perspective. Paper presented at the International Communication Association Convention, Berlin, 1977.

Barnes Richard E., & Giffin, Kim. Negative self-image in relation to balance theory. Paper presented at the International Communication Association convention, Montreal, 1973.

Barnet, A. D. Group indoctrination. In S. Fraser (Ed.), *Education and communism in China.* Hong Kong; International Studies Group, 1969, 281-298.

Barrick, James E. A cautionary note on the use of systematic desensitization. *Speech Teacher*, 1971, 20, 280-281.

Barrick, James E., McCroskey, James C., & Ralph, David. The effects of systematic desensitization on speech and test anxiety. Paper presented at the Speech Association of America convention, Chicago, December 1968.

Barrow, John, & Hayashi, Judy. Shyness clinic: A social development program for adolescents and young adults. *Personnel and Guidance Journal*, 1980, 59, 58-61.

Bashore, David N. Relationships among speech anxiety, IQ, and high school achievement. Master's thesis, Illinois State University, 1971.

Bashore, David N., McCroskey, James C., & Andersen, J. F. The relationship between communication apprehension and academic achievement among college students. *Human Communication Research*, 1976, 3, 73-81.

Bassett., Ronald, Behnke, Ralph R. Carlile, Larry W. & Roges, Jimmie. The effects on positive and negative audience responses on the automatic arousal of student speakers. *Southern Speech Communication Journal*, 1973, 38, 255-261.

Bates, Henry D., & Zimmerman, Suandra F. Toward the development of a screening scale for assertive training. *Psychological Reports*, 1971, 28, 99-107.

Baumeister, R. F., Cooper, J., & Skib, B. Interior performance as a selective response to efficacy: Taking a dive to make a point. *Journal of Personality and Social Psychology*, 1979, 37, 424-432.

Beatty, Michael Joseph. A validation study of cognitively experienced communication apprehension scales. Dissertation, Ohio State University, 1976.

Beatty, Michael J., & Beatty, Pamela J. Interpersonal communication anxiety. *Theory into Practice*, 1976, 15, 368-372.

Beatty, Michael J., & Behnke, Ralph R. An assimilation theory perspective of communication apprehension. *Human Communication Research*, 1980, 6, 319-325.

Beatty, Michael J., Behnke, Ralph R., & Henderson, Linda S. An empirical validation of the receiver apprehension test as a measure of trait listening anxiety. *Western Journal of Speech Communication*, 1980, 44, 132-136.

Beatty, Michael J., Behnke, Ralph R., & McCallum, Karen, Situational determinants of communication apprehension. *Communication Monographs*, 1978, 45, 186-191.

Beatty, Michael J., & Payne, Steven K. Receiver apprehension and cognitive complexity. *Western Journal of Speech Communication*, 1981, 45, 363-369.

Beatty, Michael J., & Payne, Steven K. Speech anxiety as a multiplicative function of audience size and social desirability. *Perceptual and Motor Skills*, 1983, 56, 792-794.

Beatty, Michael J., Springhorn, Ron G., & Kurger, Michael W. Toward the development of cognitively experience speech anxiety scales. *Central States Speech Journal*, 1976, 27, 181-186.

Beck, Aaron T. *Cognitive therapy and the emotional disorders.* New York: International Universities Press, 1976.

Becker, Ernest. *Birth and death of meaning.* New York: Free Press, 1971.

Becker, Joseph, & Finkel, Paul. Predictability and anxiety in speech by parents of female schizophrenics. *Journal of Abnormal Psychology,* 1969, 74, 517-523.

Bee John D., & Moore, Linda. The effects of speech course content on the reduction of communication apprehension. Paper presented at the Speech Communication Association convention, Louisville, 1982.

Behnke, Ralph R. Physiological measurement in speech research. *The Speech Journal,* 1970, 7, 26-31.

Behnke, Ralph R. A psychophysiological approach to the study of communication. In Robert Kibler & Larry Barker (Eds.), *Speech communication behavior.* Englewood Cliffs, N.J.: W. Prentice-Hall, 1971.

Behnke, Ralph R. An analysis of psychophysiological research in communication. *Central States Speech Journal,* 1976, 22, 16-20.

Behnke, Ralph R., & Beatty, Michael J. A cognitive-physiological model of speech anxiety. *Communication Monographs,* 1981, 48, 158-163.

Behnke, Ralph R., Beatty, Michael J., & Dabbs, Jr., J. M., Brain temperature and communication anxiety. *MENSA Research Journal,* 1983, 13, 27-29.

Behnke, Ralph R., Beatty, Michael J., & Kitchens, T. James Cognitively, experienced speech anxiety as a predictor of trembling *Western Journal of Speech Communication,* 1978, 42, 270-275.

Behnke, Ralph R., & Carlile, Larry W. Heart rate as an index of speech anxiety. *Speech Monographs,* 1971, 38, 65-69.

Behnke, Ralph R., Carlile, Larry W., & Lamb, Douglas H. A psychophysiological study of state and trait anxiety in public speaking. *Central States Speech Journal,* 1974, 25, 249-253.

Bell, R., & Daly, J. A. Affinity-seeking: Its nature and correlates. Unpublished manuscript, Department of Speech Communication, University of Texas, 1983. (a)

Bell, R., & Daly, J. A. Some communicator correlates of loneliness. Unpublished manuscript, Department of Speech Communication, University of Texas, 1983. (b)

Bem, D. J. An experimental analysis of self-persuasion. *Journal of Experimental Social Psychology,* 1965, 1, 199-218.

Bem, D. J. Self-perception theory. In L. Berkowitz (Ed.), *Advances in experimental social psychology.* (Vol. 6). New York: Academic Press, 1972.

Bem, D. J., & Allen, A. On predicting some of the people some of the time: The search for cross-situational consistencies in behavior. *Psychological Review,* 1974, 81, 506-520.

Bem, D. J., & Funder, D. C. Predicting more of the people more of the time: Assessing the personality of situations. *Psychological Review,* 1978, 85, 485-501.

Bentson, Scott B. Symbolic modeling and the effects of relevant observer-model similarity in the treatment of public-speaking anxiety. Dissertation, Southern Illinois University, 1975.

Berger, Bruce A., Baldwin, H. John, McCroskey, James C., & Richmond, Virginia P. Implementation of a systematic desensitization program and classroom instruction to reduce communication apprehension in pharmacy students. Paper presented at the Speech Communication Association convention, Louisville, 1982.

Berger, Bruce A., Baldwin, H. John, McCroskey, James C., & Richmond, Virginia P. The use of systematic desensitization and classroom instruction to reduce communication apprehension in pharmacy students. *American Journal of Pharmaceutical Education,* 1982, 46, 227-234.

Berger, Bruce A. & McCroskey, James C. Reducing communication apprehension in pharmacy students. *American Journal of Pharmaceutical Education.* 1982, 46, 132-136.

Berger, Charles R. & Calabrese, Richard J. Some explorations in initial interaction and beyond: Toward a developmental theory of interpersonal communication. Human Communication Research, 1975, 1, 99-112.

Berlo, D. K., & Lemert, J. B. A factor analytic study of the dimensions of source credibility. Paper presented at the annual convention of the Speech Association of America, New York, 1961.

Bernard, H. R., & Killworth, P. D. Informant accuracy in social network data II. *Human Communication Research,* 1977, 4 3-18.

Berrien, F. K. A super-ego for cross-cultural research. *International Journal of Psychology,* 1970, 5, 1-9.

Berry, J. W. On cross-cultural comparability. *International Journal of Psychology*, 1969, 4, 119-128.

Biggers, Thompson & Masterson, John L. A reconceptualization of communication apprehension in terms of the emotion-eliciting qualities of communication situations. Paper presented at the Speech Communication Association convention, Louisville, 1982.

Biglan, Anthony, Glaser, Susan R., & Dow, Michael G. Conversational skills training for social anxiety: An evaluation of validity. Paper presented at the Speech Communication Association convention, San Antonio, November 1979.

Birney, Sherman. Effects of verbal feedback on concept specific-anxiety. Dissertation, Colorado State University, 1971.

Bitzer, Lloyd F. The rhetorical situation,. *Philosophy and Rhetoric*, 1968, 1.

Blatt, S. J., Quinlan, D., Cherron, E. S., McDonald, C., & Zuroff, D. Dependency and self-criticism: Psychological dimensions of depression. *Journal of Consulting and Clinical Psychology*, 1982, 113-124.

Bliese, N. W., Fenton, R. J., Benhower, R., & Neff, T. D. Communication inhibition and latency of response: The chattering Syndrome. Paper presented at the International Communication Association Convention, Portland, 1976.

Blom, Bernhard E. Nonspecific determinants of speech anxiety: A methodological study. Dissertation, Pennsylvania State University, 1975.

Blom Bernhard E., & Craighead, Edward W. The effects of situational and instructional demand of indices of speech anxiety. *Journal of Abnormal Psychology*, 1974, 83, 667-674.

Blubaugh, Jon A. The effects of positive and negative feedback on selected variables of speech behavior of normal speaking college students. Dissertation, University of Kansas, 1966.

Blubaugh, Jon A. & May, Wallace R. Measurement of communication anxiety: Toward a more comprehensive conceptualization. Paper presented at the Speech Communication Association convention, Houston, December 1975.

Boak, R. T., & Conklin, R. C. The effect of teacher's levels of interpersonal skills on junior high school students' achievement and anxiety. *American Educational Research Journal*, 1975, 12, 537-549.

Bode, D. L., & Brutten, E. J. A palmar sweat investigation of the effects of audience variation upon stage fright. *Speech Monographs*, 1963, 30, 92-96.

Boman, Thomas Gerhard. An investigation of selected causes and effects of stress in a communicator-audience situation. Dissertation, University of Minnesota, 1966.

Bonner, M. R. Changes in the speech pattern under emotional tension. *American Journal of Psychology*, 1943, 50, 262-273.

Book, Virginia. Some effects of apprehension on writing performance. Paper presented at the Western Speech Communication Association Convention, San Francisco, 1976.

Borin, L. H. The construction and evaluation of a group procedure designed to raise the confidence levels of beginning students of speech. Dissertation, Northwestern University, 1949.

Borkovec, Thomas J. Physiological and cognitive processes in the maintenance and reduction of fear. In G. E. Swarz & D. Shaprio, (Eds.), *Consciousness and self-regulation.* New York: Plenum, 1976.

Borkovec, Thomas D. Fleischmann, D. J., & Caputo, J. A. The measurement of social anxiety in an analogue social situation. *Journal of Consulting and Clinical Psychology*, 1973, 41, 1957-1961.

Borkovec, Thomas D. Wall, Robert L. & Stone, Norman M. False physiological feedback and the maintenance of speech anxiety. *Journal of Abnormal Psychology*, 1974, 83, 164-168.

Bormann, E. G. & Shapiro, G. Perceived confidence as a function of self-image. *Central States Speech Journal*, 1962, 13, 253-256.

Bornstein, M. R., Bellack, A. S. & M. Hersen, Social skills training for unassertive children: A multiple-baseline analysis. *Journal of Applied Behavior Analysis*, 1977, 10, 183-195.

Bossert, George W. The relationship between expectation, belief, and anxiety in a speaking situation. Dissertation, University of Tennessee, 1975.

Boster, Franklin J., Hunter, John E., Meyer, Michael E., & Hale, Jerold L. Expanding the persuasive arguments explanation of the polarity shift: A linear discrepancy model. In D. Nimmo (Ed.), *Communication yearbook 4.* New Brunswick, NJ: Transaction Books, 1980.

Bozik, Mary. An alternative to the treatment of stage fright in the required public speaking course. Paper presented at the Speech Communication Association Convention, Louisville, 1982.

Bradac, James J., & Bell, Mae A. The effects of observer expectations, task ambiguity, and medium of presentation on low- and high-inference judgments of communicative behavior. *Human Communication Research*, 1975, 1, 123-132.

Bradac, James J., Tardy, C. H., & Hosman, L. A. Disclosure styles and a hint at their genesis. *Human Communication Research*, 1980, 6, 228-238.

Bradley, K. A study of self-perceived stage fright: Its relation to previous speaking experience, a course in fundamentals, and group counseling as a remedial approach. Master's thesis, University of Kansas, 1966.

Brady, Robert M., & Ralston, Steven M. the efficacy of modeling in the treatment of speech anxiety. Paper presented at the Speech Communication Association convention, Louisville, 1982.

Braun, P. R., & Reynolds, D. J. a factor analysis of a 100-item fear survey inventory. *Behavior Research and Therapy*, 1969, 7, 399-402.

Breland, Hunter M. Birth order, family configuration, and verbal achievement. Paper presented at the Midwestern Psychological Association Annual Meeting, Chicago, 1973.

Brenders, David. A brief therapy perspective. The Purdue University program. Paper presented at the International Communication Association convention, Boston, 1982.

Briggs, S. R., Cheek, J., & Buss, A. An analysis of the self-monitoring scale. *Journal of Personality and Social Psychology*, 1980, 38, 679-686.

Brislin, R. W., Lonner, W. J., & Thorndike, R. M. *Cross-cultural research methods.* New York: John Wiley, 1973.

Brodt, S. E., & Zimbardo, P. Modifying shyness-related social behavior through symptom misattribution. *Journal of Personality and Social Psychology*, 1981, 437-449.

Brooks, William D., & Platz, Sara M. The effects of speech training upon self-concept as a communicator. *Speech Teacher*, 1968, 17, 44-49.

Brown, J. S. *The motivation of behavior.* New York: McGraw-Hill, 1961.

Brownell, Winifred, & Katula, Richard. Communication apprehension and the speech anxiety peak experience. Paper presented at the Eastern Communication Association convention, Hartford, 1982.

Bruneau, Thomas, Cambra, Ronald E., & Klopf, Donald W. Communication apprenhension: Its incidence in Guam and elsewhere. *Communication*, 1980, 9, 46-52.

Bruskin. What are Americans afraid of? *The Bruskin Report*, No. 53, 1973.

Brutten, E. J. Palmar sweat investigation of disfluency and expectancy adaptation. *Journal of Speech and Hearing Research*, 1963, 6, 40-48.

Buchanan, Edith A., & Stirling-Hanson, Deanna. Free expression through movement. *National Elementary Principal*, 1972, 52, 46-51.

Bugg, Charles A. Systematic desensitization: A technique worth trying. *Personal & Guidance Journal*, 1972, 50, 823-828.

Burgoon, Judee K. Unwillingness to communicate and conflict as predictors of information processing behaviors. Paper presented at the Speech Communication Association convention, Chicago, 1974.

Burgoon, Judee K. Teacher strategies for coping with communication apprehension. Paper presented at the Speech Communication Association Convention, Houston, 1975.

Burgoon, Judee K. Coping with communication anxiety and reticence in the classroom. *Florida Speech Communication Journal*, 1976, 4, 13-21.

Burgoon, Judee K. The unwillingness-to-communicate scale: Development and validation. *Communication Monographs*, 1976, 43, 60-69.

Burgoon, Judee K. Unwillingess to communicate as a predictor of small group discussion behaviors and evaluations. *Central States Speech Journal*, 1977, 28, 122-133.

Burgoon, Judee K. Privacy and communication. In Michael Burgoon (Ed.), *Communication yearbook 6.* Beverly Hills, CA: Sage, 1982.

Burgoon, Judee K., & Burgoon, Michael. Unwillingness to communicate, anomia-alienation, and communication apprehension as predictors of small group communication. *Journal of Psychology*, 1974, 88, 31-38.

Burgoon, Judee K., Hale, Jerold L., & Garrison, S. Scott. Dimensions of communication avoidance and their impact on verbal encoding. Paper presented at the annual convention of the International Communication Association, Minneapolis, 1981.

Burgoon, Judee K., & Koper, Randall J. Communication reticence and relational message behavior. Paper presented at the International Communication Association convention, Dallas, 1983.

Burgoon, Judee K. & Hale, J. L. A research note on the dimensions of communication reticence. *Communication Quarterly*, 1983, *31*, 238-248.

Burnstein, K. R., Frenz, W., Bergeron, J., & Epstein, S. A comparison of skin potential and skin resistence response as measures of emotional responsivity. *Psychophysiology*, 1965, 2, 14-24.

Busch, Robert A. Facilitator's presence and locus of control in the short-term group desensitization of public speaking anxiety. Dissertation, University of Tennessee, 1979.

Bush, Janice D., & Bittner, John R. The effect of the video-tape recorder on levels of speaker anxiety, exhibitionism and reticence. Paper presented at the Speech Communication Association convention, New Orleans, 1970.

Bush, Janice D., Bittner, John R., & Brooks, William D. The effect of video-tape recorder on levels of anxiety, exhibitionism, and reticence. *Speech Teacher*, 1972, 21, 127-130.

Buss, Arnold H. *Self-consciousness and social anxiety.* San Francisco: W. H. Freeman, 1980.

Buss, Arnold H., & Plomin, R. *A temperament theory of personality development.* New York: Wiley-Interscience, 1975.

Buss, Arnold H., Iscoe, I., & Buss, E. H. The development of embarrassment. *Journal of Psychology*, 1979, 103, 227-230.

Buss, D. M., & Craik, K. H. The act frequency analysis of interpersonal dispositions: Aloofness, gregariousness, dominance, and submissiveness. *Journal of Personality*, 1981, 49, 175-192.

Butler, Pamela E. Assertive training: Teaching women not to discriminate against themselves. ERIC ED 082 103.

Cacioppo, J. T., Glass, C. R., & Merluzzi, T. V. Self-statements and self-evaluations: A cognitive response analysis of heterosocial anxiety. *Cognitive Therapy and Research*, 1979, 3, 249-262.

Cahn, Jr., Dudley Dean. An experiment based on a three factor emotion theory of state fright. Dissertation, Wayne State University, 1980.

Cahn, Dudley D. A three-factor emotion theory of stage fright. Paper presented at the annual convention of the International Communication Association, Minneapolis, 1981.

Caldwell, A. Toy, Calhoun, Karen S., Humphreys, Lewis, & Cheney Thomas. Treatment of socially anxious women by a skills training program. *Journal of Behavior Therapy and Experimental Psychiatry*, 1978, 9, 315-320.

Calef, Ruth A., & MacLean, G. Donald. A comparison of reciprocal inhibition and reactive inhibition therapies in the treatment of speech anxiety. *Behavior Therapy*, 1970, 1, 51-58.

Cambra, R., Ishii, S., & Klopf, Donald W. Four studies of Japanese speech characteristics. *Communication*, 1978, 7, 7-25.

Cambra, Ronald, & Klopf, Donald W. The relationship between apprehension about speaking and writing. Paper presented at the HCTE convention, 1979.

Cambra, Ronald, & Klopf, Donald W. Communication apprehension among Korean students: An exploratory investigation. Paper presented at the Eastern Communication Association convention, Philadelphia, 1979.

Cambra, Ronald, & Klopf, Donald W. A further study of communication apprehension among University of Hawaii students. Paper presented at the Communication Association of the Pacific — Hawaii convention, 1979.

Cambra, Ronald, & Klopf, Donald W. Communication apprehension among participants in Hawaii's high school forensics programs. Paper presented at the Communication Association of the Pacific-America conference, 1980.

Cambra, Ronald, Klopf, Donald W., & Oka, Beverly. Communication apprehension and its reduction in Hawaii. Paper presented at the Eastern Communication Association convention, Philadelphia, 1979.

Cambra, Ronald, Oka, Beverly, & Klopf, Donald W. Communication apprehension: Its extent in Hawaii and methods of reduction. Paper presented at the HCTE convention, 1978.

Campbell, D. T. Reforms as experiments. *American Psychologist*, 24, 409-429.

Campbell, J. B., & Hawley, C. W. Study habits and Eysneck's theory of extroversion-introversion. *Journal of Research in Personality*, 1982, 16, 139-146.

Cardot, Joseph J. Communication apprehension as a predictor of proxemic establishment, self-esteem, and dogmatism. Master's thesis, Western Kentucky University, 1980.

Cardot, Joseph, & Dodd, Carley. Communication apprehension as a predictor of proxemic establishment. Paper presented at the annual convention of the Speech Communication Association, San Antonio, 1979.

Carlile, Larry W., & Behnke, Ralph R. A retort to the criticism of "heart rate" as an index of speech anxiety. Speech Monographs, 1973, 40, 160-164.

Carlile, Larry, Behnke, Ralph R., & Kitchens, James T. A psychological pattern of anxiety in public speaking. Communication Quarterly, 1977, 25, 44-46.

Carlson, Robert, & Hollis, Phoebe. Rhetorical sensitivity, assertiveness and communication apprehension: Issues and affects in a basic interpersonal approach. Paper presented at the Speech Communication Association convention, New York City, November 1980.

Carp, E. A. Fear and anxiety in verbal and graphic forms of expression. Paper presented at the 7th International Congress of Psychotherapy, Wisesbaden, 1967.

Casas, Jesus M., A comparison of two mediational self-control techniques for the treatment of speech anxiety. Dissertation, Stanford University, 1976.

Cash, Thomas F., & Janda, Louis H. Evaluation of pertinent sources of volunteer bias in behavior therapy research. Journal of Consulting and Clinical Psychology, 1977, 45, 337-338.

Cassidy, Edward W. The influence of behavior rehearsal techniques on children's communicative behaviors. Dissertation, University of Maryland, 1974.

Cegala, Donald J., Fischbach, Robert M., Sokuvitz, Sydel, Maase, Shirley M., & Smitter, Roger D. A report on the development and validity of the social orientation scale. Paper presented at the Speech Communication Association convention, San Francisco, 1976.

Cegala, Donald J., Savage, Grant T., Bruner, Claire C., & Conrad, Anne B. An elaboration of the meaning of interaction involvement: Toward the development of a theoretical concept. Communication Monographs, 1982, 49, 229-248.

Cha, B. K., Choi, C. S., & Shus, C. W. A study of American's attitudes towards Koreans. Korea Journal, 1976, 16, 28-29.

Char, W. F., Tseng, W.-S., Lum, K.-Y., & Hsu, J. The Chinese. In J. F. McDermott, Jr., W.-S. Teng, & T. Maretzki (Eds.), People and cultures of Hawaii: A psychocultural profile. Honolulu: Universiy of Hawaii Press, 1980.

Cheek, J. M., & Buss, Arnold H. Shyness and sociability. Journal of Personality and Social Psychology, 1981, 41, 330-339.

Cheek, J. M., & Busch, C. M. The influence of shyness on loneliness in a new situation. Personality and Social Psychology Bulletin, 1981, 7, 572-577.

Cheek, J. M., & Buss, Arnold H. Scales of shyness, sociability and self-esteem and correlations among them. Unpublished research, University of Texas, 1979.

Chenweth, Eugene C. The adjustment of college freshmen to the speaking situation. Quarterly Journal of Speech, 1940, 26, 585-588.

Christensen, A., & Arkowitz, H. Preliminary report on practice dating and feedback as treatment for college dating problems. Journal of Counseling Psychology, 1974, 21, 92-95.

Christensen, A., Arkowitz, H., & Anderson, J. Practice dating as treatment for college dating inhibitions. Behavior Research and Therapy, 1975, 13, 321-331.

Christensen, D. The relationship between self-consciousness and interpersonal effectiveness and a new scale to measure individual differences in self-consciousness. Personality and Individual Differences, 1982, 3, 177-188.

Christensen, D., Rosenthal, R. E. Gender and nonverbal decoding skill as determinants of interpersonal expectancy effects. Journal of Personality and Social Psychology, 1982, 42, 75-86.

Clark, A. J., Weiman, L. A., & Paschall, K. A. A preliminary report of an investigation of unwillingness to communicate among physically handicapped persons. Paper presented at the Speech Communication Association convention, Louisville, 1982.

Clark, Frank, Self-administered desensitization. Behavior and Research Therapy, 1973, 11, 335-338.

Clark, J. V., & Arkowitz, H. Social anxiety and self-evaluation of interpersonal performance. Psychological Reports, 1975, 36, 211-221.

Clark, Tony, Identifying the anxious communicator. *Florida Speech Communication Journal*, 1973, 1, 17-20.

Clevenger, Theodore, Jr. An analysis of variance of the relationship of experienced stage fright to selected psychometric inventories. Dissertation, Florida State University, 1958.

Clevenger, Theodore, Jr. The effects of a physical change in the speech situation upon experienced stage fright. *Journal of Communication*, 1959, 9, 131-135.

Clevenger, Theodore, Jr. A synthesis of experimental research in stage fright. *Quarterly Journal of Speech*, 1959, 45, 134-145.

Clevenger, Theodore, Jr., & Phifer, G. What do beginning college speech tests say about stage fright. *Speech Teacher*, 1959, 8, 1-7.

Clevenger, Theordore, Jr., Motely, Michael, & Carlile, Larry W. Changes in heart rate during classroom public speaking. Unpublished research report, University of Texas, 1967.

Cohen, Herman. Teaching reticent students in a required course. *Communication Education*, 1980, 29, 222-228.

Clevenger, Theodore, Jr., & King, T. R. A factor analysis of the visible symptoms of stagefright. *Speech Monographs*, 1961, 28, 245-247.

Cole, C. W., Oetting, E. R., & Dinges, N. G. Effects of verbal interaction conditions on self-concept discrimination and anxiety. *Journal of Counseling Psychology*, 1973, 20, 431-436.

Cole, L. E. A critical evaluation of methods of controlling stage fright in the classroom. Master's thesis, Emerson College, 1964.

Cole, R. Attitudes and needs as expressed by various groups of Oral Communication I students. Master's thesis, Kansas State University, 1959.

Comadena, Mark E. Kinesic correlates of communication apprehension: An analysis of hand movements. Master's thesis, West Virginia University, 1977.

Comadena, Mark E., & Anderson, Peter A., Kinesic correlates of communication apprehension: An analysis of hand movements. Paper presented at the International Communication Association convention, Chicago, 1978.

Comrey, A. L. Scales for measuring compulsion, hostility, neuroticism, and shyness. *Psychological Reports*, 1965, 16, 697-700.

Comrey, A. L. *A first course in factor analysis*. New York: Academic Press, 1973.

Conaway, Roger N. An examination of the relationship among assertiveness, manifest anxiety, and self-esteem. Dissertation, Bowling Green State University, 1978.

Connely, Dwight W. Some effects of general anxiety and situational stress upon lexical diversity, speaking rate, speaking time, and evaluations of a speaker. Dissertation, University of Iowa, 1977.

Conville, Richard L. Linguistic nonimmediacy and communicators' anxiety. *Psychological Reports*, 1974, 35, 1104-1114.

Corey, Robert J. Preliminary bibliography on speech apprehension, communication anxiety, reticence and related speech problems. Paper presented at the Speech Communication Association convention, San Francisco, 1976.

Coles, E. M. *Clinical psychopathology: An introduction*. London: Routledge & Kegan Paul, 1982.

Cotton, J. L., Barson, R. J., & Borkovec, T. D. Caffeine injestion, misattribution therapy, and speech anxiety. *Journal of Research in Personality*, 1980, *14*, 196-206.

Coussoule, Alexandra R., & Andersen, Peter A. The perceptual world of the communication apprehensive: The effect of communication apprehension and interpersonal gaze on interpersonal perception. Paper presented at the annual convention of the Speech Communication Association, San Antonio, 1979.

Cradock, Carroll A. Behavioral prophylaxis: A test of Poser's psychological immunization hypothesis on subjects displaying sub-clinical public speaking anxiety. Dissertation, DePaul University, 1977.

Cradock, Carroll A., Cotler, Sheldon, & Jason, Leonard A. Primary prevention: Immunization of children for speech anxiety. *Cognitive Therapy and Research*, 1978, 2, 389-396.

Crocker, William C., Klopf, Donald W., & Cambra, Ronald E. Communication apprehension and its educational implication: Some initial Australian data. *Australian Journal of Education*, 1978, 23-33, 262-270.

Crocker, William C., Klopf, Donald W., & Cambra, Ronald E. Interpersonal needs of Australian students compared to those of other cultures. *Australian SCAN: Journal of Human Communication*, 1979, 3, 45-60.

Crocker, William C., Klopf, Donald W., & Cambra, Ronald E. An exploratory study of the communication style of Australian college students as compared to other Pacific national groups. *Education News*, in press.

Crowell, L., Katcher, A., & Miyamoto, S. F. Self concept of communication skill and performance in small group discussion. *Speech Monographs*, 1955, 22, 20-27.

Crowne, D. P., & Marlowe, D. *The approval motive: Studies in evaluative dependence.* New York: John Wiley, 1964.

Crozier, W. R. Shyness as a dimension of personality. *British Journal of Social and Clinical Psychology*, 1979, 18, 121-128.

Cunningham, Robert, A study of the relationship between selected student variables and speech anxiety encountered by speakers in a beginning college speech course. Dissertation, Memphis State University, 1976.

Curran, James P. Social skills training and systematic desensitization in reducing dating anxiety. *Behavior Research and Therapy*, 1975, 13, 65-68.

Curran, James P. Skills training as an approach to the treatment of heterosexual-social anxiety: A review. *Psychological Bulletin*, 1977, 84, 140-157.

Curran James P., & Gilbert, Francis S. A test of the relative effectiveness of a systematic desensitization program with date anxious subject. *Behavior Therapy*, 1975, 6, 510-521.

Curran, James P., Gilbert, Francis S., & Little, M. A comparison between behavioral replication training and interpersonal sensitivity training approaches to heterosexual dating anxiety. *Journal of Counseling Psychology*, 1976, 23, 190-196.

Curran, James P. Wallander, J. L., & Fischetti, M. The importance of behavioral and cognitive factors in heterosexual social anxiety. *Journal of Personality*, 1980, *48*, 285-292.

Daft, Richard & Pride, Paul. Preparing for Managerial careers: Communication style and academic performance. Paper presented at the Academy of Management Meetings, Kansas City, 1976.

Diabo, Ikuo, & Sugiyama, Yoshio The effects of manifest anxiety of several aspects of only one talking in dyadic communication. *Japanese Journal of Experimental Social Psychology*, 1974, 14, 1-14.

Daibo, Ikuo, Sugiyama, Yoshio, & Akama, Midori. The process of verbal activity in dyadic communication and manifest anxiety. *Japanese Journal of Experimental Social Psychology*, 1973, 13, 86-98.

Daly, John A. The effects of differential durations of time on interpersonal judgments based on vocal activity. Master's thesis, West Virginia University, 1974.

Daly, John A. Communication apprehension in the classroom: A review. Paper presented at the Speech Communication Association convention, Houston, 1975.

Daly, John A. The development of social-communicative anxiety. Paper presented at the International Communication Association convention, Berlin, 1977.

Daly, John A. The effects of writing apprehension on message encoding. *Journalism Quarterly*, 1977, 54, 566-572.

Daly, John A. The prediction of long-term changes in communication apprehension in the communication classroom. Paper presented at the Speech Communication Association convention, Washington, D.C., 1977.

Daly, John A. Communication apprehension and behavior: Applying the multiple-act criteria. Paper presented at the Speech Communication Association convention, Washington, D.C., 1977.

Daly, John A. Writing apprehension and writing competency. *Journal of Educational Research*, 1978, 72, 10-14.

Daly, John A. Writing apprehension: Correlates and consequences. Paper presented at the annual convention of the National Council of Teachers of English, Kansas City, 1978.

Daly, John A. Writing apprehension: A research review. Paper presented at the annual convention of the College Composition and Communication Association, Denver, 1978.

Daly, John A. Epistemological foundations for communication research: The case of communication apprehension. Paper presented at the Eastern Communication Association convention, Boston, 1978.

Daly, John A. The assessment of social-communicative anxiety via self-reports: A comparison of measures. *Communication Monographs*, 1978, 45, 204-218.

Daly, John A. Communication apprehension and behavior: Applying a multiple act criteria. *Human Communication Research*, 1978, 4, 208-216.

Daly, John A. The talkative-quiet dimension in person perception. Paper presented at the annual conference of the Eastern Communication Association, Philadelphia, 1979.

Daly, John A. Making sense of social-communicative anxiety. Paper presented at the International Communication Association convention, Philadelphia, 1979.

Daly, John A. Talkativeness as a central dimension in person perception. Paper presented at the Eastern Communication Association convention, Philadelphia, 1979.

Daly, John A. Writing apprehension in the classroom: Teacher role expectancies of the apprehensive student. *Research in the Teaching of English*, 1979, 72, 10-14.

Daly, John A. Writing apprehension, self-esteem and personality. *Research in the Teaching of English*, 1983.

Daly, John A. Writing apprehension: A review of theory and research. Paper presented at the American Educational Research Association convention, Boston, 1980.

Daly, John A. Broadening the writing apprehension construct. Paper presented at the Research Conference on Writing, Cinncinati, 1980.

Daly, John A. Recent research on writing apprehension. Paper presented at the annual conference on College Composition and Communication, Dallas, 1981.

Daly, John A. & Buss, A. Audience anxiety. *Communication*, 1983, 12, 27-36.

Daly, John A. & Friedrich, Gustav W. The prediction of long-term changes in communication apprehension in the communication classroom. Paper presented at the Speech Communication Association Convention, Washington, 1977.

Daly, John A. & Friedrich, Gustav The development of communication apprehension: A retrospective analysis of contributory correlates. *Communication Quarterly*, 1981, 29, 243-255.

Daly, John A. & Hailey, J. L. Putting the situation into writing research: Situational parameters of writing apprehension as disposition and state. In R. E. Beach & L. Bidwell (Eds.), *New directions in composition research.* New York: Guilford, 1983.

Daly, John A. & Lawrence, S. Self-focused attention and public speaking anxiety. Unpublished paper, Department of Speech Communication, University of Texas, 1983.

Daly, John A. & McCroskey, James C. Occupational choice and desirability as a function of communication apprehension. *Journal of Counseling Psychology*, 1975, 22, 309-313.

Daly, John A. McCroskey, James C., & Richmond, Virginia P. Judgments of quality, listening, and understanding based upon vocal activity. *Southern Speech Communication Journal*, 1976, 41, 189-197.

Daly, John A., McCroskey, James C., Richmond, Virginia P. The relationships between vocal activity and perception of communicators in small group interaction. *Western Speech Communication*, 1977, 41, 175-187.

Daly, John A. & Miller, Michael D. The empirical development of an instrument to measure writing apprehension. *Research in the Teaching of English*, 1975, 9, 242-249.

Daly, John A. & Shamo, W. Academic decisions as a function of written and oral communication apprehension. Paper presented at the annual conference of the International Communication Association, Berlin, 1977.

Daly, John A. & Street, Richard L., Jr. Measuring social-communicative anxiety: Social desirability and the fakability of responses. *Human Communication Research*, 1980, 6, 185-189.

Daly, John A. & Street, Richard L., Jr. Assessing social-communicative anxiety: Equivalence, social desirability and impression management (faking). Research report, Department of Speech communication, University of Texas, 1978.

Daly, John A. & Suite, Amy. Classroom seating choice and teacher perceptions of students. *Journal of Experimental Education*, 1982, 50, 64-69. Also paper presented at the International Communication Association convention, Philadelphia, 1979.

Daly, John A., Richmond, Virginia P., & Leth, Steven. Social communicative anxiety and the personal selection process: Testing the similarity effect in selection decisions. *Human Communication Research*, 1979, 6, 18-32.

Daly, John A. & Wilson, D. Writing apprehension, self-esteem, and personality. *Research in the Teaching of English*, 1983.

Daly, S. Behavioral correlates of social anxiety. *British Journal of Social and Clinical Psychology*, 1978, 17, 117-120.

Danileson, Gwenn M. Student needs assessment: Testing for verbal reticence. Paper presented at the Western Speech Communication Association convention, Seattle, 1975

Davey, William G. Communication performance and reticence: A diagnostic case study in the elementary classroom. Paper presented at the Western Speech Communication Association convention, Seattle, 1975

Davies, M. F. Correlates of self-consciousness and the 16 Personality Factor Questionnaire. *Journal of Psychology*, 1982, 111, 123-128.

Davis, Gary P., & Scott, Michael D. Communication apprehension, intelligence, and achievement among secondary school students. In B. D. Ruben (Ed.), *Communication yearbook 2*, New Brunswick, NJ: Transaction Books, Kaster's

Davis, M. H. Measuring individual differences in empathy: Evidence for a multidimensional approach. *Journal of Personality and Social Psychology* 1983, 44, 113-126.

Davis, R. A. A further study of the effects of stress on palmar prints. *Journal of Abnormal and Social Psychology*, 1957, 55, 130-35.

Day, H. D., Marshall, D., Hamilton, B., & Christy, J. Some cautionary notes regarding the use of aggregated scores as a measure of behavioral stability. *Journal of Research in Personality*, 1983, 17, 97-109.

DeBoer, Kathryn B., Corey, Robert J., & Metzger, Nancy J. The Pennsylvania State University speech program for reticent students—part I. Paper presented at the Speech Communication Association convention, San Francisco, 1976.

Deffenbacher, Jerry l. Hierarchies for desensitization of test and speech anxieties. *Journal of College Student Personnel*, 1974, 15, 452-54.

Deffenbacher, Jerry L., & Payne, Dennis M. J. Two procedures for relaxation as self-control in the treatment of communication apprehension. *Journal of Counseling Psychology*, 1977, 24, 255-258.

Deffenbacher, Jerry L., & Payne, Dennis M. J. Relationship of apprehension about communication to fear of negative evaluation and assertiveness. *Psychological Reports*, 1978, 42, 370.

Denny, D. A. A study of the causes and effects of microphone fright. Master's thesis, University of Tulsa, 1951.

Dibner, A. Cue-counting: A measure of anxiety in interviews. *Journal of Consulting Psychology*, 1956, 20, 475-478.

Dickens, Milton, Gibson, Francis, & Prall, Caleb, An experimental study of the overt manifestations of stage fright. *Speech Monographs*, 1950, 17, 37-47.

Dickens, Milton & Parker, William R. An experimental study of certain physiological, introspective and rating-scale techniques for the measurement of stage fright. *Speech Monographs*, 1951, 18, 251-259.

Dickey, T., Ahlgren, E. W., & Stephen, C. R. Body temperature monitoring via the tympanic membrane. *Surgery*, 1970, 67, 981-84.

DiLoreto, A. O. *comparative psychotherapy: An experimental analysis. Chicago: Aldine, 1971.*

Dixon, C. Stuttering adaption in relation to assumed level of anxiety. W. Johnson, (Ed.), *Stuttering in children and adults.* Minneapolis: University of Minnesota Press, 1955.

Dodd, Carely H., & Garman, Cecile W. The relationship of world view, communication apprehension and social participation. Paper presented at the Speech Communication Association convention, Anaheim, 1981.

Doi, L. T. The Japanese patterns of communication and the concept of Amae. *Quarterly Journal of Speech*, 1973, 59(2), 180-185.

Domenig, Kathleen M. Comparison of "self as communicator" papers as evidence of improvement in reticent speakers. Master's thesis, Pennsylvania State University 1977.

Douglass, R. L. The relation of feelings of personal security to effective public speaking. Master's thesis, University of Redlands 1947.

Dunathan, Arni T., & Powers, William G. The effect of educational level and communication apprehension upon projected instructional media utilization. Paper presented at the annual convention of the International Communication Association, Philadelphia, 1979.

Duncan, M. H. An experimental study of some of the relationships between voice and personality among students of speech. *Speech Monographs*, 1945, 12, 47-73.

Duran, Robert L., Zakahi, Walter R., & Mumper, Melanie A. Competence vs. style: A dyadic assessment of the relationship among communication performance variables and communication satisfaction. Paper presented at the Eastern Communication Association convention, Hartford, 1982.

Dymacek,l D. A. Effects of number of classroom speeches on anxiety reduction and performance improvement. Master's thesis, Illinois State University 1970.

Eakins, B. W., & Eakins, G. R. *Sex differences in human communication.* Boston: Houghton Mifflin, 1978.

Eberhard, W. *Moral and social values of the Chinese: Collected essays.* Taipei, Taiwan: Ch'eng-wen Publishing Co., 1971.

Eckert, R. G., & Keys, N. Public speaking as a cue to personality adjustment. *Journal of Applied Psychology*, 1940, 24, 144-153.

Ecroyd, Donald H. When you know what you're doing, it's easier: Communication competence and stagefright. Paper presented at the Eastern Communication Association convention, Hartford, 1982.

Eisler, R. M., Hersen, M., & Miller, P. M. Effects of modeling on components of assertive behavior, *Journal of Behavior Therapy and Experimental Psychiatry*, 1973, 4, 1-6.

Eisler, R. M., Hersen, M., Miller, P.M. & Blanchard, E. B. Situational determinants of assertive behaviors. *Journal of Consulting and Clinical Psychology*, 1975, 43, 330-340.

Ekert, R. B., & Keys, N. Public speaking as a cue to personality adjustment. *Journal of Applied Psychology*, 1940, 24, 144-153.

Elder, J., Edelstein, B., & Fremouw, W. Response acquisition and cognitive restructuring in the enhancement of social competence. *Cognitive Therapy and Research*, 1981, 5, 203-210.

Elliott, David H. The use of teacher administered systematic desensitization in reducing speech fright. Dissertation, Stanford University, 1970.

Elliot, Scott, Scott, Michael D., Jensen, Arthur D., & McDonald, Matthew. Perceptions of reticence: A cross-cultural investigation. In Michael Burgoon (Ed.), *Communication yearbook 5.* New Brunswick, NJ: Transaction Books, 1982.

Ellis, A. Outcome of employing three techniques of psychotherapy. *Journal of Clinical Psychology*, 1957, 13, 344-350.

Ellis, A. *Reason and emotion is psychotherapy.* New York: Stuart, 1962.

Ellis, D. G. Trait predictors of relational control. In B. Ruben (Ed.), *Communication yearbook 2.* New Brunswick, NJ: Transaction Books, 1978.

Emery, Richard M. An evaluation of attitudes of fear and confidence in speaking situations at the eighth and eleventh grade levels. Master's thesis, Boston University, 1950.

English, Donna D. Comparison of induced affect and systematic desensitization therapies for reduction of public speaking anxiety. Dissertation, Purdue University, 1978.

Epstein, S. The stability of behavior: I. On predicting most of the people much of the time. *Journal of Personality and Social Psychology*, 1979, 37, 1097-1126.

Ertle, Charles D. A study of the effect of homogeneous grouping on systematic desensitization for the reduction of interpersonal communication apprehension. Dissertation, Michigan State University, 1969.

Falcione, Raymond L., McCroskey, James C., & Daly, John A. Job satisfaction as a function of employees' communication apprehension, self-esteem, and perceptions of their immediate supervisor. In B. D. Ruben, (Ed.), *Communication yearbook 1.* New Brunswick, NJ: Transaction Books.

Farrell, A. D., Mariotto, M. J., Conger, A. J., Curran, J. P., & Wallander, J. L. Self-ratings and judges' ratings of heterosexual social anxiety and skill. *Journal of Clinical and Consulting Psychology*, 1979, 47, 164-175.

Fawcett, S.B., & Miller, L. K. Training public speaking behavior: An experimental analysis and social validation. *Journal of Applied Behavior Analysis*, 1975, 125-135.

Fayer, Joan M., McCroskey, James C., & Richmond, Virginia P. Communication apprehension in Puerto Rico and the United States: A preliminary report. Paper presented at the Speech Communication Association of Puerto Rico convention, San Juan, 1982.

Fedoravicius, Algirdas S. Self-instructional and relaxation variables in the systematic desensitization treatment of speech anxiety. Dissertation, University of Waterloo, Ontario, 1972.

Feldman, M. L., & Berger, C. R. Verbal dogmatism: Its explication, measurement, and relationship to interpersonal attraction. Paper presented at the annual conference of the Speech Communication Association, Chicago, 1974.

Fenigstein, A. Self-consciousness, self-attention, and social interaction. *Journal of Personality and Social Psychology*, 1979, 37, 75-86.

Fenigstein, Allan, Scheier, Michael F., & Buss, Arnold H. Public and private self-consciousness: Assessment and theory. *Journal of Consulting and Clinical Psychology*, 1975, 43, 522-527.

Fenton, Raymond J. Communication inhibition: A multi-dimensional variable affecting interpersonal communication competence. *The Communicator*, 1978, 8, 36-47.

Fenton Raymond J., & Hopf, Tim S. A conceptual explication of three common approaches to communication apprehension. Paper presented at the Western Speech Communication Association convention, Phoenix, 1977.

Fenton, Raymond J., Hopf, Tim S., & Beck, Darrell. The use of EMG biofeedback assisted relaxation training to reduce communication apprehension. Paper presented at the Western Speech Communication Association convention, Seattle, 1975.

Ferguson, G. A. *Statistical analysis in psychology and education.* New York: McGraw-Hill, 1971.

Finger, V. Study of a complex space-time pattern and its relation to stage fright. Master's thesis, Northwestern University, 1932.

Finkel, Norman J. The effects of internal and external feedback on speech fluency. Dissertation, University of Rochester, 1972.

Fisher, Jeanne Y., & Infante, Dominic A. The relation between communication anxiety and human motivation variables. *Central States Speech Journal*, 1973, 24, 246-252.

Forman, S. Hawaii's immigrants from the Philippines. In J. F. McDermott, Jr., W.-S. Teng, & T. Maretzki (Eds.), *People and cultures of Hawaii: A psychocultural profile.* Honolulu: University of Hawaii Press, 1980.

Foss, Karen A. Communication apprehension: Resources for the instructor. *Communication Education*, 1982, 31, 195-203.

Fox, Patricia. A rationale for the use of an automated program of desensitization in the treatment of speech reticence. Master's thesis, Pennsylvania State University, 1971.

Franks, C. M., & Wilson, G. T., Eds. *Annual review of behavior therapy.* (Vol. 1-7). N.Y.: Brunner/ Mazel, 1973-1979.

Franks, Cyril M., & Wilson, G. Terrence Systematic desensitization, flooding, symbolic modeling, cognitive restructuring, and assertion training. In annual review of behavior therapy (Vol. 3). New York: Brunner/Mazel, 1976.

Franks, C. M., Wilson, G. T., Kendall, P. C., & Brownell, K. D. *Annual review of behavior therapy: Theory and practice* (Vol. 8). N. Y.: Guilford, 1982.

Franks, Violet. Relaxation techniques for women. Available from BMA Audio Cassette Publications, Dept. p/200 Park Avenue South, New York, NY 10003, $10.50.

Freedman, Martin J. Treatment 1: Physiological answers for the reduction of communication apprehension. Paper presented at the Eastern Communication Association convention, Ocean City, 1980.

Freimuth, Vicki S. Communication apprehension in the classroom. In Larry Barker (Ed.), *Communication in the classroom.* Englewood Cliffs, NJ: Prentice-Hall, 1982.

Freimuth, Vicki S. Classroom identification of the apprehensive student. Paper presented at the Speech Communication Association convention, Houston, 1975.

Freimuth, Vicki S. The effects of communication apprehension on communication effectiveness. *Human Communication Research*, 1976, 2, 289-295.

Fremouw, William J. The effect of a helper role on speech anxiety. Dissertation, University of Massachusetts, 1975.

Fremouw, William J. *Client manual for integrated behavioral treatment of speech anxiety. Morgantown: West Virginia University. Catalog of Selected Documents in Psychology, February 1977, 7.*

Fremouw, William J., & Harmatz, M. G. A helper model for behavioral treatment of speech anxiety. *Journal of Consulting and Clinical Psychology*, 1975, 43, 652-660.

Fremouw, William J., & Scott, Michael D. Cognitive restructuring: An alternative method of the treatment of communication apprehension. *Communication Education*, 1979, 28, 129-133.

Fremouw, William J., & Zitter, Robert E. A comparison of skills training and cognitive restructuring-relaxation for the treatment of speech anxiety. *Behavior Therapy*, 1978, 9, 248-259.

Friedman, H. S., Prince, L. M., Riggio, R. E., & DiMatteo, M. P. Understanding and assessing nonverbal expressiveness: The affective communication test. *Journal of Personality and Social Psychology*, 1980, 39, 333-351.

Friedman, Paul G. *Shyness and reticence in students.* Washington, DC: National Education Association, 1980.

Friedman, Paul G. Procedures for one-to-one treatment of communication apprehension in college students. Paper presented at the Speech Communication Association convention, Louisville, 1982.

Fry, Dennis. *Homo Loquens: Man, the talking animal.* London: Cambridge University Press, 1977.

Friedman, Steven. A laboratory study of rational-emotive therapy as an attitude-change process. Dissertation, State University of New York–Stony Brook, 1978.

Friedrich, Gustav W. An empirical explication of a concept of self-reported speech anxiety. *Speech Monograph*, 1970, 37, 67-72.

Friedrich, Gustav W. The PRCS as a measure of self-reported speech anxiety: An empirical explication of a construct. Paper presented at the Speech Association of America convention, 1969.

Frye, Paul A. Apprehensiveness and performance in public speaking. Dissertation, University of Denver, 1979.

Gabrenya, W. K., & Arkin, R. M. Self monitoring scale: Factor structure and correlates. *Personality and Social Psychology Bulletin*, 1980, 6, 13-22.

Gadke, Laura. An examination of the relationship among performance, speech anxiety, and grades: Three field experiments. Paper presented at the Western Speech Communication Association convention, San Jose, February 1981.

Galassi, Merna D. Effect of role playing variations on assessing assertive behavior. Dissertation, West Virginia University, 1975.

Galassi, J. P., DeLo, J. S., Galassi, M. D., & Bastien, S. The college self-expression scale: A measure of assertiveness. *Behavior Therapy*, 1974, 5, 165-171.

Garrett, E. R. A study of the effect of three classroom orientations upon stagefright in beginning college speakers. Dissertation, University of Denver, 1954.

Garrison, John P., & Garrison, Karen R. Investigating communication apprehension in the elementary and secondary schools. Paper presented at Nebraska Speech Communication Association Convention, Kearney, 1975.

Garrison, John P., & Garrison, Karen. Communication apprehension and elementary school children. Paper presented at the Nebraska Speech Association convention, Omaha, 1977.

Garrison, John P. & Garrison, Karen R. Measurement of oral communication apprehension among children: A factor in the development of basic speech skills. *Communication Education*, 1979, 28, 119-128.

Garrison, John P., Seiler, W. J., & Boohar, R. K. The effects of talking apprehension on student academic achievement: Three empirical investigations in communication-restricted and traditional laboratory classes in the life sciences. In B. Ruben (Ed.), *Communication yearbook 1.* New Brunswick, NJ: Transaction Books, 1977.

Garrison, Karen R. The effect of cognitive modification on communication apprehension in children. Master's thesis, University of Nebraska, 1978.

Garrison, Karen R. Analyzing the development, treatment, and effects of communication apprehension. Paper presented at the International Communication Association convention, Philadelphia, 1979.

Garrison, Karen R., & Brown, Robert D. The effects of cognitive modification and informed teachers on communication apprehension in children. Paper presented at the American Educational Research Association convention, San Francisco, April 1979.

Garrison, Karen R., & Garrison, John P. Measurement of talking apprehension in the elementary schools. Paper presented at the annual convention of the International Communication Association, Berlin, 1977.

Garrison, Karen R., & Garrison, John P. Elementary teachers' perception of communication apprehension among their students: A research note. Paper presented at the International Communication Association convention, Philadelphia, 1979.

Garvin, H. Communication apprehension as a predictor of child abuse and neglect. Unpublished paper, West Virginia University, 1979. (Available from J.C. McCroskey)

Gatchel, Robert J., Hatch, John P., Watson, Paul J., Smith, Dan, & Gaas, Elizabeth. Comparative effectiveness of voluntary heart rate control and muscular relaxation as active coping skills for reducing speech anxiety. *Journal of Consulting and Clinical Psychology*, 1977, 45, 1093-1100.

Gatchel, Robert J., & Proctor, Janet D. Effectiveness of voluntary heart rate control in reducing speech anxiety. *Journal of Consulting and Clinical Psychology*, 1976, 44, 381-389.

Gatchel, Robert J., Hatch, John P., Maynard, Aino, Turns, Rhonad, and Taunton-Blackwood, A. Comparison of heart rate biofeedback, false biofeedback, and systematic desensitization in reducing speech anxiety: Short- and Long-term effectiveness. *Journal of Consulting and Clinical Psychology*, 1979, 47, 620-622.

Geen, Russell G. Effects of anticipation of positive and negative outcomes on audience anxiety. *Journal of Consulting and Clinical Psychology*, 1977, 45, 715-716.

Geer, J. H. Effect of fear arousal upon task performance and verbal behavior. *Journal of Abnormal Psychology*, 1966, 71, 119-123.

Germer William A. Effectiveness of cognitive modification, desensitization, and rational-emotive therapy in the treatment of speech anxiety. Dissertation, University of Texas — Austin, 1975.

Gibson, F. P. An experimental study of the measurement of auditory manifestations of stage fright by means of rating scale and film sound track techniques. *Speech Monographs*, 1955, 22, 144.

Giesen, J. Martin, & McGlynn, Dudley F. Skin conductance and heart-rate responsivity to public speaking imagery among students with high and low self-reported fear: A comparative analysis of response definition. *Journal of Clinical Psychology*, 1977, 33, 68-76.

Giffin, Kim. Interpersonal trust and speech fright: A preliminary description of a research project. *Research Monograph FR/30.0.* Lawrence: Communication Research Center, University of Kansas, 1966.

Giffin, Kim Recent research on speech anxiety. *Research Monograph P/26.* Lawrence: Communication Research Center, University of Kansas, 1967.

Giffin, Kim. Testing and counseling for speech anxiety. *Speech and Drama Service Center Bulletin of the University of Kansas*, 1967, 11, 1-22.

Giffin, Kim. A study of the relationships among four variables: Speech anxiety, self-concept, social alienation, and trust of others. *Research Report No. 24.* Lawrence: Communication Research Center, University of Kansas, 1970.

Giffin, Kim. A theory of speech anxiety in interpersonal communication. Paper presented at the National Society for the Study of Communications convention, New York, April 1968.

Giffin, Kim, & Adams, R. L. The helping relationship for speech anxiety counseling. *Research Monograph P/20.* Lawrence: Communication Research Center, University of Kansas, 1967.

Giffin, Kim, & Bradley, K. Group counseling for speech anxiety: An approach and a rationale. *Journal of Communication*, 1969, 19, 22-29.

Giffin, Kim, & Bradley, Kendall. *An exploratory study of group counseling for speech anxiety.* Research Monograph 12. Lawrence: Communication Research Center, University of Kansas, 1967.

Giffin, Kim, & Bradley, Kendall. An exploratory study of groups counseling for speech anxiety. *Journal of Clinical Psychology*, 1969, 25, 98-101.

Giffin, Kim, & Bradley, Kendall. Group counseling for speech anxiety: An approach and a rationale, *Journal of Communication*, 1969, 19, 22-29.

Giffin, Kim, & Friedrich, Gustav. *The development of a baseline for studies of speech anxiety,* Research Report 20. Lawrence: Communication Research Center, University of Kansas, 1968.

Giffin, Kim, and Gilham, S. M. Relationship between speech anxiety and motivation. *Speech Monographs,* 1971, 38, 70-73.

Giffin, Kim, & Groginsky, Barbara. A study of the relationship between social alienation and speech anxiety. Lawrence: Communication Research Center Report No. 31, University of Kansas, 1970.

Giffin, Kim, & Heider, M. The relationship between speech anxiety and the suppression of communication in childhood. *Psychiatric Quarterly* (Supplement), 1967, 2, 311-316.

Giffin, Kim, & Heider, M. An experimental program of instruction in the fundamentals of speech for students with a high degree of speech anxiety. *Research Report No. 35.* Lawrence: Communication Research Center, University of Kansas, 1970.

Gifford, R. Projected interpersonal distance and orientation choices: personality, sex, and social situation. *Social Psychology,* 1982, 45, 145-152.

Gilham. S. M. A correlational study of speaker self-confidence and motivation. Master's thesis, University of Kansas, 1968.

Gilkinson, Howard. Indexes of change in attitudes and behaviors among students enrolled in general speech courses. *Speech Monographs,* 1941, 8, 23-33.

Gilkinson, Howard. Social fears as reported by students in college speech classes. *Speech Monographs,* 1942, 9, 141-160.

Gilkinson, Howard. A questionnaire study of the causes of social fears among college speech students. *speech Monographs,* 1943, 10, 74-83.

Gilkinson, Howard, & Knower, Franklin Individual differences among students of speech as revealed by psychological tests. *Quarterly Journal of Speech,* 1940, 26, 243-255.

Gilkinson, Howard, & Knower, Franklin. A study of standardized personality tests and skills in speech. *Journal of Educational Psychology,* 1941, 32, 161-75.

Girodo, Michael *Shy?* New York: Pocket Books, 1978.

Glaser, Susan R. The development and evaluation of a course in reticence management. Paper presented at the Western Speech Communication Association convention, Los Angeles, February 1979.

Glaser, Susan R. Oral communication apprehension and avoidance: The current status of treatment research. *Communication Education,* 1981, 30, 321-341.

Glaser, Susan R. Treating oral communication apprehension and avoidance: Current research and future direction. Paper presented at the Speech Communication Association convention, Anaheim, 1981.

Glaser, Susan R., & Biglan, Anthony. Increase your confidence and skill in interpersonal situations. Unpublished manuscript, University of Oregon, 1978.

Glaser, Susan R., & Dow, Michael P. Managing communication apprehension: The design and evaluation of classroom treatment procedures. Paper presented at the Speech Communication Association convention, Anaheim, 1981.

Glass, C., Gottman, J., & Shmurak, S. Response acquisition and cognitive self statement modification approaches to dating skill training. *Journal of Counseling Psychology,* 1976, 23, 520-526.

Glass, C. R., Merluzzi, T. V., Bierer, J. L., & Larsen, K. H. Cognitive assessment of social anxiety: Development and validation of a self-statement questionnaire. *Cognitive Therapy and Research,* 1982, 6, 37-56.

Glogower, Frederic D., Fremouw, William J., & McCroskey, James C. A component analysis of cognitive restructuring. *Cognitive Therapy and Research,* 1978, 2, 209-223.

Goffman, E. *the presentation of self in everyday life.* Garden City, NY: Doubleday, 1959.

Goldberg, Joan Ratchel. A painfully shy problem comes under scrutiny. *USA Today,* Monday, March 7, 1982, 5D.

Goldfried, M. R. The use of relaxation and cognitive relabeling as copying skills. In R. B. Stuart (Ed.), *Behavioral self-management.* N.Y.: Brunner/Mazel, 1977.

Goldfried, M. R., & Goldfried, A. P. Importance of hierarchy content in the self-control of anxiety. *Journal of Consulting and Clinical Psychology,* 1977, 45, 124-134.

Goldfried, M. R., & Trier, C. S. Effectiveness of relaxation as an active coping skill. *Journal of Abnormal Psychology*, 1974, 83, 348-355.

Goldman, R. Peking University. In S. Fraser (Ed.), *Education and communism in China.* Hong Kong: International Studies Group, 1969.

Golis, A. An exploratory study of perceived values among Filipinos in Hawaii. *Speech Education*, 1979, 7, 116-122.

Gross, Blaine. The implementation of systematic desensitization in a basic course in college. Paper presented at the Central States Speech Association convention, March 1972.

Goss, Blaine, Thompson, Millie, & Olds, Stuart. Behavioral support for systematic desensitization for communication apprehension. *Human Communication Research*, 1978, 4, 158-163.

Gottschalk, Louis A., & Frank, Edward C. Estimating the magnitude anxiety from speech. *Behavior Science*, 1967, 12, 289-295.

Grande, Joseph P. The substitution of alpha-feedback for relaxation in the systematic treatment of public speaking anxiety. Dissertation, Arizona State University, 1976.

Grande, Lois H. A comparison of rational-emotive therapy, attention-placebo and no-treatment groups in the reduction of interpersonal anxiety. Dissertation, Arizona State University, 1975.

Greenblatt, Lynda, Freimuth, Vicki S., & Hasenauer, James H. Psychological sex type and androgyny in the study of communication variables: Self-disclosure and communication apprehension. *Human Communication Research*, 1980, 6, 117-129.

Greene, John O., & Sparks, Glen G. Towards a reconceptualization of communication apprehension: A cognitive approach. Paper presented at the International Communication Association convention, Boston, 1982.

Greene, John O., & Sparks, Glen G. Cognitive structures, cognitive process, and the experience of communication apprehension. Paper presented at the International Communication Association convention, Dallas, 1983.

Greene, John O., & Sparks, Glenn G. The role of outcome expectations in the experience of a state of communication apprehension. *Communication Quarterly*, 1983, 31, 212-219.

Greene, John O., & Sparks, Glenn G. Explication and test of a cognitive model of communication apprehension. *Human Communication Research*, 1983, 9, 349-366.

Greenleaf, Floyd. An experimental study of social speech fright. Master's thesis, University of Iowa, 1947.

Greenleaf, F. I. An exploratory study of stage fright. *Quarterly Journal of Speech*, 1952, 38, 326-330.

Greenstreet, Robert, & Hoover, Debra L. Cognitive modification in the small college. Paper presented at the Speech Communication Association convention, Louisville, 1982.

Grossberg, J. M. Regressive Behavior Present in a case of speech phobia ("stage fright"). *Journal of Speech and Hearing Disorders*, 1965, 30, 285-288

Gruner, C. A further note on speech fright. *Speech Teacher* 1964, 13, 223-224.

Grutzeck, Lynne F. A search for invariant characteristics of reticent elementary school children. Master's thesis, Pennsylvania State University, 1970.

Gurman, Alan S. Treatment of a case of public-speaking anxiety by invivo desensitization and cue-controlled relaxation. *Journal of Behavior Therapy and Experimental Psychiatry*, 1973, 4, 51-54.

Gustainis, J. Justin & Albone, Kenneth. the effect of communication apprehension on human bargaining behavior. Paper presented at the Eastern Communication Association convention, Pittsburgh, 1981.

Gwin, Standford, & Downey, Jennifer. The effects of communication skills training on high risk college students. Paper presented at the International Commission Association convention, Acapulco, 1980.

Gynther, R. A. The effects of anxiety and of situational stress on communication efficiency. *Journal of Abnormal and Social Psychology*, 1957, 54, 274-276.

Hain, J. D., Butcher, H. G., & Stevenson, I. Systematic desensitization therapy: An analysis of results in twenty-seven patients. *British Journal of Psychiatry*, 1966, 112, 295-307.

Hall, Adele C. Communication apprehension as a state construct: The foreign college student in the U.S. Paper presented at the Western Speech Communication Association convention, San Jose, February 1981.

Hamilton, Paul R. The effect of risk proneness on small group interaction, communication apprehension, and self-disclosure. Master's thesis, Illinois State University, 1972.

Hamilton, Peter R. An experimental investigation of the relation between internal-external locus of control of reinforcement and the systematic desensitization of communication anxiety. Paper presented at the Central States Speech Communication Association convention, Chicago, 1976.

Hamilton, Peter R. Analyzing the development, treatment, and effects of communication apprehension: A self-effiacy approach. Paper presented at the International Communication Association convention, Philadelphia, 1979.

Hamilton, Peter K., & Taylor, Stephen A. An analysis of alternative procedures in identifying and analyzing the use of systematic desensitization. Paper presented at the Central States Speech Association convention, Milwaukee, April 1974.

Hamilton, Scott B., & Bornstein, Philip H. Increasing the accuracy of self-recording in speech-anxious undergraduates through the use of self-monitoring training and reliability enhancement procedures. Journal of Consulting & Clinical Psychology, 1977, 45, 1076-1085.

Hamilton, William W. A review of experimental studies on stage fright. Pennsylvania Speech Annual, 1960, 17, 41-48.

Hansford, B. C., & Hattie, J. A. Communication apprehension: An assessment of Australian and United States data. Unpublished manuscript, University of New England, Australia, 1979.

Harper, R. G., Wiens, A. N., & Matarazzo, J. D. Nonverbal communication. New York: John Wiley, 1978.

Harris, Karen R. The sustained effects of cognitive modification and informed peachers on children's communication apprehension. Communication Quarterly, 1980, 28, 47-55.

Hart, Roderick, & Burks, Don M. Rhetorical sensitivity and social interaction. Speech Monographs, 1972, 39, 2.

Hatvany, N., & Zimbardo, P. G. Shyness, arousal, and memory: The path from discomfort to distraction to recall deficits. Unpublished manuscript, Stanford University, 1977.

Hayes, D., & Metzger, L. Interpersonal judgments based upon talkativeness: Fact or artifact. Sociometry, 1972, 35, 538-561.

Hayes, Daniel T. communication apprehension among JWCC students: Comparison with national norms for four-year college and university students. Quincy, IL: John Wood Community College, 1977.

Hayes, Dorsha. the archetypal nature of stage fright. Art Psychotherapy, 1975, 2, 279-281.

Hays, Victor, & Waddell, Kathleen. Extinguishing ineffective communication behavior: An innovative video-tape-feedback procedure. Behavioral Engineering, 1976, 3, 80.

Heald, Gary R. A comparison of systematic desensitization and conditioned relaxation in reducing speech anxiety. Paper presented at the International Communication Association convention, Portland, 1976.

Hedquist, Francis J., & Weinhold, Barry K. Behavioral group counseling with socially anxious and unassertive college students. Journal of Counseling Psychology, 1970, 17, 237-242.

Heemer, Arthur, Knutson, Tom, & Lashbrook, William B. The effect of levels of communication apprehension on perceptions of conflict. Paper presented at the Western Speech Communication Association convention, San Francisco, 1976.

Hegstrom, Tim. Speech anxiety and size of audience. Paper presented at the Central States Speech Association convention, Chicago, April 1978.

Heider, M. L. An investigation of the relationship between speech anxiety in adults and their indication of parental communication suppression during childhood. Master's thesis, University of Kansas, 1968.

Heinemann, W. The assessment of private and public self-consciousness: A German replication. European Journal of Social Psychology, 1979, 9, 331-337.

Hemme, Robert W., & Boor, Myron. Role of expectancy set in the systematic desensitization of speech anxiety: An extension of prior research. Journal of Clinical Psychology, 1976, 32, 400-404.

Henning, James H. A study of stage fright through the comparison of student reactions and instructor observations during the speech situation. Master's thesis, Northwestern University, 1935.

Henrickson, E. H. A study of stage fright and the judgment of speaking time. *Journal of Applied Psychology*, 1948, 32, 521-535.

Henrickson, E. H. Some effects of stage fright on a course in speech. *Quarterly Journal of Speech*, 1943, 29, 490-491.

Hensley, Wayne E. The inter-relationship between self-esteem and communication anxiety. Paper presented at the Conference of Basic Course Directors of Central States Universities, Ames, Iowa, April 1977.

Hensley, Wayne E., & Batty, P. The measurement of communication anxiety among students in public speaking courses. *Indiana Speech Journal*, 1974, 7-10.

Herriot, S. H. The effects of vicarious exposure to systematic desensitization on public speaking anxiety. Paper presented at the Speech Communication Association convention, New York, 1973.

Hersen, M., Eisler, R. M., Miller, P. M., Johnson, M. B., & Pinkston, S. G. Effects of practice, instructions, and modeling on components of assertive behavior. *Behaviour Research and Therapy*, 1973, 11, 443-451.

Heston, Judee K. Unwillingness to communicate and conflict as predictors of information processing behavior. Dissertation, West Virginia University, 1974.

Heston, Judee K., & Andersen, Peter, Anomie-alienation and restrained communication among high school students. Paper presented at the Western Speech Association convention, Honolulu, 1972.

Heston, Judee K., & Burgoon, Michael. Unwillingness to communicate, anomie alienation, and communication apprehension as predictors of small group communication. Paper presented at the Speech Communication Association convention, New York, 1973.

Heston, Judee K., and Paterline, E. J. Unwillingness to communicate: Explication and scale development. Paper presented at the International Communication Association convention, New Orleans, 1974.

Hewes, D., & Haight, L. The cross-situational consistency of communicative behaviors: A preliminary investigation. *Communication Research*, 1979, 6, 352-366.

Hewes, D., & Haight, L. Multiple act criteria in the validation of communication traits: What do we gain and what do we lose? *Human Communication Research*, 1980, 6, 352-366.

Hewgill, M. Typologies of anxiety responses. Paper presented at the Speech Association of America, New York City, December 1965.

Hillenberg, J. B., & Collins, F. L., Jr. A procedural analysis and review of relaxation training research. *Behaviour Research and Therapy*, 1982, 20, 251-260.

Hobbs, Tom T., & Radka, Jerome E. Modification of verbal productivity in shy adolescents during a short-term camping program. *Psychological Reports*, 1976, 39, 735-739.

Hoffman, Jan, & Sprague, Jo. A survey of reticence and communication apprehension treatment programs at U.S. colleges and universities. *Communication Education*, 1982, 31, 187.

Hoffman, Robert W. The relative effectiveness of three types of group assertive training. Dissertation, University of Texas — Austin, 1974.

Hogan, Donna. Breaking the silence barrier. *Balance Sheet*, 1978, 59, 163, 184.

Holtzman, Paul D. An experimental study of some relationships among several indices of stage fright and personality. Dissertation, University of Southern California, 1950.

Hopf, Theorodre S. Reticence and the oral interpretation teacher. *Speech Teacher*, 1970, 19, 268-271.

Horenstein, David, & Gilbert, Shirley J. Anxiety likeability, and avoidance as responses t self-disclosing communication. *Small Group Behavior*, 1976, 7, 423-431.

Horne, Arthur M., & Dougherty, A. Michael. The effects of desensitization, insight, and verbal reinforcement techniques on high and low anxious subjects with specific speech anxiety. *Catalogue of Selected Documents in Psychology*, 1974, 4, 82.

Houlihan, Keven A. The treatment of public speaking anxiety by verbal learning therapy. Dissertation, Northwestern University, 1970.

Hunter, A. D. A comparison of introverted and extroverted high school speakers. *Speech Monographs*, 1935, 2, 504-518.

Huntley, Jackson R. An investigation of the relationships between personality and types of instructor criticism in the beginning speech-communication course. Dissertation, Michigan State University, 1969.

Hurt, H. Thomas, Joseph, K., & Cook, C. D. Scales for the measurement of innovativeness. *Human Communication Research*, 1977, 4, 58-65.

Hurt, H. Thomas, & Cook, John A. The impact of communication-handicapped students on high-school teachers' expectancies, interaction anxiety, and interpersonal perceptions in regular education classes. *Communication Quarterly*, 1979, 27, 38-46. Also a paper presented at the International Communication Association convention, Philadelphia, 1979.

Hurt, H. Thomas, & Joseph, Katherine. The impact of communication apprehension in the process of social change. Paper presented at the Eastern Communication Association convention, New York, 1975.

Hurt, H. Thomas, & Preiss, Raymond. Silence isn't necessarily golden: Communication apprehension, desired social choice, and academic success among middle-school students. *Human Communication Research*, 1978, 4, 315-328.

Hurt, H. Thomas, Preiss, R., & Davis, B. The effects of communication apprehension of middle school children on sociometric choice, affective, and cognitive learning. Paper presented at the International Communication Association, conference, Portland, 1976.

Hurt, H. Thomas, Scott, Michael D., & McCroskey, James C. *Communication in the classroom*, Reading, Ma: Addison-Wesley, 1978.

Hurt, H. Thomas, & Wheeless, Lawrence R. Overview: Instructional strategies as communication systems. In D. Nimmo (ed.), *Communication yearbook 3*. New Brunswick, NJ: Transaction Books, 1979.

Hwang, J. C. Intercultural communication problems in cross-cultural research. In D. S. Hoopes (ed.), *Readings in intercultural communication, II*. Pittsburgh: Regional Council for International Education, 1973.

Hyde, Michael J. The experience of anxiety: A phenomenological investigation. *Quarterly Journal of Speech*, 1980, 66, 140-154.

Hyman, E. T., & Gale, E. N. Galvanic skin response and reported anxiety during systematic desensitization. *Journal of Consulting and Clinical Psychology*, 1973, 15, 108-114.

Ickes, William K. A classical conditioning model for reticence. *Western Speech*, 1971, 35, 48-55.

Illig, David. Treatment of speech anxiety through the use of a self-administered modified systematic desensitization program. Master's thesis, Pennsylvania State University, 1974.

Infante, Dominic A., & Fisher, Jeanne J. Anticipated credibility and message strategy intentions as predictors of trait and state speech anxiety. *Central States Speech Journal*, 1978, 29, 1-10.

Infante, Dominic A., & Rancer, A. S. A conceptualization and measure of argumentativeness. *Journal of Personality Assessment*, 1982, 46, 72-80.

Innes, John M. & Young, Roger F. The effect on presence of an audience, evaluation apprehension and objective self-awareness on learning. *Journal of Experimental Social Psychology*, 1975, 11, 35-42.

Ishii, Satoshi, Cambra, Ronald E., & Klopf, Donald H. Communication anxiety: A comparison of Japanese and American college students. *Psychological Reports*, 1980, 46, 1194.

Ishii, Satoshi, Cambra, Ronald E. & Klopf, Donald. Communication apprehension of Japanese and Americans in three speaking situations. Paper presented at the International Communication Association convention, Chicago, April 1978.

Ishii, Satoshi, Cambra, Ronald E., & Klopf, Donald. The fear of speaking and the fear of writing among Japanese college students. *Speech Education*, 1979, 7-1, 55-59.

Ishii, Satoshi, Cambra, Ronald E. & Klopf, Donald. Oral and written apprehension: Japan compared to the U.S.A. Japanese Association of Current English, 1979.

Ishii, Satoshi, & Klopf, Donald W. Increasing instructional effectiveness: Reducing communication apprehension. *Otsuma Review*, 1981, 14, 61-80.

Iverson, N. E. A descriptive study of some personality relationships underlying a range of speaker confidence as determined by the thematic apperception test. Dissertation, University of Denver, 1952.

Jablin, Frederic M. Cultivating imagination: factors that enhance and inhibit creativity in brainstorming groups. *Human Communication Research*, 1981, 7, 245-258.

Jablin, Frederic M., Seibold, David R., & Sorenson, Ritch L. Potential inhibitory effects of group participation on brainstorming performance. *Central States Speech Journal*, 1977, 28, 113-121.

Jablin, Frederic M., Sorenson, R., & Seibold, D. Interpersonal perception and group brainstorming performance. *Communication Quarterly*, 1978, 26, 36-44.

Jablin, Frederic & Sussman, L. Correlates of individual productivity in real brainstorming groups. Paper presented at the annual conference of the Speech Communication Association, San Francisco, 1976.

Jablin, Frederic M. & Sussman, Lyle. An exploration of communication and productivity in real brainstorming groups. *Human Communication Research*, 1978, 4, 329-337.

Jaccard, J. Predicting social behavior from personality. *Journal of Research in Personality*, 1974, 7, 358-367.

Jaccard, J., & Daly, John A. Personality traits and multiple-act criteria. *Human Communication Research*, 1980, 6, 367-377.

Jackson, J. M., & Latané, B. All alone in front of all those people: Stage fright as a function of number and type of co-performers and audience. *Journal of Personality and Social Psychology*, 1981, 40, 73-85.

Jacobson, E. *Progressive relaxation*. Chicago: University of Chicago Press, 1938.

Jaremko, Matt E. The use of stress inoculation training in the reduction of public speaking anxiety. *Journal of Clinical Psychology*, 1980, 36, 735-738.

Jaremko, Matt E., Hadfield, R., & Walker, W. E. Contribution of an educational phase to stress inoculation of speech anxiety. *Perceptual and Motor Skills*, 1980, 50, 495-501.

Jaremko, Matt E., & Wenrich, W. W. A prophylactic usage of systematic desensitization. *Journal of Behavior Therapy & Experimental Psychiatry*, 1973, 4, 103-106.

Jarmon, David G. Differential effectiveness of rational-emotive therapy, bibliotherapy, and attention-placebo in the treatment of speech anxiety. Dissertation, Southern Illinois University, 1973.

Jeger, Abraham M., & Goldried, Marvin R. A comparison of situation tests of speech anxiety. *Behavior Therapy*, 1976, 7, 252-255.

Jenkins, Vivian Y. The Montana State University reticent program. Paper presented at the Speech Communication Association convention, Louisville, 1982.

Jensen, Arthur D. The relationship among communication traits, communication behaviors and person perception variables. Master's thesis, West Virginia University, 1978.

Jensen, Arthur D. & Tsou, Benny T. Community size, social class, family decision-making patterns and the development of communication apprehension. Paper presented at the Eastern Communication Association convention, Pittsburgh, 1981.

Jensen, Jon Keith. An empirical investigation of the effects of speech anxiety on the perception of audience feedback. Dissertation, University of Iowa, 1973.

Jensen, Keith. The effects of speech anxiety on the perception of audience feedback. Paper presented at the Speech Communication Association convention, Houston, 1975.

Jensen, Keith. Self-reported speech anxiety and selected demographic variables. *Central States Speech Journal*, 1976, 27, 102-108.

Johnson, Carl. *Speech reticence: Sounds and silence*. Fort Collins: Shields, 1973.

Johnson, Tom, Tyler, Vernon, Thompson, Richard, & Jones, Elvet. Systematic desensitization and assertive training in the treatment of speech anxiety in middle-school students. *Psychology in the Schools*, 1971, 8, 263-267.

Jones, M. M. The relationships of certain personality traits to stage fright. Master's thesis, Stanford University, 1947.

Jones, W. H., Freemon, J. E., & Goswick, R. A. The persistence of loneliness: Self and other determinants. *Journal of Personality*, 1981, 49, 27-48.

Jones, W. H., & Russell, D. W. The social reticence scale: A measure of shyness. *Journal of Personality Assessment*, 1982, 46, 629-631.

Jordan, William J., & Powers, William G. Verbal behavior as a function of apprehension and social context. *Human Communication Research*, 1978, 4, 294-300.

Kandel, Henry J., Ayllon, Teodoro, & Rosenbaum, Michael S. Flooding or systematic exposure in the treatment of extreme social withdrawal in children. *Journal of Behavior Therapy & Experimental Psychiatry* 1977, 8, 75-81.

Kanfer, F. H., & Phillips, J. S. *Learning foundations of behavior therapy*. New York: John Wiley, 1970.

Kang, Kyung-What. The meaning of reticence: A cross-cultural study. Paper presented at the Speech Communication Association convention, New York City, November 1980.

Kanter, Norman J. & Goldried, Marvin R. Relative effectiveness of rational restructuring and self-control desensitization in the reduction of interpersonal anxiety. *Behavior Therapy*, 1979, 10, 472-490.

Karst, Thomas O., & Most, Robert. A comparison of stress measures in an experimental analogue of public speaking. *Journal of Consulting & Clinical Psychology*, 1973, 41, 342-348.

Karst, Thomas O., Trexler, Larry D. Initial study using fixed role and rational emotive therapy in treating public speaking anxiety. *Journal of Consulting and Clinical Psychology*, 1970, 34, 360-366.

Karst, Thomas O., & Trexler, Larry. Rational emotive therapy, placebo, and no treatment effects on public anxiety. *Journal of Abnormal Psychology*, 1972, 70, 60-67.

Kasl, S. V., & Mahl, G. F. The relationship of disturbances and hesitations in spontaneous speech to anxiety. *journal of Applied Behavioral Analysis*, 1965, 1, 425-433.

Katz, Alan Marvin. The rationale, nature, and evaluation of a group-centered approach to the treatment of speech anxiety. Dissertation University of Illinois at Urbana-Champaign, 1976.

Kazdin, Alan E. Effects of covert modeling and model reinforcement on assertive behavior. *Journal of Abnormal Psychology*, 1974, 8, 240-252.

Kazdin, Alan E., & Wilcoxon, Linda A. Systematic desensitization and nonspecific treatment effects: A methodological evaluation. *Psychological Bulletin*, 1976, 83, 729-758.

Kearney, Patricia, & McCroskey, James C. Relationships among teacher communication style, trait and state communication apprehension and teacher effectiveness. In Dan Nimmo (Ed.), *Communication yearbook 4*. New Brunswick, NJ: Transaction Books, 1980. Also a paper presented at the International Communication convention, Acapulco, 1980.

Kelly, D., Brown, C. C., & Shaffer, J. W. A comparison of physiological and psychological measurements of anxious patients and normal controls. *Psychophysiology*, 1970, 6, 429-441.

Kelly, J. A. *Social-skills training: A practical guide for interventions*. New York: Springer, 1982.

Kelly, J. A., Furman, W., Phillips, J., Hathorn, S., & Wilson, T. Teaching conversational skills to retarded adolescents. *Child Behavior Therapy*, 1979, 1, 85-97.

Kelly, Lynn. "Pennsylvania State University's program in reticence: An alternative to assessment. Paper presented at the Speech Communication Association convention, Anaheim, 1981.

Kelly, Lynn. Treating reticent students: The Pennsylvania State University program. Paper presented at the International Communication Association convention, Boston, 1982.

Kelly, Lynn. A rose by any other name is still a rose: A comparative analysis of reticence, communication apprehension, unwillingness to communicate, and shyness. *Human Communication Research*, 1982, 8, 99-113.

Kelly, Lynn. Observers' comparisons of the interpersonal communication skills of reticent and non-reticent students. Paper presented at the Speech Communication Association convention, Louisville, 1982.

Kelly, Lynn, & Copeland, Gary. A comparison of the availability of adequacy of relationships of reticent and non-reticent persons. Paper presented at the International Communication Association Convention, Dallas, 1983.

Kelly, Lynn, & Phillips, Gerald. A program to reduce shyness: Antithesis to the medical model. Paper presented at the International Communication Association convention, Acapulco, 1980.

Kelly, Lynn, Phillips, Gerald M., & McKinney, Bruce. Reprise: Farewell reticence, goodbye apprehension! Building a practical nosology of speech communication problems. *Communication Education*, 1982, 31, 211-222.

King, T. R. An experiment to determine the relationship between individual visible manifestations of stage fright and the degree of stage fright reported by the individual. Master's thesis, Florida State University, 1958.

Kinsley, W. A. An investigation of the phenomenon of stage fright in certain prominent speakers. *Speech Monographs*, 1951, 18, 125.

Kirsch, Irving, & Henry, David. Extinction versus credibility in the desensitization of speech anxiety. *Journal of Consulting and Clinical Psychology*, 1977, 45, 1052-1059.

Kirsch, Irving, & Henry, David. Self-desensitization and meditation in the reduction of public speaking anxiety. *Journal of Consulting & Clinical Psychology*, 1979, 47, 536-541.

Kirsch, Irving, Wolpin, M., & Knutson, J. L. A comparison of in vivo methods for rapid reduction of "stage fright" in the college classroom: A field experiment. *Behavior Therapy*, 1975, 6, 165-171.

Kleinsasser, Dennis. The reduction of performance anxiety as a function of desensitization, pretherapy vicarious learning and vicarious learning alone. Master's thesis, Pennsylvania State University, 1968.

Klopf, Donald W. Communication apprehension: Its incidence in Guam and elsewhere. *Communication*, 1980, 92, 46-52.

Klopf, Donald W. Alter, Jason, & Cambra, Ronald. The educational impact of communication apprehension: An exploratory study in the People's Republic of China. *Waiyn Jaiouxue Yu Yanjiu*, 1980, 3, 45-51.

Klopf, Donald W., & Cambra, Ronald. Apprehension about speaking in organizational settings. *Psychological Reports*, 1979, 45, 58.

Klopf Donald W. & Cambra, Ronald. Apprehension about speaking among college students in the People's Republic of China. *Psychological Reports*, 1980, 46, 1194.

Klopf, Donald W. & Cambra, Ronald E. Apprehension about writing and speaking." *Psychological Reports*, 1979, 45, 530.

Klopf, Donald W. & Cambra, Ronald E. Communication apprehension among college students in America, Australia, Japan, and Korea. *Journal of Psychology*, 1979, 102, 27-31.

Klopf, Donald W. & Cambra, Ronald. Apprehension about speaking among college students in the Philippines. *Perceptual and Motor Skills*, 1980, 51-128.

Klopf, Donald W., Cambra, Ronald E., & Satoshi, Ishii, The typical Japanese university student as an oral communicator: A preliminary profile. Communication Association of the Pacific seminar paper, Tokyo, July 1983.

Klopf, Donald W. Crocker, William, & Cambra, Ronald. Communication apprehension and its educational implications: Some initial Australian data. *Australian Journal of Education*, 1978, 23-33, 262-270.

Klopf, Donald W., & Ishii, Sotashi. *Toward better communication across cultures: Problems and solutions.* Tokyo: Nanbundo, 1983.

Klopf, Donald W., Ishii, Satoshi. & Cambra, Ronald E. Patterns of oral communication among the Japanese. *Cross-Currents*, 1978, 5, 37-49.

Klopf, Donald W., Ishii, Satoshi, & Cambra, Ronald. The fear of speaking and the fear of writing among Japanese college students. *Speech Education*, 1979, 7-1, 55-59.

Klopf, Donald W., Ishii, Satoshi, & Cambra, Ronald. Oral communication apprehension among students in Japan, Korea, and the United States. *Current English Studies*, 1979, 18, 12-26.

Knapp, Mark L., Hart, R. P., and Dennis, H. S. An exploration of deception as a communication construct. *Human Communication Research*, 1974, 1, 15-29.

Knower, Franklin H. A study of speech attitudes and adjustments. *Speech Monographs*, 1938, 5, 130-203.

Knutson, Patricia K. Relationships among teacher communication style, trait and state communication apprehension, and teacher effectiveness. Dissertation, West Virginia University, 1979.

Knutson, Patricia K., Lashbrook, William B. Communication apprehension as an antecedent to social style. Paper presented at the Speech Communication Association convention, San Francisco, 1976.

Kondas, Ondrej. Reduction of examination anxiety and stage fright by group desensitization and relaxation. *Behavior Research and Therapy*, 1967, 5, 275-280.

Kondas, Ondrej. Stage fright as a form of learned fear. *Psycholoigia a Patopsycholoigia Diet7at7a*, 1967, 2, 67-77.

Kordinak, Stanley. The relationship between cognitive rehearsal and the reduction of measured anxiety in college students. Dissertation, Texas A&M University, 1974.

Kougl, Kathleen M. Dealing with quiet students in the basic college speech course. *Communication Education*, 1980, 29, 234-238.

Kovac, Damian. Structure of fear in pupils of various types of schools. *Studia Psychologica*, 1972, 14, 90-93.

Krapfl, J., & Nawas, M. Differential ordering of stimulus presentation in systematic desensitization. *Journal of Abnormal Psychology*, 1970, 75, 333-337.

Krause, M., & Pilisuk, M. Anxiety in verbal behavior: A validation study. *Journal of Consulting Psychology*, 1961, 25, 419.

Krayer, Karl, Cherry-O-Hair, Mary John, O-Hair, Dan, & Furio, Brian. Instructional implications for cognitive restructuring treatment of communication apprehension: preferences and perceived usefulness of task and context coping statements. Paper presented at the International Communication Association convention, Dallas, 1983.

Kuno, Y. The physiology of human perspiration. London: J. & J. Churchill, 1934.

Lacey, J. L. The evaluation of autonomic responses: Toward a general solution. *Annals of the New York Academy of Sciences*, 1956, 67, 125-164.

Laemmle, Paul E. A psysiological investigation of desensitization therapy with public speaking anxiety. Dissertation, Michigan State University, 1969.

LaGreca, Annette M. Teaching children how to interact with peers: Evaluating the effectiveness of social-skills training with low accepted elementary school children. Dissertation, Purdue University, 1978.

Lamb, Douglas H. The effects on public speaking of self-report, physiological, and behavioral measures of anxiety. Dissertation, Florida State University, 1970.

Lamb, Douglas H. Speech anxiety: Towards a theoretical conceptualization and preliminary scale development. *Speech Monographs*, 1972, 39, 62-67.

Lamb, Douglas H. The effects of the stressors on state anxiety for students who differ in trait-anxiety. *Journal of Research in Personality*, 1973, 7, 116-126.

Lamb, Douglas H. Usefulness of situation-specific trait and state measures of anxiety. *Psychological Reports*, 1976, 38, 188-190.

Lamb, Douglas H. Use of behavioral measures in anxiety research. *Psychology Reports*, 1978, 43, 1079-1085.

Larson, C. E., Backlund, P. M., Redmond, M. K., & Barbour, A. *Assessing communicative competence.* Falls Church, VA: Speech Communication Association and ERIC. 1978.

Lasch, Christopher. *The culture of narcissism.* New York: W. W. Norton, 1978.

Lashbrook, Velma J. The implementation of systematic desensitization in a basic course in high school. Paper presented at the Central Speech Association convention, Minneapolis, 1973.

Lashbrook, Velma J., Lashbrook, William B., & McCroskey, James C. Improving self-esteem: overcoming communication anxiety. Paper presented to the Training 1978 Conference, New York, 1978.

Lashbrook, William B., Lashbrook, Velma J., Bacon, Connie, & Salinger, Steve. An empirical examination of the relationship between communication apprehension and tolerance of ambiguity. *Southern Speech Communication Journal*, 1979, 44, 244-251.

Latané, Bibb, & Harkins, Stephen. Cross-modality matches suggest anticipated stage fright a multiplicative power function of audience size and status. *Perception & Psychophysics*, 1976, 20, 482-488.

Lazarus, A. A. On assertive behavior: A brief note. *Behavior Therapy*, 1973, *4*, 697-699.

Lazarus, P. J. Correlation of shyness and self-esteem for elementary school children. *Perceptual and Motor Skills*, 1982, 55, 8-10. (a)

Lazarus, P. J. Incidence of shyness in elementary school age children. *Psychological Reports*, 1982, 51, 904-906. (b)

Leary, Mark R. The social psychology of shyness: Testing a self-presentational model. Dissertation, University of Florida, 1980.

Leary, Mark R. Social anxiety. In L. Wheeler (Ed.), *Review of personality and social psychology*, (Vol. 3). Beverly Hills, CA: Sage, 1982.

Leary, Mark R. Problems with the construct and measurement of social anxiety. Paper presented at the annual meeting of the American Psychological Association, Washington, D.C., 1982.

Leary, Mark R. Social anxiousness: The construct and its measurement. *Journal of Personality Assessment*, 1983, 47, 65-75.

Leary, Mark R., & Schlenker, Barry R. The social psychology of shyness: A presentational model. In J. T. Tedeschi (Ed.), *Impression management and social psychological research.* New York: Academic Press, 1981.

Leavy, P. Situational and dispositional antecedents of shyness. Unpublished paper.

Lebra, T. S. *Japanese patterns of behavior.* Honolulu: University of Hawaii Press, 1976.

Lederman, Linda C. High communication apprehensives talk about communication apprehension and its effects on their behavior. *Communication Quarterly,* 1983, 31, 233-237.

Lee, M., Zimbardo, P., & Bertholf, M. J. The sudden murderer syndrome: Overcontrolled, shy, and feminine. (Report described in D. Dempsey & P. Zimbardo, *Psychology and you.* Glenview, IL: Scott, Forseman, 1978.)

Lee, Y.-H. The Korean people's national consciousness: An analysis of survey data. *Korea Journal,* 1978, 18, 47.

Leone, Susan D., & Gumaer, Jim. Group assertiveness training of shy children. *Social Counselor,* November, 1973, 27, XXX

Lerea, L. A preliminary study of the verbal behavior or speech fright. *Speech Monographs,* 1956, 23, 220-233.

Lesser, G. & Kandel, D. Cross-cultural research: Advantages and problems. Unpublished paper, 1968.

Levin, Harry, Baldwin, Alfred L., Gallwey, Mary, & Paivio, Allen. Audience stress personality and speech. *Journal of Abnormal and Social Psychology,* 1960, 61, 469-473.

Levine, Bruce, Sherry, Gail S., & Gorman, Shepard B. Degree of reported speech anxiety under two descriptive conditions. *Journal of Psychology,* 1978, 98, 171-173.

Lillywhite, H. Symposium of "A broader concept of communication disorders." *Journal of Communication,* 1964, 14, 3.

Levison, Gayle. Communication apprehension/communication competency: isolation and measurement of communication competencies. Paper presented at the Eastern Communication Association convention, Philadelphia, 1979.

Lima, Paul P. A comparison of induced anxiety and flooding in the modification of speech anxiety. Dissertation, University of Georgia, 1975.

Lind, A. W. Communication: A problem of island youth. *Social Process in Hawaii,* 1960, 24, 44-45.

Lindquist, Douglas S. Videotape feedback and self-regulatory processes in the modification of classroom speech anxiety and classroom discussion behavior. Dissertation, Miami University, 1975.

Lipper, Steven, & McNair, Douglas M. Simulated public speaking and anxiety. *Journal of Experimental Research in Personality,* 1972, 6, 237-240.

Little, Jacqueline M. The relative contribution of thought stopping and covert assertion in the treatment of speech anxiety. Dissertation, University of Maryland, 1977.

Lohr, James W., & McManus, Marianne L. The development of an audio-taped treatment for systematic desensitization of speech anxiety. *Central States Speech Journal,* 1975, 26, 215-220.

Lohr, Jeffrey M., Rea, Richard G., Porter, Becky B., & Hamburger, L. Kevin. Communication fear: A correlational study of trait generality. *Human Communication Research,* 1980, 6, 280-284.

Lomas, Charles W. A study of stage fright as measured by student reactions to the speaking situation. Master's thesis, Northwestern University, 1934.

Lomas, Charles W. The psychology of stagefright. *Quarterly Journal of Speech,* 1937, 23, 35-44.

Lomas, Charles W. Stagefright. *Quarterly Journal of Speech,* 1944, 30, 479-485.

Low, Gordon M., & Sheets, B. V. The relation of psychometric factors to stage fright. *Speech Monographs,* 1951, 18, 266-271.

Ludwig, R. P., & Lazarus, P. J. Differences in cognitive style between shy and nonshy children. *Preceedings of the National Association of School Psychologists,* 1982, 236-237 (summary).

Lujan, Philip D., & Dobkins, Dave. Communicative reticence: Native Americans in the college classroom. Paper presented at the Speech Communication Association convention, Minneapolis, November 1978.

Lundgren, David C. Public esteem, self-esteem, and interpersonal stress. *Social Psychology,* 1978, 41, 68-73.

Lungren, David C., & Schwab, Mary R. Perceived appraisals by others, self-esteem, and anxiety. *Journal of Psychology,* 1977, 97, 205-213.

Lustig, Myron W. Verbal reticence: A reconceptualization and preliminary scale development. Paper presented to the Speech Communication Association convention, Chicago, 1974.

Lustig, Myron W. The relationship between verbal reticence and verbal interaction in triads. Dissertation, University of Wisconsin-Madison, 1977.

Lustig, Myron W. Computer analysis of talk-silence patterns in triads. *Communication Quarterly*, 1980, 28, 3-12.

Lustig, Myron W. Communication apprehension and idea generation: Nonsignificant relationship. Paper presented at the Western Speech Communication convention, San Jose, February 1981.

Lustig, Myron W., & Grove, Theodore G. Interaction analysis of small problem-solving groups containing reticent and non-reticent members. *Western Speech Communication*, 1975, 39, 155-64.

Lustig, Myron W., & King, Stephen W. The effects of communication apprehension and situation on communication strategy choices. *Human Communication Research*, 1980, 7, 74-82.

Lustig, Myron W., & Zucker, Jackie H. Communication interviews with high-, moderate-, and low-verbal subjects: An exploratory study. Paper presented at the Western Speech Communication Association convention Los Angeles, 1979.

Lynd, Robert S. Anxiety relief, progressive muscle relaxation, and expectancy relaxation in the treatment of speech phobia. Dissertation, North Texas State University, 1976.

Mahl, G. F. Disturbances and silences in the patients' speech in psychotherapy. *Journal of Abnormal and Social Psychology*, 1956, 53, 1-15.

Main, Charles V. Helping shrinking violent blossoms. *American Way*, 1982, 50-55.

MacDonald, M. L., Lindquist, C. U., Kramer, J. A., McGrath, R. A., & Rhyne, L. D. Social skills training: Behavior rehearsal in groups and dating skills. *Journal of Counseling Psychology*, 1975, 22, 224-230.

Mager, Robert. *Goal analysis.* Belmont, CA: Fearon Publishers, 1972.

Magnusson, D., & Endler, N. S. *Personality at the crossroads: Current issues in interactional psychology.* Hillsdale, NJ: Lawrence Erlbaum, 1977.

Mahl, G. F. Measuring the patient's anxiety during interviews from "expressive" aspects of speech. *Transactions of the New York Academy of Sciences*, 1959, 21, 249-257.

Maiuro, Roland D. The effects of self versus externally attributed behavior change in the treatment of speech anxiety: Outcome, maintenance, and generalization. Dissertation, Washington University, St. Louis, 1978.

Maleski, E. F. Effects of contingency awareness and suggestion on systematic desensitization: Unplanned therapist differences. *Journal of Consulting and Clinical Psychology*, 1971, 37, 446.

Malkiewich, L. E., & Merluzzi, T. V. Rational restructuring versus desensitization with clients of diverse conceptual level: A test of client-treatment matching model. *Journal of Counseling Psychology*, 1980, 27, 453-461.

Marinelli, R. P. State anxiety in interactions with visibly disabled persons. *Rehabilitation Counseling Bulletin*, 1974, 18, 72-77.

Maroldo, G. K., Eisenreick, B. J., & Hall, P. Reliability of a modified Stanford shyness survey. *Psychological Reports*, 1979, 44, 706.

Marshall, W. L., & Andrews, W. R. *A manual for the self-management of public speaking anxiety.* Kingston, Ontario, Canada: Queen's University, n.d.

Marshall, W. L., Presse, Lucinda, & Andrews, W. R. A self-administered program for public speacking anxiety. *Behavior Research & Therapy*, 1976, 14, 33-39.

Marshall, W. L., Stoian, M. & ANdrews, W. R. Skills training and self-administered desensitization in the reduction of public speaking anxiety. *Behavior Research & Therapy*, 1977, 15, 115-117.

Martens, Rainer. Palmar sweating and the presence of an audience. *Journal of Experimental Social Psychology*, 1969, 5, 371-374.

Martinson, W. D., & Zerface, J. P. Comparison of individual counseling and a social program with nondaters. *Journal of Counseling Psychology*, 1970, 17, 36-40.

Marzillier, J. S., Lambert, C., & Kellett, J. A. A controlled evaluation of systematic desensitization and social skills training for socially inadequate psychiatric patients. *Behaviour Research and Therapy*, 1976, 14, 225-238.

Matsumoto, G. M. Meredith, G. M., & Masuda, M. Ethnic identification: Honolulu and Seattle Japanese-Americans. *Journal of Cross-Cultural Psychology*, 1970, 1, 63-76.

McCann, Lynn. Measuring foreign students' communication apprehension. Paper presented at the Speech Communication Association convention, Louisville, 1982.

McClintock, C. C., and Hunt, R. C. Nonverbal indicators of affect and deception in an interview setting. *Journal of Applied Social Psychology*, 1975, 5, 54-67.

McCroskey, James C. The effects of the basic speech course on students' attitudes. *Speech Teacher*, 1967, 16, 115-117.

McCroskey, James C. The effect of systematic desensitization on speech anxiety. *Speech Teacher*, 1970, 19, 32-36.

McCroskey, James C. Measures of communication-bound anxiety. *Speech Monographs*, 1970, 37, 269-277.

McCroskey, James C. The implementation of a large-scale program of systematic desensitization for communication apprehension. *Speech Teacher*, 1972, 21, 255-264.

McCroskey, James C. The effects of communication apprehension on nonverbal behavior. *Communication Quarterly*, 1976, 24, 39-44.

McCroskey, James C. Classroom consequences of communication apprehension. *Communication Education*, 1977, 26, 27-33.

McCroskey, James C. Validity of the PRCA as an index of oral communication apprehension. *Communication Monographs*, 1978, 45, 192-203.

McCroskey, James C. The problems of communication apprehension in the classroom. *The Florida Speech Communication Journal*, 1976, 4, 1-12.

McCroskey, James C., The problems of communication apprehensive in the classroom. *Florida Speech Communication Journal*, 1976, 4, 1-12.

McCroskey, James C., *Quiet children and the classroom teacher.* Falls Church, VA: Speech Communication Associated, 1977.

McCroskey, James C., Aspects of communication apprehension. Paper presented at the Eastern Communication Associated convention, New York City, March 1977.

McCroskey, James C., Oral communication apprehension: A summary of recent theory and research. *Human Communication Research*, 1977, 4, 78-96. Also in Ben W. Morse & Lynn A. Phelps (Eds.), *Interpersonal communication: A relational perspective. Minneapolis: Burgess, 1979.*

McCroskey, James C., On communication competence and communication apprehension: A response to Page. *Communication Education*, 1980, 29, 109-111.

McCroskey, James C., Overview of the communication apprehension problem. Paper presented at the Eastern Communication Associated convention, Ocean City, 1980.

McCroskey, James C., Quiet children in the classroom: On helping not hurting. *Communication Education*, 1980, 29, 239-244.

McCroskey, James C., The relationships between assertiveness and communication apprehension: What do we have to gain and lose?" Paper presented at the Eastern Communication Associated convention, Pittsburgh, 1981.

McCroskey, James C., *Introduction to rhetorical communication* (4th ed.). New Brunswick, NJ: Prentice-Hall, 1982.

McCroskey, James C., Oral communication apprehensive: A reconceptualization, In Michael Burgoon (Ed.), *Communication yearbook 6.* Beverley Hills, CA: Sage, 1982.

McCroskey, James C., Cross-situational consistency of the PRCA: Another view. Paper presented at the Western Speech Communication Association convention, Albuquerque, 1982.

McCroskey, James C., Deep muscular relaxation. Annandale, A: Speech Communication Association.

McCroskey, James C., & Andersen, Janis F. The relationship between communication apprehension and academic achievement among college students. *Human Communication Research*, 1976, 3, 73-81.

McCroskey, James C., Andersen, Janis F., Richmond, Virginia P., & Wheeless, Lawrence R. Communication apprehension of elementary and secondary students and teachers. *Communication Education*, 1981, 30, 122-132.

McCroskey, James C., Andersen, Janis F., Richmond, Virginia P., & Wheeless, Lawrence R. Teacher orientations and the development of communication orientations among elementary school children: A modeling explanation. Paper presented at the International Communication Association convention, Philadelphia, 1979.

McCroskey, James C., & Daly, John A. Teachers' expectations of the communication apprehensive child in the elementary school. *Human Communication Research, 2976, 3, 67-72.*

McCroskey, James C., Daly, John A., Hurt, H. Thomas, Jordan, William, Lashbrook, Velma J., Powers, William G. & Todd-de-Mancillas, William, Communication competencies for teachers: Preschool-college and adult education. Report prepared by the Instructional Communication Competencies Committee of the International Communication Association, 1978.

McCroskey, James C., Daly, John A., Richmond, Virginia P., & Cox, Barbara G. The effects of communication apprehensive on interpersonal attraction. *Human Communication Research,* 1975, 2, 51-65.

McCroskey, James C., Daly, John A., Richmond, Virginia P., & Falcione, Raymond L. Studies of the relationship between communication apprehension and self-esteem. *Human Communication Research* 1977, 3, 264-277.

McCroskey, James C., Daly, John A., & Sorensen, Gail A. Personality correlates of communication apprehension. *Human Communication Research, 1976, 2, 376-380.*

McCroskey, James C., Hamilton, Paul. :R., & Weiner, Allen N. The effect of interaction behavior on source credibility, homophily, and interpersonal attraction. *Human Communication Research,* 1974, 1, 42-52.

McCroskey, James C., & Kretzechmar, Monika M., Communication apprehension and marital relationships of college graduates: An exploratory investigation. Paper presented at the Eastern Communication Association convention, New York, 1977.

McCroskey, James C., & McVetta, Rod W. The relationship between communication apprehensive and classroom seating references. *Communication Education,* 1978, 27, 99-111.

McCroskey, James C., Ralph, David C., & Barrick, James E. The effect of systematic desensitization on speech anxiety. *Speech Teacher,* 1970, 19, 32-36.

McCroskey, James C., & Richmond, Virginia P. Communication apprehensive and shyness: Validation of two constructs and measures. Paper presented at the annual convention of the International Communication Association, Minneapolis, 1981.

McCroskey, James C., & Richmond, Virginia P. Communication apprehension as a predictor of self-disclosure. *Communication Quarterly,* 1978, 25, 40-43. Paper presented at the Western Speech Communication Association convention, San Francisco, 1976.

McCroskey, James C., & Richmond, Virginia P. Community size as a predictor of development of communication apprehension: Replication and extension. *Communication Education,* 1978, 27, 212-219.

McCroskey, James C., & Richmond, Virginia P. Communication apprehension and shyness: Conceptual and operational distinctions. *Central States Speech Journal,* 1982, 33, 458-468.

McCroskey, James C., & Richmond, Virginia P. *The quiet ones: Communication apprehensive and shyness*(2nd ed.). Dubuqe: Gorsuch-Scarisbrick, 1982.

McCroskey, James C., & Richmond, Virginia P. The effects of communication apprehension on the perception of peers. *Western Speech Communication Journal,* 1976, 40, 14-21.

McCroskey, James C., & Richmond, Virginia P. The etiology and effects of communication apprehension: Cross-cultural implications. Paper presented at the Puerto Rico Speech Communication Association convention, San Juan, 1981.

McCroskey, James C., & Richmond, Virginia P. The impact of communication apprehension on individuals in organizations. *Communication Quarterly,* 1979, 27, 55-61.

McCroskey, James C., & Richmond, Virginia P. Self-credibility as an index of self-esteem. Paper presented at the Speech Communication Association convention, Houston, 1975.

McCroskey, James C., Richmond, Virginia P., Berger, Bruce A., & Baldwin, H. John. A study of communication apprehensives in pharmacy students in 51 colleges and universities. Paper presented at the International Communication Association convention, Dallas, 1983.

McCroskey, James C., & Sheahan, Michael E. Communication apprehension social behavior in a college environment *Communication Quarterly*, 1978, 26, 41-50.

McCroskey, James C., & Sheahan, Michael E. Seating position and participation: An alternative theoretical/explanation. Paper presented at the International Communication Association convention, Portland, 1976.

McCroskey, James C., Simpson, Timothy, & Richmond, Virginia P. Biological sex and communication apprehension. *Communication Quarterly*, 1982, 30, 129-133.

McCroskey, James C., & Wheeless, Lawrence R. *Introduction to human communication* (2nd ed.) Boston: Allyn & Bacon, 1979.

McCroskey, James C., & Wright, D. W. The development of an instrument for measuring interaction behaviors in small groups. *Speech Monographs*, 1971, *38*, 335-340.

McCroskey, James C., Young, Thomas J. & Richmond, Virginia P. A simulation methodology for proxemic research. *Sign Language Studies*, 1978, 17, 357-368.

McDowell, Carlene E., McDowell, Earl E., & Lohr, James W. Adapting and testing audio-taped systematic desensitization for high school students. Paper presented at the Central States Speech Association Convention, Chicago, 1976.

McDowell, Earl E., & McDowell, Charlene E. An investigation of source and receiver apprehension at the junior high, senior high and college levels. *Central States Speech Journal*, 1978, 29, 11-19.

McDowell, Earl E., & McDowell, Charlene E. An investigation of ideal teacher immediacy, unwillingness-to-communicate, and ideal student attentiveness at the junior high and senior high levels. Papers presented at the Speech Communication Association convention, Anaheim, 1981.

McDowell, Earl E., McDowell, Charlene E., Hyerdahl, Janet, & Steil, Lyman K. A multivariate study of demographics, psychological sex-roles and communication apprehension. *Resources in Education*, 1978, 1-18.

McDowell, Earl E., McDowell, Carlene E., Pullan, Geoffrey, & Lindbergs, K. An investigation of source and receiver apprehensive between United States and Australian students at the high school and college level. Paper presented at the annual convention of the International Communication Association, Minneapolis, 1981.

McFall, R. M., & Lillesand, D. B. Behavior rehearsal with modeling and coaching in assertion training. *Journal of Abnormal Psychology, 1971, 77, 313-323.*

McFall, R. M., & Marston, A. R. An experimental investigation of behavior rehearsal in assertive training. *Journal of Abnormal Psychology*, 1970, 76, 295-303.

McFall, R. M., & Twentyman, C. T. Four experiments on the relative contributions of rehearsal, modeling, and coaching to assertion training. *Journal of Abnormal Psychology*, 1973, 81, 199-218.

McGary, Lois J., & Parts, Arlie Muller. Communication anxiety, self-image and locus of control. Paper presented at the Basic Course Conference of the Western Communication Association, Denver, 1982.

McGovern, K. B., Arkowitz, H., & Gilmore, S. K. Evaluation of social skill training programs for college dating inhibitions. *Journal of Counseling Psychology*, 1975, 22, 505-512.

McGowan, J., & Gormly, J. Validation of personality traits: A multicriteria approach. *Journal of Personality and Social Psychology*, 1976, 34, 791-795.

McKinney, B. C. Comparison of students in self-selected speech options on four measures of reticence and cognate problems. Master's thesis, Pennsylvania State University, 1980.

McKinney, B. C. The effects of reticence on group interaction. *Communication Quarterly*, 1982, 30, 124-125.

McKinney, Mark E., Gatchels, Robert J., & Paulus, Paul B. The effects of audience size on high and low speech-anxious subjects during an actual speaking task. *Basic and Applied Social Psychology*, 1983, 4, 73-87.

McManus, Marianne, & Lohr, James. Automated desensitization for the clinical treatment of speech anxiety. *Journal of the American College Health Association, 1976, 24, 218-220.*

McQuerry, B. Koreans, a rapidly assimilated group. In *Asian Americans in Hawaii*. Honolulu: General Assistance Center for the Pacific, 1975.

Mead, N. A. Issues related to a National Assessment of speaking and listening skills. Paper presented at the Speech Communication Association convention, Washington, D.C., December 1977.

Mehrabian, A. Some referents and measures of nonverbal behavior. *Behavior Research Methods and Instrumentation,* 1969, 1, 203-207. (a)

Mehrabian, A. Significance of posture and position in the communication of attitude and status relationships. *Psychological Bulletin,* 1969, 71, 359-372. (b)

Mehrabian, A. Nonverbal betrayal of feelings. *Journal of Experimental Research in Personality,* 1971, 5, 64-73. (a)

Mehrabian, A. Verbal and nonverbal interaction of strangers in a waiting situation. *Journal of Experimental Research in Personality,* 1971, 5, 127-138. (b)

Mehrabian, A. *Nonverbal communication.* Chicago: Aldline, 1972.

Mehrabian, A. *Silent messages* (2nd ed.). Belmont, CA: Wadsworth, 1981.

Mehrabian, A., & Ksionsky, S. Categories of social behavior. *Comparative Group Studies,* 1972, 3, 425-436. (a)

Mehrabian, A., & Ksionsky, S. Some determiners of social interaction. *Sociometry,* 1972, 35, 588-609. (b)

Mehrabian, A., & Williams, M. Nonverbal concomitants of perceived and intended persuasiveness. *Journal of Personality and Social Psychology,* 1969, 13, 37-58.

Meichenbaum, D. An examination of model characteristics in reducing avoidance behavior. *Journal of Personality and Social Psychology,* 1971, 17, 298-307.

Meichenbaum, D. Applications of cognitive behavioral therapy: An overview. Available from BMA Audio Cassette Publications, Dept. P/200 Park Avenue South, New York, NY 10003, $10.50.

Meichenbaum, D. Clinical implication of modifying what clients say to themselves. Unpublished manuscript, University of Waterloo, 1973.

Meichenbaum, D. Toward a cognitive theory of self-control. In G. Schwartz & D. Shapiro (Eds.), *Consciousness and self-regulation: Advances in research.* New York: Plenum, 1976.

Meichenbaum, D. *Cognitive behavior modification.* New York: Plenum, 1977.

Meichenbaum, D., Gilmore, J. B. & Fedoravicious, A. Group insight versus group desensitization in treating speech anxiety. *Journal of Consulting and Clinical Psychology,* 1971, 36, 410-421.

Melnic, Joseph, & Wicher, Donna. Social risk taking propensity and anxiety as predictors of group performance. *Journal of Counseling Psychology,* 1977, 24, 415-419.

Menchofer, J. D. Cause and cure of stage fright. *Western Speech,* 1938, 3, 9-11.

Meredith, G. Personality correlates of Pidgin English usage among Japanese American college students in Hawaii. *Japanese Psychological Research,* 1964, 6, 176-183.

Metzger, N. J. Description and diagnosis of reticent speakers: Who, what, and shy. Paper presented at the Speech Communication Association convention, New York, 1973.

Metzger, N. J. The effects of a rhetorical method of instruction on a selected population of reticent students. Dissertation, Pennsylvania State University, 1974.

Metzger, Nancy J. The effects of a rhetorical method of instruction on a selected population of reticent students. *Pacific Speech Journal,* 1976, 4, 92-103.

Metzger, Nancy. Helping the reticent student. Distributed by the Speech Communication module, 1976, ERIC Clearing-house on Reading and Communication Skills, 5105 Backlick Road, Annandale, VA 22003.

Meyer, Mary E., & Berg-Cross, Linda. Helping the withdrawn child. *Theory into Practice,* 1976, 15, 332-336.

Meyers, R. M. Validation of systematic desensitization of speech anxiety through galvanic skin response. *Speech Monographs,* 1974, 41, 233-235.

Millar, Dan Pyle, & Yerby, Janet. Regression analysis of selected personal characteristics as predictors of small group leadership. Paper presented at the Speech Communication Association, Louisville, 1982.

Miller, L., Berg, J. H., & Archer, R. L. Openers: Individuals who elicit intimate self disclosure. *Journal of Personality and Social Psychology,* 1983, 44, 1234-1244.

Mimas, L. A study of the relations of Dominance-Submission to speech participation. Master's thesis, University of Denver, 1939.

Mingler, B. & Wolpe, J. Automated self-desensitization: A case report. *Behavior Research and Therapy,* 1967, 5, 133-135.

Mino, Mary. Oral reading as a prelude to public speaking for the communication apprehensive student. Paper presented at the Communication Association of the Pacific — America Conference, Honolulu, 1982.

Mino, Mary. The effects of oral interpretation training on public speaking effectiveness of reticent and non-reticent students. Unpublished manuscript, 1982.

Mischel, W. *Personality and assessment.* New York: John Wiley, 1968.

Mitchell, K. R., & Orr, T. E. Note on treatment of heterosexual anxiety using short-term massed desensitization. *Psychological Reports,* 1974, 35, 1093-1094.

Miyamoto, S. F., Crowell, L. & Katcher, A. Self-concepts of communicative skills among beginning speech students. *Speech Monographs,* 1956, 23, 66-74.

Monson, T. C., & Hesley, J. W. Causal attributions for behaviors consistent or inconsistent with an actor's personality trait: Differences between those offered by actors and observers. *Journal of Experimental Social Psychology,* 1982, 18, 416-432.

Monson, T., Hesley, J. W., & Chernick, L. Specifying when personality can and cannot predict behavior: An alternative to abandoning the attempt to predict single-act criteria. *Journal of Personality and Social Psychology,* 1982, 43, 385-299.

Moore, Dennis L. The effects of systematic desensitization on communication apprehension in an aged population. Master's thesis, Illinois State University, 1972.

Moore, Meredith Ann. Language, correlates of communication apprehension. Dissertation, Purdue University, 1972.

Moore, W. E. Factor related to achievement and improvement in public speaking. *Quarterly Journal of Speech,* 1943, 29, 213-217.

Mordeno, J., Cambra, Ronald E., & Klopf, Donald W. Communication apprehension: Its incidence in the Philippines and elsewhere. Paper presented at the Communication Association of the Pacific, Manilla, 1980.

Mordeno, J., Cambra, Ronald E., & Klopf, Donald W. Communication style: College students in the Philippines compared to those from elsewhere. Paper presented at the Communication Association of the Pacific conference, November, Manila, 1980.

Mordey, T. Conditioning of appropriate behavior to anxiety producing stimuli: Hypnotherapy of a stage fright case. *American Journal of Clinical Hypnosis,* 1965, 8, 117-121.

Morgan, John M. Self-modeling versus other-modeling versus practice in the reduction of public speaking anxiety. Dissertation, University of Arizona, 1970.

Morganstern, Barry F., & Wheeless, Lawrence R. The relationship of nonverbal anxiety, status-self-control, and affective behaviors to relational anxiety. Paper presented at the Speech Communication Associated convention, New York, 1980.

Moroney, W. F., & Zenhausern, R. J. Detection of deception as a function of galvanic skin response recording methodology. *Journal of Psychology,* 1972, 80, 255-262.

Morris, L. W., Harris, E. W., & Rovins, D. S. Interactive effects of generalized and situational expectancies on the arousal of cognitive and emotional components of social anxiety. *Journal of Research in Personality,* 1981, 15, 302-311.

Morsbach, H. Aspects of nonverbal communication in Japan. In L. E. Samovar & R. E. Porter (Eds.) *Intercultural communication: A reader* (2nd ed.). Belmont, CA: Wadsworth, 1976.

Morse, Ben W. The reduction of communication apprehension. Paper presented at the Eastern Communication Association convention, Philadelphia, 1979.

Mortensen, D., & Arnston, P. The effects of predispositions toward verbal behavior in interaction patterns in dyads. *Quarterly Journal of Speech,* 1974, 61, 421-430.

Mortensen, David C., Arntson, Paul H., & Lustig, Myron. The measurement of verbal predispositions: Scale development and application. *Human Communication Research,* 1977, 3, 146-158.

Moscu, Judith. Experimental study of actors' state fright. *Revue Roumaine des Sciences Sociales — Serie de Psychologie,* 1973, 17, 145-158.

Moskowitz, D. S. Coherence and cross-situational generality in personality: A new analysis of old problems. *Journal of Personality and Social Psychology,* 1982, 43, 754-768.

Motley, Michael T. Stage fright manipulation by (false) Heart Rate Feedback. *Central States Speech Journal*, 1976, 186-191. Also paper presented at the Western Speech Communication Association convention, Newport Beach, 1974.

Mowrer, O. H. Stage fright and self regard. *Western Speech*, 1965, 29, 197-201.

Moxnes, Paul. Verbal communication level and anxiety in psychotherapeutic groups. *Journal of Counseling Psychology*, 1974, 21, 399-403.

Muehleman, Jacob T. The effects of cognitive rehearsal and cognitive reappraisal on fearful behavior. Dissertation, Southern Illinois University, 1972.

Muir, Francis, L. Case studies of selected examples of reticence and fluency. Master's thesis, Washington State University, 1964.

Mulac, Anthony, & Sherman, A. Robert. Behavioral assessment of speech anxiety. *Quarterly Journal of Speech*, 1974, 60, 134-143.

Mulac, Anthony, & Sherman, A. Robert. Relationships among four parameters of speaker evaluation: Speech skill, source credibility, subjective speech anxiety, and behavioral speech anxiety. *Speech Monographs*, 1975, 42, 302-310.

Mulac, Anthony, & Sherman, A. Robert. Conceptual foundations of the behavioral assessment of speech anxiety. *Western Journal of Speech Communication*, 1975, 39, 176-180.

Munger, Daniel I. *A decade of stage fright research (1960-1969): A synthesis.* ERIC ED 099 934.

Murray, D. C. Talk, silence, and anxiety. *Psychological Bulletin*, 1971, 75, 244-260.

Murray, E. A study of factors contributing to the maldevelopment of the speech personality. *Speech Monographs*, 1936, 3, 95-108.

Muse, R. Allen, & Hurt, H. Thomas. The effect of communication apprehensive on foreign language learning. Paper presented at the International Communication Association convention, Philadelphia, 1979.

Myers, Russel M. Validation of systematic desensitization of speech anxiety through galvanic skin response. *Speech Monographs*, 1974, 41, 233-235.

Mylar, J. L., & Clement, P. W. Prediction and comparison of outcome in systematic desensitization and implosion. *Behaviour Research and Therapy*, 1972, 10, 235-236.

Naruse, Gosaku, Hypnotic treatment of stage fright in champion athletes. *Psychologia: An International Journal of Psychology in the Orient*, 1964, 7, 199-205.

Natale, M., Entine, E., & Joffe, J. Vocal interruptions in dydadic communication as a function of speech and social anxiety. *Journal of Personality and Social Psychology*, 1979, 37, 865-878.

Neer, Michael R. Learning how to cope with the fear of speaking. Paper presented at the Communication Associated of the Pacific-America conference, Honolulu, 1981.

Neer, Michael R. Enrolling students in communication apprehension laboratories, *Communication Education* 1982, 205-210.

Neer, Michael R. A multi-method laboratory for the treatment of communication apprehension. Paper presented at the Western Speech Communication Association convention, Denver, 1982.

Neer, Michael R., & Cambra, Ronald E. Reducing apprehension about class discussion: Methods of facilitating student participation. Paper presented at the Communication association of the Pacific-American conference, Honolulu, 1982.

Neer, Michael R., & Hudson, David D. Role behavior of the apprehensive communicator: A preliminary scale development. Paper presented at the Speech Communication Association convention, Anaheim, 1981.

Neer, Michael R., Hudson, David D., & Warren, Clay. Instructional methods for managing speech anxiety in the classroom. Paper presented at the Speech Communication Associated convention, Louisville, 1982.

Nelsen, C. D. The problem of stage fright as related to family and school adjustment in clinical autobiographies. Master's thesis, University of Utah, 1965.

Nelsen, D. D. Student speaking disorders — beyond the symptoms. *Journal of Communication*, 1964, 14, 6-9.

Neter, Michael R., & Cambra, Ronald E. Reducing apprehension about class discussion: Methods of facilitating student participation. Paper presented at the Western Speech Communication Association convention, Albuquerque, 1983.

Newburger, Craig Alan. Student self-concept modification in communication: An exploration of the sources of conflicting findings. Paper presented at the Speech Communication Association convention, Louisville, 1982.

Newhouse, T. L., & Spooner, E. W. A skills development and apprehension reduction program for communication apprehensive reticent studentS: An alternative to basic course instruction. Paper presented at the Western Speech Communication Association convention, Denver, 1982.

Newlund, Sam. Public speaking often brings out the butterflies: The trick is to train them to fly information. *Minneapolis Tribune*, October 24, 1982, page 5, section K.

Nichols, Jack G. An investigation of the effects of varied rates of training on systematic desensitization for interpersonal communication apprehension. Dissertation, Michigan State University, 1969.

Nicholls, J. G., Licht, B. G., & Pearl, R. A. Some dangers of using personality questionnaires to study personality. *Psychological Bulletin*, 1982, 92, 572-580.

Nida, Richard A. The double bind theory of communication as it relates to communication apprehension and associated personality development. Dissertation, Ohio University, 1977.

Norman, William H. The efficacy of self-instructional training in the treatment of speech anxiety. Dissertation, Pennsylvania State University, 1975.

Norton, G. R., MacLean, Lynne, & Wachna, Elaine. The use of cognitive desensitization and self-directed mastery training for treating state fright. *Cognitive Therapy & Research*, 1978, 2, 61-64.

Norton, Robert, & Warnick, Barbara. Assertiveness as a communication construct. *Human Communication Research*, 1976, 3, 62-71.

Nuttal, E. C., & Scheidel, T. Stutterers' estimates of normal apprehensiveness toward speaking. *Speech Monographs*, 1965, 32, 455-457.

O'Bannion, K., & Arkowitz, H. Social anxiety and selective memory for affective information about the self. *Social Behavior and Personality*, 1977, 5, 321-328.

O'Connor, M. C. Nervousness in public speaking. Master's thesis, Cornell University, 1937.

O'Donnell Clifford R. The measurement of anxiety and evaluative components in exam and speech concepts for males. *Journal of Clinical Psychology*, 1973, 29, 326-327.

Oerkvitz, Susan K. Reports of continuing effects of instruction in a specially designed speech course for reticent students. Master's thesis, Pennsylvania State University, 1975.

Oerkvitz, Susan K. Continuing effects of a rhetorical method of instruction[?] for reticent students. *Pacific Speech Journal*, 1976, 4, 104-114.

O'Hair, Henry D., & Goss, Blaine. Dealing with students' communication apprehension: The University of Oklahoma program. Paper presented at the International Communication Association convention, Boston, 1982.

Oliver, R. *Korea: Forgotten nation*. Washington, DC: Public Affairs Press, 1944.

Orr, F. E., Mitchell, K. R., & Hall, R. F. Effects of reductions in social anxiety on behavior in heterosexual situations. *American Psychologist*, 1975, 30, 139-148.

Osberg, J. W. The effectiveness of applied relaxation in the treatment of speech anxiety. *Behavior Therapy*, 1981, *12*, 723-729.

Osborn, Lynn R. The Indian pupil in the high school speech class. *Speech Teacher*, 1967, 16, 187-189.

Page, William T. The development of a test to measure anticipated communicative anxiety. Dissertation, University of Illinois, 1970.

Page, William T. Some notes on measurement of observable speech anxiety. *Western Speech Communication*, 1975, 39, 271-275.

Page, William T. Recent research on the treatment of speech anxiety. Paper presented at the International Communication Association convention, Chicago, 1978.

Page, William T. Rhetoritherapy versus behavior therapy: Issues and evidence. *Communication Education*, 1980, 29, 95-104.

Paivio, Allan. A study of stage fright. Master's thesis, McGill University, 1957.

Paivio, Allan. Audience influence, social isolation and speech. *Journal of Abnormal and Social Psychology*, 1963, 67, 247-253.

Paivio, Allan. Personality and audience influence. In *Progress in experimental personality research*. (Ed.), B. Maher, New York: Academic Press, 1965.

Paivio, Allan. Childrearing antecedents of audience sensitivity. *Child Development*, 1964, 35, 397-416.

Paivio, Allan, & Lambert, Wallace E. Measures and correlates of audience anxiety ("stage fright"). *Journal of Personality*, 1959, 27, 1-17.

Paivio, Allan, Baldwin, ALfred L. & Berger, Seymour M. Measurement of children's sensitivity to audiences. *Child Development*, 1961, 32, 721-730.

Park, M.-S. *Communication styles in two different cultures: Korean and American*. Seoul: Han Shin Publishing, 1979.

Park, M.-S, Cambra, Ronald E., & Klopf, Donald W. Characteristics of Korean oral communication patterns. *Korea Journal*, 1979, 19, 4-8.

Park, Terry P. Covert positive reinforcement: Contribution of the reinforcing stimulus in reducing public speaking anxiety. Dissertation, University of South Dakota, 1979.

Parks, Arlie Muller, & Swift, Louisa H. W. Behavioral self evaluations as a measure of communication apprehension. Paper presented at the International Communication Association convention, Minneapolis, 1981.

Parks, Malcolm R. Shyness and sensation-seeking as predictors of communication patterns among close friends. Paper presented at the Western Speech Communication Association convention, Los Angeles, 1979.

Parks, Malcolm R. A dynamic analysis of the impact of communication apprehension on group satisfaction and leadership emergence. Paper presented at the annual convention of the Western Speech Communication Association, Portland, 1980.

Parks, Malcolm R. A test of the cross-situational consistency of communication apprehension. *Communication Monographs*, 1980, 47, 220-232.

Parks, Malcolm R., Dindia, Kathryn, Adams, John, Berlin, Eileen, & Larson, Kirby. Communication apprehension and student dating patterns: A replication and extension. *Communication Quarterly*, 1980, 28, 3-9.

Patton, B. R. An experimental study of the effects of the beginning speech course at the University of Kansas on student attitudes and abilities. Dissertation, University of Kansas, 1966.

Paul, Gordon L. *Insight vs. desensitization in psychotherapy: An experiment in anxiety reduction*. Stanford: Stanford University Press, 1966.

Paul, Gordon L. Insight versus desensitization in psychotherapy two years after termination. *Journal of Consulting Psychology*, 1967, 31, 333-348.

Paul, Gordon L. Two-year follow-up systematic desensitization in therapy groups. *Journal of Abnormal Psychology*, 1968, 73, 119-130.

Paul, Gordon L. Outcome of systematic desensitization. I. Background and procedures, and uncontrolled reports of individual treatments. In C. M. Franks (Ed.), *Behavior therapy: Appraisal and status*. New York: McGraw-Hill, 1969.

Paul, Gordon L., & Bernstein, D. Anxiety and clinical problems: Systematic desensitization and related techniques. In J. Spence, R. Carson, & J. Thibaut (Eds.), *Behavioral approaches to therapy*. Morristown, NJ: General Learning Press, 1976.

Paul, Gordon L., Marquis, J., & Morgan, G. W. *A guidebook for systematic desensitization*. Palo Alto, CA: Palo Alto Veterans Administration, 1968.

Paul, Gordon L., & Shannon, D. Treatment of anxiety through systematic desensitization in therapy groups. *Journal of Abnormal Psychology*, 1966, 71, 124-135.

Paulson, S. F. Changes in confidence during a period of speech training: Transfer of training and comparison of improved and non-improved groups on the Bell Adjustment Inventory. *Speech Monographs*, 1951, 18, 260-265.

Paulus, P. B., & Murdoch, P. Anticipated evaluation and audience presence in the enhancement of dominant responses. *Journal of Experimental Social Psychology*, 1971, 7, 280-291.

Pearce, W. Barnett. Generality and necessity in understanding communication apprehension: A theoretical analysis of a research construct. Paper presented at Eastern Communication Association convention, Boston, 1978.

Pearson, D. A. The diagnostic manifestations of stage fright. Master's thesis, University of Denver, 1951.

Pearson, Judy C. A factor-analytic study of the items in the personal report of communication apprehension and the Rathus Assertiveness Schedule. Paper presented at the International Communication Association convention, Acapulco, 1980.

Pearson, Judy C. The relationship between communication apprehension and assertiveness. Paper presented at the Eastern Communication Association convention, Ocean City, 1980.

Pearson, Judy C. The relationship between psychological sex type and communication apprehension. Paper presented at the Western Speech Communication Association convention, Denver, 1982.

Pearson, Judy C., & Yoder, Donald D. Public speaking or interpersonal communication: The perspective of the high communication apprehension student. Paper presented at the Eastern Communication Association Convention, Philadelphia, 1979.

Pedersen, Douglas J. *Report to the Alameda County school district and Title III, area J. Of Pennsylvania of the incidence of reticence in their respective school district.* Alameda County: Pace Center, 1968.

Pedersen, Douglas J. Systematic desensitization as a model for dealing with the reticent student. *Communication Education*, 1980, 29, 229-233.

Peters, Ruth A. The effects of anxiety, curiosity, and instructor threat on student verbal behavior in the college classroom. Dissertation, University of South Florida, 1976.

Petrucci, Ralph J. An investigation of a support group technique designed to lower interpersonal anxiety and improve self-concept for medical students. Dissertation, Temple University, 1978.

Phelps, Ann T. Development and evaluation of an instructional counseling procedure for the treatment of reticence. Dissertation, University of California, Los Angeles, 1979.

Phifer, L. G., & Clevenger, T. A semantogenic theory of stage fright. *ETC: A Review of General Semantics*, 1958, 15, 284-287.

Phillips, Gerald M. The problem of reticence. *Pennsylvania Speech Annual*, 1965, 22, 22-38.

Phillips, Gerald M. Reticence: Pathology of the normal speaker. *Speech Monographs*, 1968, 35, 39-49.

Phillips, Gerald M. A new direction for the speech profession. In Johnnye Akin et al., (Eds.), *Language behavior.* The Hague: Mouton, 1970.

Phillips, Gerald M. Theory and research concerning reticence: Where, when, whither. Paper presented at the Speech Communication Association convention, New York, 1973.

Phillips, Gerald M. The reticent speaker: Etiology and treatment. *Journal of Communication Disorders*, 6, 1973, 210-218.

Phillips, Gerald M. The friendship clinic: The treatment of reticence. Paper presented at the Eastern Communication Association convention, New York, March 1975.

Phillips, Gerald M. The noncommunicator. Paper prepared for the special edition of *Communication*, Journal of the Communication Association of the Pacific, compiled for the Communication Association of the Pacific convention, Kobe, Japan, June 1976.

Phillips, Gerald M. Rhetoritherapy versus the medical model: Dealing with reticence. *Communication Education*, 1977, 26, 34-43.

Phillips, Gerald M. "On apples and onions": A reply to Page. *Communication Education*, 1980, 29, 105-108.

Phillips, Gerald M. (Ed.). The practical teacher's symposium on shyness, communication apprehension, reticence and a variety of other common problems. *Communication Education*, 1980, 29, 213-263.

Phillips, Gerald M. Science and the study of human communication: An inquiry from the other side of the two cultures. *Human Communication Research*, 1981, 7, 361-370.

Phillips, Gerald M. *Help for shy people: And anyone else who ever felt ill at ease on entering a room full of strangers.* Englewood Cliffs, NJ: Prentice-Hall, 1981.

Phillips, Gerald M. Shyness: Ways to conquer it. Interview in *U.S. News & World Report*, 1981, May 18, p. 56-57.

Phillips, Gerald M. The nature of contemporary relationships: A study in impending sociopathology. Paper presented at the Speech Communication Association Convention, Louisville, 1982.

Phillips, Gerald M. (Ed.). Symposium. *Communication Education*. 1982, 31.

Phillips, Gerald M. Coming of age in the academy. *Communication Education*, 1982, 31, 177-183.

Phillips, Gerald M., & Butt, David. Reticence re-visited. *Pennsylvania Speech Annual*, 1966, 23, 40-57.

Phillips, Gerald M., Butt, David E. & Metzger Nancy J. *Communication in Education: A rhetoric of schooling and learning.* New York: Holt, Rinehart & Winston, 1974.

Phillips, Gerald M., Dunham, Robert E., Brubaker, Robert, & Butt, David. *The development of oral communication in the classroom.* Indianapolis: Bobbs-Merrill, 1970.

Phillips, Gerald M., & McCroskey, James C. Postscript. *Communication Education*, 1982, 31, 223.

Phillips, Gerald M. & Metzger, Nancy J. The reticent syndrome: Some theoretical considerations about etiology and treatment. *Speech Monographs*, 1973, 40, 220-230.

Phillips, Gerald M. & Sokoloff, Kent A. A refinement of the concept of reticence. *Journal of Communication Disorders*, 1976, 9, 331-347.

Phillips, Gerald M., & Sokoloff, Kent A. An end to anxiety: Treating speech problems with rhetoritherapy. *Journal of Communication Disorders*, 1979, 12, 385-397.

Pilkonis, Paul. Shyness, public and private, and its relationship to other measures of social behavior. *Journal of Personality*, 1977, 45, 585-595. (a)

Pilkonis, Paul. The behavioral consequences of shyness. *Journal of Personality*, 1977, 45, 596-611. (b)

Pilkonis, Paul. Shyness: Public behavior and private experience. Dissertation, Stanford University, 1976.

Pilkonis, Paul, & Zimbardo, P. The personal and social dynamics of shyness. In C. E. Izard (Ed.), *Emotions in personality and psychotherapy.* New York: Plenum, 1979.

Pilkonis, Paul, Heape, Carol, & Klein, Robert H. Treating shyness and other relationship difficulties in psychiatric outpatient. *Communication Education*, 1980, 29, 250-255.

Ponce, D. E. Introduction: The Philippine background. In J. F. McDermott, Jr. W.-S. Teng & T. Maretzki (Eds.), *People and cultures of Hawaii: A psychocultural profile.* Honolulu: University of Hawaii Press, 1980.

Popper, K. R., & Eccles, J. C. *The self and its brain.* New York: Springer, 1977.

Porter, D. Thomas. An empirical appraisal of the PRCA for measuring oral communication. *Human Communication Research*, 1981, 8, 58-71. Also paper presented at the Speech Communication Association convention, New York City, November 1980.

Porter, D. Thomas. Communication apprehension causation: Toward an empirical answer. Paper presented at the International Communication Association convention, Chicago, 1978.

Porter, D. Thomas. Communication apprehension: Communication's latest artifact. In Dan Nimmo (Ed.), *Communication Yearbook 3.* New Brunswick, NJ: Transaction Books, 1979.

Porter, D. Thomas. Communication apprehension context: Toward an empirical appraisal of etiology. Paper presented at the International Communication Association convention, Dallas, 1983.

Porter, D. Thomas. Communicator style perceptions as a function of communication apprehension. *Communication Quarterly*, 1982, 30, 237-244.

Porter, D. Thomas. A multivariate analysis of the effects of communication apprehension upon language behavior. Dissertation, Florida State University, 1974.

Porter, D. Thomas. Self-report scales of communication apprehension and autonomic arousal (heart rate): A test of construct validity. *Speech Monographs*, 1974, 41, 267-276.

Porter, D. Thomas, & Burns, Gerald P., Jr. A criticism of "heart rate as an index of speech anxiety." *Speech Monographs*, 1973, 40, 156-159.

Porter, D. Thomas, & Freimuth, Vicki S. Classroom identification of the apprehensive student. Paper presented at the Speech Communication Association convention, Houston, 1975.

Porter, D. Thomas, Kibler, Robert J. & Freimuth, Vicki S. An empirical evaluation of the construct "communication apprehension." Paper presented at the Speech Communication Association convention, Chicago, 1974.

Post, A. L., Wittmaier, B. C. & Rabin, M. E. Self-disclosure as a function of state and trait anxiety. *Journal of Clinical and Consulting Psychology*, 1978, 46, 12-19.

Potter, Ellen F. Correlates of children's initiation of oral participation in classroom. *Journal of Instructional Psychology*, 1978, 5, 23-34.

Powell, Barbara. *Overcoming shyness.* New York: McGraw-Hill, 1979.

Powell Robert G., & Johnson, John R. Cognitive complexity, unwillingness to communicate and perceived situational effectiveness. Paper presented at the Western Speech Communication Association convention, Denver, 1981.

Powers, William G. The rhetorical interrogative: Anxiety or control?" *Human Communication Research*, 1977, 4, 44-47.

Powers, William G., & Dunathan, A. T. Student teacher success expectancies for communication apprehension students. Paper presented at the International Communication Association convention, Chicago, 1978.

Powers, William G. & Hutchinson, Kevin. The measurement of communication apprehension in the marriage relationship. *Journal of Marriage and the Family*, 1979, 89-95.

Powers, William G., & Smythe, Mary Jeanette. Communication apprehension and achievement in a performance-oriented basic communication course. *Human Communication Research*, 1980, 6, 146-152.

Prall, C. W. An experimental study of the measurement of certain aspects of stage fright by means of rating scale and motion picture techniques. Dissertation, University of Southern California, 1950.

Price, W. K. The University of Wisconsin speech attainment test. Dissertation, University of Wisconsin, Madison, 1964.

Prisbell, Marshall. Heterosocial communicative behavior and communication apprehension. *Communication Quarterly*, 1982, 30, 251-258.

Prince, R., & Mombour, W. A technique for improving linguistic equivalence in cross-cultural surveys. *International Journal of Social Psychiatry*, 1967, 13, 229-237.

Prisbell, Marshall. The relationships among dating behavior, shyness, and loneliness in college students. Paper presented at the Western Speech Communication Association convention, Albuquerque, 1983.

Prisbell, Marshall, & Dallinger, Judith. Trait and state communication apprehension and level of uncertainty over time. Paper presented at the Western Speech Communication Association convention, San Jose, February 1981. TOP LINE OF DATA MISSING A cross-cultural study of stress behavior, Speech Communication Association convention paper, November, 1982, Louisville.

Quiggins, James G. An attributional analysis of communication anxiety. *Journal of the Tennessee Speech Communication Association*. 1979, 5, 4-30.

Quiggins, James G. A multi-dimensional conceptualization and measurement of communication anxiety. Dissertation, University of Kansas, 1977.

Quiggins, James G. Effects of high and low communication apprehension on small group member source credibility and interpersonal attraction. Master's thesis, Illinois State University, 1972.

Ragsdale, J. Donald. Relationships between hesitation phenomena, anxiety, and self-control in a normal communication situation. *Language & Speech*, 1976, 19, 257-265.

Rakos, Richard, & Schroeder, Harold E. Self-directed assertiveness training. Available from BMA Audio Cassette Publications, Dept. E1/200 Park Avenue South, New York, NY 10003 (4 cassettes, workbook, and manual), $45.00.

Ralph, David C., & Goss, Blaine. Implementing a systematic desensitization laboratory. Paper presented at the Speech Communication Association convention, New Orleans, December 1970.

Ralston, Steven M. Social modeling as a treatment for public speaking anxiety: A critical review. Master's thesis, University of Tennessee, 1981.

Randolph, Fred L. The relationship between family configuration and the development of oral communication apprehension. Master's thesis, West Virginia University, 1979.

Randolph, Fred L. & McCroskey, James C. Oral communication apprehension as a function of family size: A preliminary investigation. Paper presented at the Eastern Communication Association convention, New York, 1977.

Randolph, Fred L., & McCroskey, James C. The cause(s) of oral communication apprehension: Failure of a theory. Paper presented at the Eastern Communication Association convention, Boston, 1978.

Rathus, S. A. A thirty item schedule for assessing assertive behavior. *Behavior Therapy*, 1973, 4, 398-406.

Redding, Charles W. The psychogalvanometer as a laboratory instrument in the basic course in speech. Master's thesis, University of Denver, 1936.

Reedy, Jackie. Helpingtalk project. *California Speech Bulletin*, 1976, 12, 10-21.

Rehm, Lynn P. & Marston, Albert R. Reduction of social anxiety through modification of self-reinforcement: An instigation technique. *Journal of Consulting and Clinical Psychology*, 1968, 565-574.

Reinsch, Lamar. Communication apprehension as a determinant of channel preferences. Paper presented at the International Communication Association convention, Dallas, 1983.

Ribordy, Sheila C., Holmes, David S., & Bucksbaum, Helen K. Effects of affective and cognitive distractions on anxiety reduction. *Journal of Social Psychology*, 1980, 112, 121-127.

Rich, A. R. & Schroeder, H. E. Research issues in assertiveness training. Psychological Bulletin, 1976, 83, 1081-96.

Richards, W. Please take the hatchett: Why Japanese are uncomfortable with words and what to do about it. *Speech Education*, 1982, 9.

Richmond, Virginia P. Communication apprehension and success in the job applicant screening process. Paper presented at the Western Speech Communication Association convention, San Francisco, 1976.

Richmond, Virginia P. Communication apprehension and success on the job applicant screening process. Paper presented at the International Communication Association convention, Berlin, 1977.

Richmond, Virginia P. An investigation of the relationship between trait and state communication apprehension and interpersonal perceptions during initial and later acquaintance stages of dyadic linkages. Dissertation, University of Nebraska, 1977.

Richmond, Virginia P. The relationship between trait and state communication apprehension and interpersonal perception during acquaintance stages. *Human Communication Research*, 1978, 4, 338-349.

Richmond, Virginia P. A study of the relationship among opinion leadership, tolerance for disagreement, communication apprehension, innovativeness, and self-evaluation. Paper presented at the Eastern Communication Association convention, Philadelphia, 1979.

Richmond, Virginia P. Monomorphic and polymorphic opinion leadership within a relatively closed communication system. *Human Communication Research*, 1980, 6, 111-116.

Richmond, Virginia P., McCroskey, J. C., & Davis, L. Individual differences among employees, management, communicator style, and employee satisfaction: Replication and extension. *Human Communication Research*, 1982, 8, 170-188.

Richmond, Virginia P., & Robinson, Lynn D. Communication apprehension as a function of being raised in an urban or rural environment. Paper presented at the annual convention of the Western Speech Communication Association, Phoenix, 1977.

Richmond, Virginia P., Wagner, J. P., & McCroskey, James C. The impact of perceptions of leadership style, use of power, and conflict management style on organizational outcomes. *Communication Quarterly*, 1983, 31, 27-36.

Richter, Martin O. Systematic Desensitization of social anxiety in junior college students. Dissertation, University of Pennsylvania, 1975.

Rihani, Sulaiman T. The comparative effects of implosive therapy and systematic desensitization upon counselor trainees' anxiety and ability to communicate emotions. Dissertation, Michigan State University, 1973.

Rimm, D. C., & Masters, J. C. *Behavior therapy: Techniques and empirical findings* (2nd ed.). New York: Academic Press, 1979.

Rimm, David C., Snyder, J. J., Depue, R. A., Haanstad, M. J., & Armstrong, D. P. Assertive training versus rehearsal and the importance of making an assertive response. *Behavior Research and Therapy*, 1976, 14, 315-321.

Roberts, Charles V. Psychological arousal as a variable in communication research. Paper presented at the Southern Speech Communication Association convention, Birmingham, 1980.

Robinson, Edward Ray. An experimental investigation of certain commonly suggested methods for the development of confidence in beginning students of public speaking. *Speech Monographs*, 1956, 23, 97-98.

Rocklin, T., & Revelle, W. The measurement of extraversion: A comparison of the Eysenck Personality Inventory and the Eysenck Personality Questionnaire. *British Journal of Social Psychology*, 1981, 20, 279-284.

Rogers, R. Groups in two cultures. *Personnel and Guidance Journal*, 1979, 58, 11-15.

Rogers, T., & Izutsu, S. The Japanese. In J. F. McDermott, Jr., W.-S. Teng, & T. Maretzki (Eds.), *People and cultures of Hawaii: A psychocultural profile.* Honolulu: University of Hawaii Press, 1980.

Romero, Gloria. An experimental study of the effect of counterattitudinal messages on decreasing communication apprehension. Paper presented at the Speech Communication Association convention, Louisville, 1982.

Rosenfeld, Lawrence B., & Frandsen, Kenneth D. The other speech student: An empirical analysis of some interpersonal relations orientations of the reticent student. *Speech Teacher*, 1972, 21, 296-302.

Rosenfeld, Lawrence B., & Plax, Timothy G. Personality discriminants of reticence. *Western Journal of Speech Communication*, 1976, 40, 22-31.

Ross, F. Susan Ackerman. Physician reticence: Detection and treatment. Paper presented at the International Communication Association convention, Chicago, April 1978.

Ross, Raymond S. Speech fright problems of grade school students. Detroit, MI: Wayne State University, 1966.

Rowe, Harold F. A comparative study of stage fright as evidenced by subjective reports among speech, music, and physical education students. Master's thesis, University of Redlands, 1951.

Ruben, Brent. Stress and assertiveness training: Theoretical and pragmatic perspectives for the consultant to the corporation. Paper presented at the Eastern Communication Association convention, Pittsburgh, 1981.

Russell, Richard K. The use of systematic desensitization and conditioned relaxation in the treatment of public speaking anxiety. Dissertation, University of Illinois Urbana-Champaign, 1973.

Russell, Richard K., & Wise, Fred. Treatment of speech anxiety by cue-controlled relaxation and desensitization with professional and paraprofessional counselors. *Journal of Counseling Psychology*, 1976, 23, 583-86.

Ryan, G. F. Preliminary studies for an experiment in the psychodramatic treatment of stage fright. Master's thesis, University of Wisconsin, 1948.

Saidel, Madelaine N. Effects of false feedback and relaxation on an experimental analogue of public speaking anxiety. Dissertation, University of Rochester, 1976.

Sanders, Bruce D. Behavior rehearsal and imaginal desensitization in reducing public speaking anxiety. Dissertation, Stanford University, 1968.

Saral, T. Intercultural communication theory and research: Am overview. In B. D. Ruben (Ed.), *Communication yearbook 1.* New Brunswick, NJ: Transaction Books, 1977.

Sarnoff, I., & Zimbardo, Phillip G. Anxiety, fear and social affiliation. *Journal of Abnormal and Social Psychology*, 1961, 62, 356-363.

Schachter, S. The interaction of cognitive and physiological determinants of emotional state. In L. Berkowitz (Ed.), *Advances in experimental social psychology* (Vol. 1). New York: Academic Press, 1964.

Schachter, S., & Singer, J. F. Cognitive, social and physiological determinants of emotional state. *Psychological Review*, 1962, 69, 379-399.

Schleifer, Lawrence M. The effectiveness of group administered cue-controlled relaxation in the reduction of public speaking anxiety. Dissertation, State University of New York — Albany, 1978.

Schlenker, Barry R., & Leary, Mark R. Social anxiety and self-presentation: A conceptual model. *Psychological Bulletin*, 1982, 92, 641-669.

Schmitt, Connie. Oral interpretation as a catalyst for the reticent. *Pennsylvania Speech Communication Annual*, 1975, 31, 46-56.

Schneider, D. J., Hastorf, A. H., & Ellsworth, P. C. *Person perception* (2nd ed.). Reading, MA: Addison-Wesley, 1979.

Schumlowitz, Jay S. Effectiveness of group counseling as a function of state/trait anxiety in reducing problematic speech in children. Dissertation, Hofstra University, 1976.

Schwalb, Geraldine. Police-specific communication training: A practice approach to family crisis mediation. Dissertation University of California at Los Angeles, 1976.

Scott, Michael D., McCroskey, James C., & Sheahan, Michael E. Measuring communication apprehension in the organization setting. *Journal of Communication*, 1978, 28, 104-111.

Scott, Michael D., & Wheeless, Lawrence R. Communication apprehension, student attitudes, and levels of satisfaction. *Western Journal of Speech Communication*, 1977, 44, 188-198.

Scott, Michael D., & Wheeless, L. R. The relationship of three types of communication apprehension to classroom achievement. *Southern Speech Communication Journal*, 1977, 3, 246-255.

Scott, Michael D., & Wheeless, Lawrence R. Towards reconceptualization of the relationship between communication apprehension and learning: A critical review. Paper presented at the International Communication Association convention, Chicago, 1978.

Scott, Michael D., Wheeless, Lawrence R., Yates, M. P., & Frandolph, F. L. The effects of communication apprehension and test anxiety on three indicants of achievement in alternative systems of instruction: A follow-up study. In B. D. Ruben (Ed.), *Communication Yearbook 1*. New Brunswick, NJ: Transaction Books, 1977.

Scott, Michael D., Yates, Michael, & Wheeless, Lawrence R. An exploratory investigation of the effects of communication apprehension in alternative systems of instruction. Paper presented at the International Communication Association convention, Chicago, 1975.

Seiler, William J. et al. Communication apprehension, student assistance outside the classroom, and academic achievement: Some practical implications for the classroom teacher. Paper presented at the Central States Speech Association convention, Chicago, April 1978.

Seigman, A. W. & Pope, B. (Eds.). *Studies in dyadic communication. New York: Pergamon, 1972.*

Seiler, William J. Reduction of communication apprehension and self-awareness. Paper presented at the Speech Communication Association convention, Anaheim, CA. 1982.

Seligman, M. E. *Helplessness: On depression, development and death.* San Francisco: W. H. Freeman, 1975.

Sharma, S. Cross-cultural comparisons of anxiety: Methodological problems. *Topics in cultural learning*, 1977, 5, 166-173.

Shaw, I. R. Speech fright in the elementary school, its relationship to speech ability and its possible implications for speech readiness. *Speech Monographs*, 1967, 34, 319.

Sheehan, Angela M. The effects of systematic desensitization and communication exposure on speech anxious students. Master's of Science thesis, Illinois State University, 1971.

Sheahan, Michael E. Communication apprehension and electoral participation. Master's thesis, West Virginia University, 1976.

Shepherd, J. R. An experimental study of the responses of stage frightened students to certain scoring categories of the group Rorschach test. Dissertation, University of Southern California, 1952.

Sherman, Robert A., Mulac, Anthony, & McCann, Michael J. Synergistic effect of self-relaxation and rehearsal feedback in the treatment of subjective and behavioral dimensions of speech anxiety. *Journal of Consulting and Clinical Psychology*, 1974, 42, 819-827.

Shyness. Available from, BMA Cassette Publications, 200 Park Avenue South, New York, NY 10003, $10.50.

Siegman, A. W. & Pope, B. Effects of question specificity and anxiety producing messages on verbal fluency in the initial interview. *Journal of Personality and Social Psychology*, 1965, 2. 522-530.

Sikkink, D. E. An experimental study comparing improvers and nonimprovers in the beginning speech course, *Western Speech*, 1955, 19, 201-205.

Slivken, K. E., & Buss, A. H. Misattribution and speech anxiety. Unpublished paper, Department of Psychology, University of Texas, 1983.

Slutsky, Jeffrey M. & Allen, George J. Influence of contextual cues on the efficacy of desensitization and a credible placebo in alleviating public speaking anxiety. *Journal of Consulting and Clinical Psychology*, 1978, 46, 119-125.

Smith, R. E. & Campbell, A. L. Social anxiety and strain toward symmetry in dyadic attraction. *Journal of Personality and Social Psychology*, 1975, 43, 429.

Smith, R. E. & Sarason, I. G. Social anxiety and the evaluation of negative interpersonal feedback. *Journal of Consulting and Clinical Psychology*, 1975, 43, 429.

Smith, T. W., Ingram, R. E., & Brehm, S. S. Social anxiety, anxious self-perceptions, and recall of self relevant information. *Journal of Personality and Social Psychology*, 1983, 44, 1276-1283.

Smythe, Mary-Jeanette, & Powers, William G. When galatea is apprehensive: The effect of communication apprehension on teacher expectations. In B. D. Ruben (Ed.), *Communication yearbook 2*. New Brunswick, NJ: Transaction Books, 1978.

Smythe, Mary-Jeanette, & Schleuter, David, A comparison of the effects of reward-cost orientation and communication apprehension on academic achievement. Paper presented at the Speech Communication Association convention, Louisville, 1982.

Snavely, William B. & Phelps, Lynn A. Homophily, attraction, and self-esteem as predictors of situational communication apprehension in the acquaintance context. Paper presented at the Speech Communication Association convention, New York City, November 1980.

Snavely, William, Merker, George E., Becker Linda L., & Book, Virginia. Predictors of interpersonal communication apprehension in the acquaintance context. Paper presented at the Speech Communication Association convention, San Francisco, 1976.

Snavely, William & Sullivan, Daniel L. Components of self-esteem as predicators of oral communication apprehension. Paper presented at the Western Speech Communication Association convention, San Francisco, 1976.

Sokoloff, Kent A. Developing a reticence program, Paper prepared for the special edition of *Communication*, journal of the Communication Association of the Pacific. Compiled for the Communication Association of the Pacific convention, Kobe, Japan, June, 1976.

Sokoloff, Kent A. The treatment of the reticent person. *Pacific Speech Journal*, 1976, 4, 81-92.

Sokoloff, Kent A. Treatment of the reticent in a private clinical setting. *Communication Eduction*, 1980, 29, 245-249.

Sokoloff, Kent A. & Phillips, Gerald M. A refinement of the "reticence." *Journal of Communication Disorders*, 1976, 9, 331-347.

Sorenson, Gail A. A review of communication apprehension treatments with recommendations and warnings. Paper presented at the Eastern Region Basic Course Director's Conference, Stroudsburg, 1979.

Sorenson, Gail. Treatment II: Cognitive restructuring for the reduction of communication apprehension. Paper presented at the Eastern Communication Association convention, Ocean City, 1980.

Sorenson, Gail A. The use of personality traits and communication apprehension in predicting interaction behavior in small groups. Master's thesis, Illinois State University, 1972.

Sorenson, Gail, & McCroskey, James C. The prediction of interaction behavior in small groups: Zero history vs. intact groups. *Communication Monographs*, 1977, 44, 73-80.

Sours, David. Comparison of direct interview and instructor diagnosis in reticence. Master's thesis, Pennsylvania State University, 1979.

Spitzberg, Brian H. Interpersonal competence and loneliness. Paper presented at the Western Speech Communication Association, convention, Portland, 1980.

Spitzberg, Brian H. Loneliness and communication apprehension. Paper presented at the Western Speech Communication Association convention, San Jose, February 1981.

Spicer, Christopher H. The comment-provoking potential of T-shirts: A nonverbal dimension of communication apprehension. Paper presented at the Western Speech Communication Association convention, San Jose, 1981.

Spielberger, Charles D. (Ed.). *Anxiety and behavior.* New York: Academic Press, 1966.

Spielberger, C. D. Theory and research on anxiety. In C. D. Spielberger (Ed.), *Anxiety and behavior* New York: Academic Press, 1966.

Spock, Linda C. Instructional sets and treatment credibility as influences on analogue speech anxiety. Dissertation, University of Connecticut, 1977.

Sroufe, L. A. Wariness of strangers and the study of infant development. *Child Psychology*, 1977, 48, 731-746.

Stacks, Don W., & Stone, John D. The effect of self-concept, self-disclosure, and type of basic speech course on communication apprehension. Paper presented at the Speech Communication Association convention, Louisville, 1982.

Starr, B. J. & Wilson, S. F. Some epistemological and methodological issues in the design of cross-cultural research. *Topics in Cultural Learning*, 1977, 5, 125-135.

Stafford, L., & Daly, John A. Conversational memory: Effects of recall mode and instruction set on memory for naturally occuring conversations. Paper presented at the International Communication Association convention, Dallas, 1983.

Steffen, J. J., & Redden, J. Assessment of social competence in an evaluation-interaction analogue. *Human Communication Research*, 1977, *4*, 30-37.

Stewar, Larry A. Attitudes toward communication: The content analysis of interviews with eight reticent and eight non-reticent college students. Dissertation, Pennsylvania State University, 1968.

Stodolsky, David et al. Automatic facilitation of dialogue in shy and not shy problem solving teams. Paper presented at the Western Psychological Association convention, San Diego, April 1979.

Straatmeyer, Alvin J. The effectiveness of rational-emotive therapy in the reduction of speech anxiety. Dissertation, University of South Dakota, 1974.

Straatmeyer, Alvin J. & Walkins, John T. Rational-emotive therapy and the reduction of speech anxiety. *Rational Living*, 1974, 9, 33-37.

Strahan, Robert F. A study of speech anxiety. Dissertation, University of Minnesota, 1968.

Strahan, Robert F. Situational dimensions of self-reported nervousness, *Journal of Personality Assessment*, 1974, 38, 341-352.

Street, Richard L., Jr., Street, Nancy James, & Kleeck, Anne Van. Noncontent speech convergence among talkative and reticent three-year-olds. Paper presented at the International Communication Association convention, Minneapolis, 1981.

Streibel, B. J. The implications of selected personality factors and perceptions of communication for the diagnosis and instruction of reticent students. Dissertation, Pennsylvania State University, 1978.

Sullican, Chesna R., & Jordan, William. Solidarity, apprehension, and juvenile delinquents. Paper presented at the International Communication Association convention, Philadelphia, 1979.

Snyder, M., & Gangestad, E. Choosing social situations: Two investigations of self-monitoring processes. *Journal of Personality and Social Psychology*, 1982, 43, 123-135.

Snyder, M., & Swann, W. B. Hypothesis testing processes in social interaction. *Journal of Personality and Social Psychology*, 1978, 36, 1202-1212.

Snyder, M., Tanke, E. D., & Bersheid, E. Social perception and interpersonal behavior: On the self-fulfilling nature of social stereotypes. *Journal of Personality and Social Psychology*, 1977, 35, 656-666.

Swann, W. B., Giuliano, T., & Wegner, D. M. Where leading questions can lead: The power of conjecture in social interaction. *Journal of Personality and Social Psychology*, 1982, 42, 1025-1035.

Talent, Barbara K. Differential effects of systematic desensitization and cognitive modification on subjects with two kinds of speech anxiety. Dissertation, Washington University, 1979.

Talley, Mary A. & Richmond, Virginia P. The relationship between psychological gender orientation and communication style. *Human Communication Research*, 1980, 6, 326-339.

Taugher, David. Measuring communication apprehension as an individual difference among organizational personnel. Paper presented at the Speech Communication Association convention, San Antonio, 1979.

Taugher, C. David, & Koehler, Jerry W. An instructor's guide to understanding and treating the communication apprehensive student: a practical alternative. Paper presented at the International Communication Association convention, Minneapolis, 1981.

Taylor, Steven A., & Hamilton, Peter K. The effects of the basic speech course on anxiety, dogmatism, cognitive ability, and communicative ability. Paper presented at the International Communication Association convention, New Orleans, 1974.

Teglasi, H., & Hoffman, M. A. Causal attributions of shy subjects. *Journal of Research in Personality*, 1982, 16, 376-385.

Teigen, C. Ward. The relationship between communication apprehension, tolerance for conflict, and specific communication behaviors. Master's thesis, West Virginia University, 1977.

Tesser, A., Leone, C., & Clary, E. G. Affect control: Process constraints versus catharsis. *Cognitive Therapy and Research*, 1978, *2*, 265-274.

Thoreson, C. E. Oral non-participation in college students: A survey of characteristics. *American Educational Research Journal*, 1966, 8, 199.

Thorne, B., & Henley, N. (Eds.), *Language and sex: Differences and dominance.* Rowley, Ma: Newbury House, 1975.

Thorpe, G. L. Desensitization, behavior rehearsal, self-instructional training and placebo effects on assertive-refusal behavior. *European Journal of Behavioural Analysis and Modification*, 1975, 1, 30-44.

Thorpe, G., Amatu, H., Blakey, R., & Burns, L. Contribution of overt instructional rehearsal and "specific insight" to the effectiveness of self-instructional training: A preliminary study. *Behavior Therapy*, 1976, 7, 501-511.

Trexler, Larry D. & Karst, Thomas O. Rational-emotive therapy, placebo and no treatment effects on public speaking anxiety. *Journal of Abnormal Psychology*, 1972, 60-67.

Trier, Christine S. Effectiveness of two versions of rational restructuring in reducing speech anxiety. Dissertation, State University of New York — Stony Brook, 1975.

Trower, P., Bryant, B., & Argyle, M. *Social skills and mental health.* Pittsburgh University of Pittsburgh Press, 1978.

Trussel, Richard P. Speech anxiety reduction: Program development and evaluation. Dissertation, University of Utah, 1977.

Trussel, Richard P. Use of graduated behavior rehearsal, feedback, and systematic desensitization for speech anxiety. *Journal of Counseling Psychology*, 1978, 25, 14-20.

Tuccy, J. T-test procedure. In N. H. Nie, C. H. Hall, J. G. Jenkins, K. Steinbrenner, & D. H. Brent (Eds.), *Statistical package for the social sciences.* New York: McGraw-Hill, 1975.

Tucker, Ann J. The effects of audience size of self-report and behavioral measures of anxiety of male and female students in a public speaking class. Dissertation, Florida State University, 1971.

Twentyman, C. T. & McFall, R. M. Behavioral training of social skills in shy males. *Journal of Consulting and Clinical Psychology*, 1975, 43, 324-395.

Ullman, M. K. A note on overcoming stage fright among musicians. *Journal of Applied Psychology*, 1940, 24, 82-84.

Urey, J. R., Laughlin, C. S., & Kelly, J. A. Teaching heterosexual conversational skills to male psychiatric patients. *Journal of Behavior Therapy and Experimental Psychiatry*, 1979, 10, 323-328.

Van Kleeck, A., & Daly, John A. Instructional communication research and theory: Communication development and instructional communication — A review. In M. Burgoon (Ed.), *Communication yearbook 5.* New Brunswick, N.J.: Transaction Books, 1982.

Varela, Jacoba A. Solving human problems with human science. *Human Nature* 1978, 1, 10.

Vicker, Lauren Anne. The speech anxiety reduction program: implementation of a large-scale program for reducing fear of public speaking. Paper presented at the Eastern Communication Association convention, Hartford, 1982.

Vrolijk, A. A comparison of several strategies for the reduction of speech anxiety. *Nederlands Tijdschrift voor de Psychologie en haar Grensgebieden*, 1975, 30, 149-169.

Vrolijk, A. Habituation as a mode of treatment of speaking anxiety. *Gedrag*: Tidjschrift voor Pschologie, 1974 2, 332-338.

Vrolijk, A. Training public speaking behavior: The effect of model and manual. *Gedrag: Tijdschrift voor Psychologie*, 1977, 5, 95-105.

Waggener, J. O. A comparative galvanomeric study of the behavior of inferior and superior speakers. Master's thesis, University of Denver, 1934.

Walk, R. D. Self-ratings of fear in a fear-invoking situation. *Journal of Abnormal and Social Psychology*, 1956, 52, 171-178.

Wampler, Larry D. & Amira, Stephen B. Transcendental meditation and assertive training in the treatment of social anxiety. Paper presented at the Western Psychological Association convention, Honolulu, May, 1980.

Watson, Arden K. *Handbook with activities for confidence in speaking.* Bowling Green: Western Kentucky University Press, 1979.

Watson, Arden K. An explorative study of relationships of characteristics and test scores among communication apprehensive and underprepared college students. Paper presented at the Eastern Communication Association, Hartford, 1982.

Watson, Arden K. The confidence model: an alternative approach to alleviating communication apprehension. Paper presented at the Speech Communication Association convention, Louisville, 1982.

Watts, F. Habituation model of systematic desensitization. *Psychological Bulletin*, 1979, 86, 627-637.

Watson, David & Friend, Ronald. Measurement of social- evaluative anxiety. *Journal of Consulting and Clinical Psychology*, 1969, 33, 448-457.

Way, J. R. & Efran, J. S. Systematic desensitization and expectancy in the treatment of speaking anxiety. *Journal of Behavior Research and Therapy*, 1972, 10, 43-49.

Webb, R. A. J. Fear and communication. *Journal of Drug Education*, 1974, 4, 97-103.

Weerts, Theodore C. & Lang, Peter J. Psychophysiology of fear imagery: differences between focal phobia and social performance anxiety. *Journal of Consulting and Clinical Psychology*, 1978, 46, 1157-1159.

Weinberger, Alex, and Engelhart, Roland S. Three group treatments for reduction of speech anxiety among students. *Perceptual and Motor Skills*, 1976, 43, 1317-1318.

Weiner, Allen N. Machiavellianism as a predictor of group interaction and cohension. Masters thesis, West Virginia University, 1973.

Weingarten, Charles J. Systematic desensitization vs. accelerated mass desensitization with speech anxious subjects. Dissertation, Purdue University, 1973.

Weissberg, M. A. A comparison of direct and vicarious treatments of speech anxiety: Desensitization, desensitization with coping imagery, and cognitive modification. *Behavior Therapy*. 1977, 8, 606-620.

Weissberg, Michael; Anxiety-inhibiting statements and relaxation combined in two cases of speech anxiety. *Journal of Behavior Therapy and Experimental Psychiatry*, 1975, 6, 163-164.

Weissberg, Michael & Lamb, Douglas. Comparative effects of cognitive modification, systematic desensitization, and speech preparation in the reduction of speech and general anxiety. *Communication monographs*, 1977, 44, 27-36.

Welke, J. W. The effects of intentional and existential audiences on communicator anxiety. *Central States Speech Journal*, 1968, 19, 14-18.

Wells, Judith. A study of the effects of systematic desensitization on the communicative anxiety of individuals in small groups. Master's thesis, San Jose State College, 1970.

Wenzlaff, Velma J. The prediction of leadership: A consideration of selected communication variables. Master's thesis, Illinois State University, 1972.

Werner, O. & Campbell, D. Translating, working through interpreters, and the problem of decentering. In R. Naroll & R. Cohen (Eds.), *A handbook of method in cultural anthropology*. New York: American Museum of Natural History, 1970.

Wheeless, Lawrence R. *Pilot study: A physiological measure of speech fright in elementary school children*. Project No. S-936-63; on file with the U.S. Office of Education, Washington, D.C., 1967.

Wheeless, Lawrence R. Communication apprehension in the elementary school. *Speech Teacher*, 1971, 20, 297-299.

Wheeless, Lawrence R. An investigation of receiver apprehension and social context dimensions of communication apprehension. *Speech Teacher*, 1975, 24, 261-268.

Wheeless, Lawrence R. & Morganstern, Barry F. The relationship of perceived anxiety, status/self-control, and affective behaviors to self-reported relational anxiety and interpersonal solidarity. Paper presented at the Speech Communication Association convention, Anaheim, 1981.

Wheeless, Lawrence R. Nesser, Kathryn & McCroskey, James C. The relationship among self-disclosure, disclosiveness, and communication apprehension. Paper presented at the Western Speech Communication Association, San Francisco, 1976.

Wiemann, J. M. Explication and test of a model of communicative competence. *Human Communication Research*, 1977, 3, 195-213.

Wiemann, J. M. Effects of laboratory videotaping procedures on selected conversation behaviors. *Human Communication Research*, 1981, 7, 302-311.

Wiggins, J. S. A psychological taxonomy of trait descriptive terms. *Journal of Personality and Social Psychology*, 1979, 37, 395-412.

Wilder, J. The law of initial value in neurology and psychiatry: Facts and problems. *Journal of Nervous and Mental Disorders*, 1957, 125, 73-86.

Wilkinson, E. R. A study of disintegrating background factors in the development of effective speech participation. Master's thesis, University of Denver, 1938.

Williams, N. G. An investigation of maladjustment to a speaking situation shown by seventh, eighth, ninth, and tenth grade students in a secondary school. Master's thesis, University of Iowa, 1950.

Wilson, Barbara J. Relationship between self-esteem and communication problems in the classroom. Master's thesis, Pennsylvania State University, 1969.

Wilson, G. D. & Cox, D. N. Personality of paedophile club members. *Personality and Individual Differences*, 1983, 4, 323-329.

Wilson, John & Arnold, Carroll. *Public speaking as a liberal art.* Boston: Allyn & Bacon, 1974.

Winans, James. *Speech making.* New York: D. Appleton, 1938.

Winch, R. F. *Mate selection: A study of complementary needs.* New York: Harper, 1958.

Wischner, G. J. Behavior theory, behavior therapy, and speech deviations. *Folia Phoniatrica*, 1972, 24, 105-49.

Wissmiller, Andrew P. & Merker, George E. Communication apprehension, social distance and interpersonal judgments in small groups. Paper presented at the Speech Communication Association convention, San Francisco, 1976.

Witteman, Hal R. The relationship of communication apprehension to opinion leadership and innovativeness. Master's thesis, West Virginia University, 1976.

Wolfe, Janet. Assertiveness training for women. Available from BMA Audio Cassette Publication, Dept. P/200 Park Avenue South, New York, NY 10003, $10.50.

Wolff, James, & Desiderato, Otello. Transfer of assertion-training effects to roommates of program participants. *Journal of Counseling Psychology*, 1980, 27 484-491.

Wolpe, J. *Psychotherapy by reciprocal inhibition.* Stanford: Stanford University Press, 1958.

Wolpe, Joseph L. & Fodoer, I. G. Modifying assertive behavior in women: A comparison of three approaches. *Behavior Therapy*, 1977, 8, 567-574.

Wong, Kenneth B. Measurement of the propensity to communicate. Unpublished monograph, School of Business, Queen's University at Kingston, 1975.

Work, William. On communication apprehension: Everything you've wanted to know but have been afraid to ask. *Communication Education*, 1982 31, 248-257.

Woy, John R. Effects of expectation on the outcome of systematic desensitization. Dissertation, University of Rochester, 1971.

Woy, John R. & Efran, J. S. Systematic desensitization and expectancy in the treatment of speaking anxiety. *Behavior Research and Therapy*, 1972, 10, 43-49.

Wrenchly, E. D. O. A study of stage fright attacks in a selected group of speakers. Master's thesis, University of Denver, 1948.

Wright, J. C. A comparison of systematic desensitization and social skill acquisition in the modification of a social fear. *Behavior Therapy*, 1976, 7, 205-210.

Wright, John W. II & Cara, Arthur J. An analysis of the interpersonal dimensions of high anxiety communication. Paper presented at the Speech Communication Association convention, Louisville, 1982.

Yankelovich, Daniel. *New Rules.* New York: Random House, 1981.

Yates, A. *Behavior therapy.* New York: John Wiley, 1970.

Yates, A. *Theory and practice in behavior therapy.* New York: John Wiley, 1975.

Yoshikawa, M. Implications of Martin Buber's philosophy of dialogue in Japanese and American intercultural communication. *Communication*, 1977, 6, 103-104.

Young, Stephen Lee. An experimental investigation of the effects of positive and negative reinforcement on students with different levels of self-confidence as a communicator. Dissertation, Purdue University, 1974.

Zajonc, R. B. Social facilitation. *Science*, 1965, 149, 269-274.

Zakahi, Walter R. & Duran, Robert L. All the lonely people: The relationship among loneliness, communicative competence, and communication anxiety. *Communication Quarterly*, 1982, 30, 203-209.

Zakahi, Walter R. & Duran, Robert L. Loneliness, communicative competence and communication apprehension: Replication and extension. Paper presented at the Eastern Communication Association convention, Hartford, 1982.

Zemore, R. Systematic desensitization as a method of teaching a general anxiety-reducing skill. *Journal of Consulting and Clinical Psychology*, 1975, 157-161.

Zimbardo, Phillip G. *The shy child.* New York: McGraw-Hill, 1981.

Zimbardo, Phillip G. Shyness can be a quiet yet devastating problem. *Learning*, 1977, 6, 68-72.

Zimbardo, Phillip G. Shyness clinic. Available from BMA Audio Cassette Publication, Dept. P/200 Park Avenue South, New York, NY 10003, $10.50.

Zimbardo, Phillip G. Shyness — The people phobia. *Today's Education*, 1977, 47-49.

Zimbardo, Phillip G. The social disease called "shyness". *Psychology Today*, 1975, 8, 68ff.

Zimbardo, Phillip G. *Shyness: What it is, what to do about it.* Reading, MA: Addison-Wesley, 1977.

Zimmerman, Gary W. Augmented systematic desensitization versus systematic desensitization for reduction of speech anxiety. Dissertation, Washington State University, 1974.

Zolten, J. Jerome & Mino, Mary. Oral reading as a prelude to public speaking for reticent students. Paper presented at the International Communication Association convention, 1981.

Zweig, Paul. *The heresy of self love: A study of subversive individualism.* Princeton: Princeton University Press, 1980.

About the Contributors

Michael Beatty received his Ph.D. from Ohio State University. He has taught at Texas Christian University and West Virginia University.

Arnold Buss is Professor of Psychology at the University of Texas at Austin. He is a fellow of the American Psychological Association. He received his doctorate in psychology from Indiana University.

Theodore Clevenger, Jr. is Professor and Dean of the College of Communication at Florida State University. Among other honors, he has served as president of the Speech Communication Association. He received his Ph.D. from the University of Illinois.

John A. Daly is an associate professor in the College of Communication at the University of Texas. He is currently co-editor of *Written Communication* and editor-elect of *Communication Education*. He received his Ph.D. from Purdue University.

William Fremouw is an associate professor in the Department of Psychology at West Virginia University. He received his Ph.D. from the University of Massachusetts.

Gustav Friedrich is Chair of the Communication Department at the University of Oklahoma. He is a former editor of *Communication Education*. Friedrich received his doctorate from the University of Kansas.

Blaine Goss is on the faculty at the University of Oklahoma. He has published in a number of scholarly journals. He received his Ph.D. from Michigan State University.

Lynne Kelly is Assistant Professor in the Department of Speech Communication at the University of Hartford. She received her Ph.D. from the Pennsylvania State University.

Donald Klopf was, until recently, Professor and Chair of the Department of Speech at the University of Hawaii. He is a former president of the Pacific Communication Association. He received his Ph.D. from the University of Washington.

James McCroskey is Professor and Chair of the Department of Speech Communication at West Virginia University. A fellow of the International Communication Association, he is a former editor of *Human Communication Research* and former president of the Eastern Communication Association. He received his doctorate from Pennsylvania State University.

Gerald Miller is Professor of Communication at Michigan State University. A fellow and former president of the International Communication Association, he received his Ph.D. from the University of Iowa. He is currently editor of *Communication Monographs* and former editor of *Human Communication Research*.

Anthony Mulac is a professor in the Department of Speech at the University of California, Santa Barbara. He received his doctorate from the University of Michigan.

Steven Payne is a doctoral student at West Virginia University. He received his M.A. from Texas Christian University in 1982.

Gerald Phillips is a professor in the Department of Speech Communication at Pennsylvania State University. He is currently editor of *Communication Quarterly*. He received his doctorate from Case Western Reserve University.

Virginia Richmond is Associate Professor and Director of Graduate Study at West Virginia University. She received her Ph.D. from the University of Nebraska, Lincoln.

Laura Stafford is a graduate fellow in the Department of Speech Communication at the University of Texas. She received her M.A. in speech communication from the University of Texas in 1982.

John Wiemann is an associate professor in the Department of Speech at the University of California, Santa Barbara. He received his doctorate in Communication from Purdue University.